'In his absorbing book about the lost and the gone,
Peter Ross takes us from Flanders Fields to Milltown to
Kensal Green, to melancholy islands and surprisingly lively
ossuaries ... a considered and moving book on the timely
subject of how the dead are remembered, and how they
go on working below the surface of our lives'
HILARY MANTEL

'Ross is a wonderfully evocative writer, deftly capturing a
sense of place and history, while bringing a deep humanity
to his subject. He has written a delightful book'
Guardian

'The pages burst with life and anecdote while also
examining our relationship with remembrance'
Financial Times

'Among the year's most surprising "sleeper" successes is
A Tomb with a View. In a year with so much death, it may
have initially seemed a hard sell, but the author's humanity
has instead acted as a beacon of light in the darkness'
The Sunday Times

'Never has a book about death been so full of life.
James Joyce and Charles Dickens would've loved it – a book
that reveals much gravity in the humour and many stories
in the graveyard. It also reveals Peter Ross to be among
the best non-fiction writers in the country'
ANDREW O'HAGAN

'Fascinating ... Ross makes a likeably idiosyncratic guide
and one finishes the book feeling strangely optimistic
about the inevitable'
Observer

A TOMB WITH A VIEW

PETER ROSS is an award-winning journalist.
A nine-times winner at the Scottish Press Awards
and shortlisted for the Orwell journalism prize, he is
a regular contributor to the *Guardian* and *The Times*.
He is the author of the non-fiction collections
Daunderlust and *The Passion Of Harry Bingo*, the latter
shortlisted as non-fiction book of the year at the
Saltire Society literary awards. He lives in
Glasgow with a view of the tombs.

A TOMB WITH A VIEW

The Stories & Glories of Graveyards

PETER ROSS

HEADLINE

First published in 2020 by
HEADLINE PUBLISHING GROUP

First published in paperback in 2021 by
HEADLINE PUBLISHING GROUP

1

Cataloguing in Publication Data is available from the British Library

ISBN 978 1 4722 6778 8

Designed and typeset by EM&EN
Printed and bound in Great Britain by Clays Ltd, Elcograf S.p.A.

HEADLINE PUBLISHING GROUP
An Hachette UK Company
Carmelite House
50 Victoria Embankment
London EC4Y 0DZ

www.headline.co.uk
www.hachette.co.uk

For David and Michael
– and for Liam

But why all this racket in the dirty dust?

– Máirtín Ó Cadhain, *Cré na Cille*

Can you hear things when you are dead?
Perhaps the dead hear all sorts.

– Jackie Kay, *Red Dust Road*

Do you realize that everyone you know
someday will die?

– The Flaming Lips

Contents

Author's Note xiii

IVY *1*

The Old Town Cemetery, Stirling; Mark Sheridan, Comedian;
love and death in Whitby

ANGELS *21*

London: Brompton; Queerly Departed; Kensal Green;
Graveyard Walker; Medi's Island

CHERUBS *51*

Edinburgh: Greyfriars Bobby; the Mackenzie poltergeist;
the man from Valhalla; Warriston

LILIES *67*

Belfast: Milltown Cemetery; Easter parades; Friar's Bush; City
Cemetery; Lyra McKee

PHOEBE *95*

The long and dramatic life of Phoebe Hessel, the Stepney Amazon

CEDAR *103*

Highgate: Lizzie Siddal; Karl Marx; a gravedigger speaks;
death-masks; the sentinel tree

Contents

UNMARKED *133*

The outcast dead: Crossbones Graveyard; the cillíní *of Ireland;
the last vigil of John Crow*

ANCHOR *161*

*War graves: St Finnan's Isle; conscientious objectors in Yorkshire;
Belgium and France*

ANKH *193*

*Graves of ghost-story writers: M. R. James; Amelia B. Edwards;
Joseph Sheridan Le Fanu*

DUBLINERS *217*

*Glasnevin Cemetery: the extraordinary life and death of
Shane MacThomáis*

LILIAS *241*

In search of the grave of Lilias Adie, the Witch of Torryburn

CRESCENT *247*

*In Whitechapel with Haji Taslim, the oldest firm of
Muslim funeral directors in Britain*

SKULLS *265*

*The Bone Crypt, Rothwell; mummies of St Michan's;
the ossuary of St Leonard's, Hythe*

Contents

PETER 289

*At the grave of Peter the Wild Boy in Northchurch,
Hertfordshire*

CROWS 299

*Natural burial; meet the green undertakers;
Bridgitt and Wayne – a love story*

BELOVED 313

*Arnos Vale, Bristol; the man who grew up in a graveyard;
Shaun and Liz get married*

Selected Sources 327

Acknowledgements 339

Picture Credits 342

Index 343

Author's Note

I finished writing *A Tomb with a View* on 1 March 2020. Eleven days later, everything changed. 'I must level with the British public,' the prime minister said. 'Many more families are going to lose loved ones before their time.'

They did. Nurses and doctors. Bus drivers. Carers and those in care. Hilda, aged 108, who survived the so-called Spanish flu that, in 1918, had killed her baby sister. Ismail, a thirteen-year-old from Brixton, the first child in the UK to die of coronavirus. William, who had been a child in Bergen-Belsen concentration camp. Harold, a war veteran who had been among those to burn the camp down. By Easter Sunday, more than 13,000 had died; by Whitsun, three times that. Mortuaries ran out of body bags. A lone piper greeted a wicker coffin at an Edinburgh crematorium; the widow and daughter were unable, for fear of contagion, to give each other a hug.

I had tried, in a year of writing, to reckon death in ink; Death, though, keeps his ledger in blood.

During the lockdown, the cemetery behind my house – the cemetery which had first inspired this book – became a sanctuary. I walked there most days. It might seem counter-intuitive to seek escape, and escapism, from a killer disease in a graveyard, but I found it a vaccine against gloom; exposure to a particle of darkness means one does not sicken with it.

Glasgow is known as 'the dear green place' on account of its many parks. However, these were now so busy that it had become difficult to keep the regulation two metres apart. A tumbledown cemetery, though? Much better. From the highest point, where some of the grandest stones still stand, though many have been toppled, one has a view of the city centre a few miles north. Just visible is the huge pink sign overlooking George Square, and the words: People Make Glasgow. This is a marketing slogan that happens to be true. So, too, does the reverse: Glasgow makes people. It makes them funny often, and chippy sometimes, and, most of all, resilient. That resilience was on full display in the graveyard.

Joggers, dog-walkers, amblers, we nodded and waved from safe removes, glad to feel the sun and wind on our faces. A young woman, bike laid in leaf-litter, sketched a stone angel. For years this cemetery had felt almost entirely abandoned, the haunt of users and boozers, vandals with spray paint and hammers, but now it was experiencing a new life. Covid's metamorphosis – the place was transformed.

A number of UK cemeteries had closed their gates to visitors in response to the coronavirus outbreak. This I thought a great shame. Graveyards had been functioning as an important overflow, relieving the pressure on parks. More than that, though, they provided a comforting feeling of arm-around-the-shoulders solidarity with those who had gone before. All these folk in my cemetery had delights and troubles of their own. They had lived through world wars, through depressions economic and personal. They were made by Glasgow, and remade it in their turn, and now they were fading names on cracked stones.

One of the central ideas of *A Tomb with a View* is that the dead and the living are close kin. We think of them, visit them, sometimes speak with them, and will, one day, join them. In Philip Pullman's *The Amber Spyglass*, everyone is born with their own death present, a quiet and kindly companion, invisible, who draws near as the end approaches: 'Your death taps you on the shoulder, or takes your hand, and says, come along o' me, it's time.' The coronavirus outbreak intensified this feeling I have that we are always in the company of the dead; that the outstretched palm is only a handspan away.

The weeks passed. Flowers bloomed and faded. Snow-drops, crocuses, wild garlic.

Funerals were, by law, restricted to close family only, but how this worked in practice seemed to vary, depending on the undertaker. One day, I saw an Islamic burial taking place. There must have been twenty people around the grave. Social distancing was not being observed. The men, some of whom wore masks over their noses and mouths, looked on as a mechanical digger pushed soil into the hole. Women, who, according to religious tradition, do not attend the burial, stood silent behind a low wall which separates the cemetery from the road. They held their headscarves over the lower part of their faces.

Dandelions, daffodils, daisies.

At the top of the hill were three men in their fifties, two of them seated on fallen stones, red-faced with sun and beer; the third had a golf club and was skelping balls as hard as he could down the slope and over the graves. I asked him to stop; said that it was dangerous and disrespectful. He squared up, ready to fight, told me: 'Get to fuck.' In a time of sickness, rude health.

Primroses, cuckoo flowers, celandine.

I followed the sound of 'Auld Lang Syne' and found a musician – Brian was his name – playing the bagpipes in a clearing. I thought perhaps that he, like the piper at the Edinburgh crem, was lamenting the lost, but no. 'I'm giving my neighbours peace,' he said. The cemetery, during lock-down, was simply a good place to practise. His motives may have been pragmatic rather than poetic, but the old ballad of comradeship and nostalgia, carried by the wind across hundreds of graves, was in harmony with the national mood.

We were at once looking backwards to an impossibly distant life before Covid-19 – auld lang syne – and forwards to some indefinite point, which had come to be known, yearningly, as 'When this is all over . . .'

This book finds you, I hope, in those better days. May you read in peace.

IVY

I GREW UP IN GRAVEYARDS. The dead were my babysitters, my quiet companions. Not silent, though. They announced themselves with great formality. You only had to read the stones.

Here Lays
The Corps Of Mary Dickie
Who Died Dec 18th 1740
Aged 3 Years & 9 Months
Suffer The Little Children
To Come Unto Me

That's one I remember from the Old Town Cemetery in Stirling. I'd spend whole summers there, a little-ish child myself, trying to catch tadpoles, those living commas, in the small pond called the Pithy Mary, or taking a poke of penny sweets up on to the Ladies' Rock, a steep outcrop in the centre of the cemetery, where one could enjoy flying saucers and foam shrimps while looking out over the panorama of graves.

Those graves. Laid out in rows, they were shelves full of stories. I was a shy boy; wary, watchful, living inside myself, living in books. *Treasure Island, The Hound of the Baskervilles*, adventures from an earlier age. Headstones, in that company, were just more tales. Jim Tipton, founder of the Find A Grave website, calls cemeteries 'parks for introverts', which sounds about right. I would wander among the headstones, reading the inscriptions, gawping at the eighteenth-century carvings, poking a soft finger into the socket of a stone skull, or into the pits left by musket balls in the walls of the medieval church. If the imagination is a muscle, graveyards are a gym. I'd look at the names and wonder. Did John Barnes, Hairdresser, who died aged sixty-seven in January 1891, ever, in his youth, take comb and scissors to Ebenezer Gentleman, who died at Christmas 1868 and whose crooked stone lies just a step or two away?

It never felt frightening to be surrounded by dead people. In those days – the late seventies, early eighties – the living seemed much more of a threat. The cemetery was in poor repair. Lots of vandalism. Worst of all was the monument to a pair of women, Margaret McLachlan and Margaret Wilson, put to death in Wigtown in 1685 for refusing to give up their Protestant religion. They had been tied to stakes and drowned in the rising tide of the Solway Firth. Now, here in Stirling, they had suffered a second martyrdom, the glass of their memorial smashed, the heads and hands of the marble statues broken off and stolen.

Who would do that? The sad truth is it could have been anyone. The cemetery was haunted by ne'er-do-wells: junkies, punk dafties, solvent-huffers with fairy rings of zits around chafed lips. I lived in mortal fear of a lad known as Tommy Gluebag who was rumoured to have inhaled so much solvent that a pouch of the stuff had mushroomed on the back of his head, pushing tight and milky through his short ginger hair. Nobody wanted to get close enough to verify this. Tommy had a reputation for recreational violence. One day, while I was playing alone on the Ladies' Rock, he saw me and began, cursing, to climb. But his legs were rubbery beneath him, and about halfway up, he became – rather appropriately for a glue-sniffer – stuck. Still, it was a bad moment. I felt like Jim Hawkins in the rigging, looking down in terror as Israel Hands climbed, dagger in teeth, towards him.

That was the thing about graveyards, though: they felt like – feel like – treasure-houses of stories. Some of these stories are international bestsellers. George Eliot and George Michael in Highgate, Oscar Wilde and Jim Morrison in Père Lachaise. Others, though, are known only locally, if at all.

This book, like the best sort of funeral, will be a celebration, not a lament. It will uncover the stories and glories of the best graveyards, from grand city cemeteries to couthy country churchyards. I love all these places. I love the bones of them. I want to make you love them too.

'Burial grounds are like libraries of the dead, indexes to lives long gone,' Sheldon K. Goodman, founder of Cemetery Club, told me. Goodman offers deeply researched tours of graveyards, including Hampstead, where the music hall star Marie Lloyd is buried. It feels like time travel to stand by Lloyd's grave and play on one's phone – as I once did – her 1915 recording, 'A Little of What You Fancy Does You Good'; her voice was a ghost floating between the surface noise and the caw of the London crows.

When we first spoke, Sheldon was busy prepping for his Queerly Departed tour of Brompton Cemetery, exploring the history of the gay and lesbian Londoners buried there. He was enthusiastic, even giddy, on the subject of cemeteries. 'Millions of people have ended up in these remarkable places,' he said. 'Heroes and villains, inventors and actors, people who once lived, laughed, loved and cried. I think it's important to resurrect their stories and memories and achievements, which highlight the importance of the past and its effect on the future.'

True; but what draws me, personally, to these old stones is not so much the famous dead as extraordinary tales of ordinary folk. Deep within the cracked stone ribs of Dundrennan Abbey, a beautiful medieval ruin in Galloway, southern Scotland, there lies a graveyard which, though now old itself, grew up in the centuries since the church was abandoned and the roof fell in. 'This is the British Empire squashed into one little place,' said Glyn Machon, the sixty-year-old custodian of the abbey, pointing out the graves of this young man who died at Gallipoli in 1915, that young woman who died at sea – as her stone says, with an E. M. Forster touch – 'on her passage from India' in 1852.

Glyn is a bricklayer by trade, a Yorkshireman by profession, and though he appears as unsentimental as one of his own walls, it was clear when we met, one bright morning, that he loves this place deeply. His wife says that the abbey is the other woman in their marriage.

One small grave sheltered in the north-east corner of the dyke caught his eye: 'This is the little lad, here, look.' Within the top-curve of the headstone, a cherub; wind and rain and time had worn away its colours, but enough paint remained to show that its hair was blond, its wings white, its smiling face a boyish pink. This is the resting place of Douglas Crosby, who died shortly before the Christmas of 1789, aged seven, of a broken heart – or so the story goes.

How does the story go? 'This grave is known as "the boy and the snake",' Glyn said. Squinting in the autumn sun, he read a verse carved into the stone: 'He was a manly pritty boy / His father's hope, his mother's joy / But death did call, and he must go / Whither his parents would or no.'

Douglas Crosby lived at Newlaw Farm, a little inland from Dundrennan. Every morning that summer it was his habit to take his bowl of porridge and eat in the garden. His mother, Jane, thought little of it until one day she overheard him say, with amused crossness, 'Keep tae yer ain side o' the plate.' She went outside and saw the boy sitting on the grass. An adder was coiled beside him, eating from the bowl, and – as she watched – Douglas reached out his spoon and tapped it gently on the top of the head, at which the creature moved to the other side of the bowl and the pair continued, companionably, to share breakfast.

Horrified, she called the boy in, and shouted for her husband. The adder had slithered off into the longer grass, but the farmer, beating around with a stick, found it and clubbed it to death. Young Douglas grieved for his best friend, and did not live long without it. He shed this life like an old skin and was buried where he lies. There is nothing on his stone to connect the grave to the story – no mention at all of a snake, never mind porridge – and yet the story clings to it like lichen, a living thing growing on the dead.

Tales like that are everywhere, lying beneath the moss and leaves. Sometimes you need only walk out your door.

Stan Laurel's mother lies in an unmarked grave a little way behind my house. Visiting Cathcart Cemetery, looking for the spot, I chanced instead upon a pink granite stone marked with these words: 'Mark Sheridan, Comedian'.

Sheridan was a music hall star. His real name was Frederick Shaw and he came from County Durham. A faded photograph shows a man in heavy make-up wearing bell-bottoms and a comically oversized bowler hat. That we all know 'I Do Like to Be Beside the Seaside' is because of the popularity of his 1909 recording. Nine years later he was dead, having taken his own life in Kelvingrove Park while on tour in Glasgow. He was buried in the far south of the city two days later.

Cathcart is the least celebrated of Glasgow's historic cemeteries. It doesn't look as dramatic as the Necropolis in the city centre, with its huge glowering effigy of John Knox, the religious reformer, which functions as a sort of Statue of Illiberty, representing all that is stern and joyless and unbending about Scotland. And it doesn't have the disquieting air of urban gothic that characterises the Southern Necropolis,

where tower blocks loom, brute and mute, over the eerie marble figure known as the White Lady. That monument, which marks the grave of two women killed by a tramcar in 1933, is said to turn its head to gaze – blank and implacable – at passers-by. The cemetery is also said to be home to the legendary Gorbals Vampire, a creature with iron teeth and a taste for the blood of local boys. Between the watchful eyes and the monstrous teeth it's a wonder that anyone ever walks their dog there, yet they do. Glesga dugs have sceptical bladders. They will happily cock a leg in the Southern Necropolis, never cocking an ear to the stories.

What can I tell you about Cathcart? It is mine. It is inside me as, perhaps, one day, I will be inside it. When you find a graveyard that you enjoy, it can become like a favourite beach or woodland walk; the pleasure is in familiarity, belonging, a sense of home. One summer evening, my wife and children and I climbed a green hill to the highest point in the cemetery, and, sitting on a tartan picnic rug, listened to the Arctic Monkeys drifting over from their concert four miles away on Glasgow Green. On Hogmanay, we followed our ears and discovered a woodpecker rat-a-tatting high in a beech. Head a blur of white and red, it was knocking on the new day, on the new year, on the old wood, asking to come in.

If a tree can look haughty, this beech did. Around its foot were several headstones, some rather crooked, others so overgrown with ivy that they seemed more like topiary. When ivy is carved on a gravestone it symbolises eternal life, but in Cathcart, as in so many old cemeteries, the plant has made the figurative literal, smothering what must once have been beautiful carving as if to show its distaste for metaphor. Ivy in a graveyard is disgustingly, ostentatiously alive. It strikes names from stone as, below, flesh strips from bone.

Still, as the woodpecker kept time on the trunk above, I could make out some of the names. The most recent carving was from 1976, a death in the long hot summer, but the others were a good bit older. One granite cross, erected by a William Fulton Young, marked the resting place of his wife, Isabella, and their sons, Alexander, John and Robert, all of whom died as a result of their war service. Only Alexander appears to have been killed in action, on 26 September 1916; the others survived the fighting but succumbed, eventually, to their injuries. Robert, 'BADLY GASSED IN FRANCE', lingered on until 2 February 1921, and what a universe of suffering must be contained within those four capitalised words. Poor Sandy, John and Rab – as their parents may well have known them – who went to war as boys and came back with lungs full of death, if they came back at all. To visit that grave on New Year's Eve, drawn there by the bird, was to experience a jumpcut: from the rattle of guns to the beat of beak on wood.

In an old graveyard the mind snags on stories, just as a fox, pushing between overgrown tombs, might catch on the undergrowth and carry away burrs in its coat. Walking through Cathcart Cemetery, the eye is caught by a French name:

Jean-Baptiste Louis Janton
Bachelier ès Arts et ès Sciences Paris
Né à Versailles France
Mort à Glasgow le 28 Octobre 1925

Here, if you like, is the opposite story to that of the Young family – a Frenchman who came to Scotland and died here. How, one wonders, did our smoke-black city seem after Paris and Versailles? What sort of man was Jean-Baptiste and what made him settle here? Did the Glaswegian dialect, with its glottal stops and guttural fricatives, feel ugly in his mouth, or did he enjoy the rough sounds, the way one might take pleasure in tonguing a broken tooth? A cemetery is a place of questions, tantalisingly so.

Mark Sheridan – that one got under my skin, a burr snagged deep. It was such a simple stone; pink marble, just his name and dates, and that word: comedian. I had to know more.

A visit to the Mitchell, the city's grand Edwardian library, furnished a report from the *Glasgow Herald* newspaper, dated 16 January 1918: 'There was a bullet wound in his forehead and a Browning revolver was lying beside the body.' Sheridan had left his hotel in time to attend a noon rehearsal, but never arrived. At 2.20 p.m., his corpse was discovered by two men out walking: 'The spot where the tragedy occurred is an unfrequented part of the park on the west side of the Kelvin. The body was lying on the footpath.'

Sheridan's burlesque *Gay Paree*, in which he played Napoleon, had just opened at the Coliseum on Eglinton Street. His daughter and two sons had parts in the show, and his wife, Ethel, was on the road too. Shortly before 7 p.m., the curtain was about to be raised when police informed the theatre manager of his leading man's death. He made a sombre announcement and the audience filed quietly out.

Received wisdom has it that this desperate act was prompted by bad notices for *Gay Paree*, which is odd as the *Herald*'s review on the day of his death observed that it 'admirably fulfils its purpose of mirthmaking, and is in every way an attractive entertainment'. The following November, in a court battle with an insurance company, lawyers for Sheridan's widow argued, unsuccessfully, that he had not intended to end his life. Ethel Shaw claimed her husband had gone into the park to rehearse a scene in which he had to fire a pistol, and – while doing so – 'the unfortunate accident' occurred. George Robey, 'the Prime Minister of Mirth', later famous as Falstaff in Olivier's film of *Henry V*, gave his view that Sheridan 'was not the man to commit suicide because his play was not a success the first night'. All very curious.

A fellow performer once recalled: 'When you saw Mark Sheridan sing "I Do Like to Be Beside the Seaside", it was something more than someone singing a good, rousing song ... As he strode across the stage, singing lustily in his Tyneside voice and slapping the back-cloth with his stick, he was a man full of fresh air and vigour and health, striding along the promenade.'

It is queer – and more than a little sad – to think of this fellow of infinite jest buried so far from home, beyond the sound of the silvery sea.

*

To the taphophile – a lover of graves – Sheridan's lair is the equivalent of a rare bird to the twitcher. The thrill is discovering something in a place where it should not be. A Blackburnian Warbler, blown off course by an Atlantic storm to St Kilda, doesn't mean much to people like me, but give us a weird ersatz graveyard in some unlikely nook and we're delighted.

When you get your eye in, you begin to notice these everywhere. In York, coming away from a family wedding, heading for the train, I spotted a few old stones, shaded beneath trees, on a patch of grass hemmed in between two busy roads. This, it turned out, was a burial ground for some of the 185 people who died from 'a plague of cholera' – as a small sign has it – during the summer and autumn of 1832.

It had been a panic. No one knew how it was caused, or how it could be cured. Citizens were dying in Castlegate and Coppergate, in Fossgate and Friargate, and especially in the fetid, ill-fated slum known as the Hagworm's Nest. The Privy Council decreed that the funerals of victims could not be held in church and that they should not be buried in the churchyards. This was done from fear of further contagion, and, it seems, out of some sense that these deaths were, as one contemporary account has it, 'Divine chastisements' – God's vengeance on the sinful. We know now, thanks to the work of the York-born doctor John Snow (whose grave can be found in Brompton, one of London's grand cemeteries), that their only sin was drinking infected water. But back then they were, literally, outcasts. A patch of wasteland just outside the city walls, between Thief Lane and some dog kennels, was identified as a suitably isolated spot for the disposal of the wretched corpses, and that is where they remain today, paid little if any mind by those hurrying for trains north and south.

There are an estimated 14,000 cemeteries and churchyards in the UK, of which approximately 3,500 predate the First World War. Nobody knows the numbers for sure, and it is unlikely that a near-forgotten oddity such as York's cholera graves appear in the statistics.

The same goes for the Navvies' Graveyard. A forlorn and little-known spot between the South Lanarkshire villages of

Elvanfoot and Crawford, at the side of the fledgling River Clyde, it goes unnoticed by those who roar past on the M74. Yet turn off the motorway, park up on a back road, pick your way down a steep bank and you are there – one of the secret sites of Scotland's industrial history. A circle of cairns linked by rusty chains encloses a rickle of stones from the river bed, worn and mossy and sinking into the sodden earth. These mark the graves of the thirty-seven Irish workers – known as navigators, hence 'navvies' – who died here, in 1847, of typhus, while building the Caledonian Railway, connecting London to Glasgow and Edinburgh through many hard miles of bleak countryside. We do not know their names.

I found this place a few years ago and now, whenever driving south, glance left as it blurs past. It feels important to acknowledge it. These men, whoever they were, made a sacrifice of sorts to the future of the country, and this crude memorial is their Cenotaph, dandelions and bracken their only poppies.

Many of Britain's burial grounds are full, or close to full, with new interments no longer permitted. Without fresh dead, a cemetery dies, or so some believe. 'Highgate Cemetery is reaching capacity and will run out of available space for new burials within the next decade,' a recent report warned. 'Unless additional grave space can be provided it will cease to be a working cemetery, harming its significance and threatening the conservation of the historic memorial landscape.'

If cemeteries are filling up, closing down, it is also true that fewer and fewer people actually want to be buried in them. Three-quarters of us in the UK are cremated, and our remains are often scattered in a favourite spot rather than being interred. As a result, the habit of visiting and tending the grave of a loved one is becoming less and less common. In that cemetery behind my house, fresh flowers are a rare sight, fresh graffiti all too familiar. Only in the Muslim and Jewish sections are there any signs of recent visits; in the latter, I am always moved to notice new pebbles placed on headstones, the most humble imaginable indicator of love.

There are, however, many other reasons to visit. Tombstone tourism is on the rise. There are guided tours around some of the country's most famous cemeteries – Highgate in London, the Necropolis in Glasgow, Arnos Vale in Bristol – but we taphophiles enjoy seeking out the lesser-known. Whenever I am in a place I have never visited before, and have a little time to spare, I will look for the oldest graveyard in town. There's a deep joy in finding an interesting headstone. The churchyard of St Mary's in Banff, Aberdeenshire, has an incredibly cute grim reaper holding an hourglass and scythe, and wearing not the famous cowl and bony scowl, but a half-smile and what appears to be a tiny pair of pants. How this appeared in 1765 goodness only knows, but in the twenty-first century it manages to be both deeply sinister and deeply camp: not an easy combination, but one it achieves with aplomb.

In the grounds of Malmesbury Abbey, Wiltshire, is another of my favourite graves: a rather ordinary-looking stone, much weathered and hard to read. It is worth the effort, though, for here lies Hannah Twynnoy, a maid at a nearby inn, who – on 23 October 1703 – became the first person in England to be killed by a tiger:

> *In bloom of Life*
> *She's snatched from hence.*
> *She had not room*
> *To make defence;*
> *For Tyger fierce*
> *Took Life away.*

IVY

And here she lies
In a bed of Clay
Until the Resurrection Day.

The Old White Lion dates from at least the 1200s. It was already very old by the time Hannah Twynnoy was serving ale. It hasn't been a working inn since 1970, but Paul and Frances Smith, who live there, open to the public a few times each year as a pop-up pub – including a Hallowe'en re-enactment of the bloody mauling. I had missed that by a week, but they were good enough to show me around their home and out into the back garden, where Hannah met her end. The story, they said, is that the yard of the inn was being used by a travelling circus, and that it was the maid's habit, as she passed the tiger's cage, to rattle a stick along the bars – out of pure mischief. One day, the catch broke, the beast sprang out, and it was all over in moments. She was thirty-three. The incident must have been awful, a claret horror, but the passing of time has given it a folklorish air; it feels like a cautionary tale for children. The headstone makes it real, though. Poor Hannah.

The smallest graveyards sometimes tell the tallest tales. In the village of Leadhills, South Lanarkshire, there is buried an old miner – John Taylor – said to have lived until he was 137, though some argue that's totally ridiculous and he actually died at 133. Either way, his was not a long retirement: he put down his pick at the age of 117. The year of his death was 1770. In his idle moments, which were not many, he liked – locals say – to reminisce about the eclipse of 1652.

Amid these disputable claims, an indisputable fact: Leadhills is home to the world's oldest subscription library, founded in 1741. The Miners Library was established for the elevation of the minds of men who worked underground.

John Taylor very líkely used it. One wall is lined with brown leather-bound volumes, mostly religious and scientific titles, the air smells pleasantly musty, and against the opposite wall stands a wooden pulpit with 'Learning Makes The Genius Bright' painted in gold along the top.

Graveyards, as Sheldon K. Goodman said, are libraries of sorts; their stories bound in stone. Council libraries may be closing, or shrinking, but graveyards – those which remain active – are forever replenishing their stock of spines. One of my own cherished libraries of this kind is in the town of Whitby on the North Yorkshire coast.

On days when Whitby gets too hot and busy, I like to climb the famous 199 steps and walk the cliffs. In Bram Stoker's novel *Dracula*, inspired by the author's stay in the town, the vampire bounded up these steps in the form of a black dog. The human visitor, or at least this one, prefers a more leisurely pace. You rise from the pleasant reek of pubs and sweet shops to the fresh wind off the sea. A sign on a farm gate up there used to warn, in fading red paint, that 'Trespassers will be shot'. Happily, there is a place nearby where trespasses are not only forgiven (that being part of the whole Christian deal) but visitors actively welcomed: St Mary the Virgin, the town's parish church.

Nineteenth-century box pews, one marked 'For Strangers Only', bring to mind a ship's galley. Philip Larkin might have considered this a serious house on serious earth, but the seriousness of the latter is open to question. Landslips have exposed bones. At night, St Mary's is spotlit; light bouncing off its old walls casts a milky glow over the churchyard, picking out certain graves. Thomas Boynton, Master Mariner of the eighteenth century, is buried beneath a stone rich with carving: lawless ivy; a jawless skull, sockets deeply shadowed.

I was fortunate, one Sunday morning, to be shown around

the church by Bob Franks, tower captain; the boss of the bellringers. He was eighty-four, but you wouldn't know it. They stood in a circle at the foot of the belltower, ten men and women, pulling candytwist ropes in suffragette colours. Mr Franks, a small gentleman with white hair and an air of gentle amusement, called the changes – 'Seven on five, five leading!' – rising to the very tips of his black loafers as the rope ascended. A plaque on the wall commemorated the summer day in 1935 on which the bells were rung to mark the Silver Jubilee of King George V. There was, in every peal and echo, a sense of the eternal, a thing being done because it had always been done and would always be done. No dusty duty, though. The bellringers love the music and the ritual, and calling Whitby folk to worship is, for them, a sort of hallowed pleasure.

Once the churchgoers were nicely settled in their pews, Mr Franks led the way up narrow stone stairs to the belfry. He undid a padlock, slid a bolt. The sound of the choir rose from far below. We were among the bells. They hung, still and heavy in the darkness, like ripe fruit. He asked: 'Do you want to have a quick pop upstairs for the best view in Whitby?'

The tower captain led the way along a beam, between the bells, and we stooped through a tiny door on the other side of the belfry. 'This is where I like to come to watch the Red Arrers do their stunts,' he said, sweeping his arm around the roof. 'They fly right over the top of the church here.' He was right about the view. The outlook north – flat blue sea, flat blue sky – was pure Rothko. South-west, a Turner-ish smear of smoke, rising from the moors, showed the position of the steam train chuffing towards Goathland.

The churchyard below had the look of a Hornby model. We were too high up to read the graves; even close to, many are illegible, scoured by clifftop wind. I could see some black-clad figures picking their way between the stones. One wore a top hat, another a crinoline skirt and bustle. Goths.

Whitby, thanks to its *Dracula* connection, has become the spiritual home for this particular tribe. The 'velvet pound' is important to the local economy. Goths in fishnets can, these days, generate more income than trawlermen with fishing nets. There is even a goth B&B, Bats & Broomsticks, where guests breakfast by candlelight and enjoy the music of The Damned with their cornflakes. As one local told me: 'Whitby needs goths to keep it in the black.'

St Mary's is catnip for goths – batnip, I suppose. It has long been a favourite spot for photographs, but this has now been restricted. As John Hemson, the churchwarden, had once explained to me: 'Some women were photographed lying on the tombstones and exposing quite a bit of themselves that you wouldn't normally expect in the street, never mind a churchyard. We still have a lot of people in Whitby who have relatives buried here, and they objected to what was going on.'

Photography per se is not banned, just people posing on the graves, but there has, nevertheless, been some resistance to the new rule. 'No one has been buried in that graveyard since 1851,' Carole Platts, a goth in her thirties, had said. 'And if they died in the nineteenth century then they've seen corsets like ours before.'

From the roof of St Mary's, my impression was that the goths had no intention of draping themselves provocatively over tombs. Too busy reading. They were round the back of the church, and I thought I knew what they were looking at. It was a tombstone I had often admired myself:

Here lies the bodies of FRANCIS HUNTRODDS and MARY his wife who were both born on the same day of the week month and year — Septr ye 19th 1600 marry'd on the day of their birth and after having had 12 children born to them died aged 80 years on the same day of the year they were born September ye 19th 1680 the one not above five hours before ye other

A love story, no less, in the library of the dead.

ANGELS

Son Of A Tutu, a British-Nigerian drag queen, is getting on for seven feet tall from headdress to heels. Between these poles she is entirely fabulous, entirely gift-of-the-gabulous, and seemingly entirely at home among the dead.

Golden evening light cascaded through the cupola of the Anglican Chapel, sparkling on scarlet fingernails as she lifted her hands towards the dome at the climax of 'This is Me', a defiant anthem of self-acceptance from *The Greatest Showman*, and sang: *I won't let them break me down to dust / I know that there's a place for us* . . . In her company, this graveyard didn't seem so grave.

We were in Brompton, a beautiful Victorian cemetery, for Queerly Departed — a tour of those plots in which are buried people who are known, or thought, to have been gay, lesbian, bisexual or some shade in between. It was early July, the evening before Pride, when 30,000 Londoners were expected out marching on the streets, and this tour was being conducted in the same spirit of solidarity and celebration.

It isn't about outing people posthumously, the guide, Sheldon K. Goodman, had told me earlier. 'We are their ambassadors,' he said. 'They can now have their life stories told without fear of retribution or ostracisation. In their own lifetimes, they couldn't fully be themselves.'

Sheldon, who is thirty-two, was wearing heavy black and silver make-up around his eyes. His T-shirt had a drawing of a skull on it. I was curious about how to characterise his thing for cemeteries. Was it a fascination, or perhaps even an obsession? The word 'hobby' seemed inadequate.

'An obsession, definitely,' he laughed.

Graves are just so tantalising. Those basic facts – a name and dates – are the entrance to a wormhole for anyone armed with a curious mind and a well-charged phone. Start with Google and take it from there.

'See that big obelisk?' he pointed. 'That's Lionel Monckton. He was a composer and songwriter, and all his stuff is on Spotify for streaming. Probably only three people a month listen to it, but I'm one of them. Some of the songs are delightfully of their time.' He started to sing one, about horse racing, from 1909: *Back your fancy, back your fancy, come and have a gamble* . . . He is also keen on Sir Montague Fowler, an eminent priest, and always gives his stone a clean whenever he is in Brompton. 'This sounds weird, but it feels like I know him,' he said. 'It's a shame he died in the thirties. I would love to take him out for a pint.'

Brompton is the most central of the grand Victorian cemeteries which encircle London, a bracelet around bone, and which are known as 'The Magnificent Seven'. The others are, clockwise, Abney Park, Tower Hamlets, Nunhead, West Norwood, Kensal Green and Highgate. Brompton, which opened in 1840, is on the western fringe of Kensington; Stamford Bridge, Chelsea's ground, looms over one of the cemetery walls.

On that summer afternoon when I first walked through the great arch of its gatehouse on Old Brompton Road, the cemetery seemed especially gorgeous. The architect, Benjamin Baud, had conceived of it as an open-air cathedral, and even though his design was never fully realised, Brompton does feel serenely elegant and church-like.

The 600-metre central avenue, lined by trees, is a nave running to the high altar represented by the Anglican Chapel. The Great Circle, through which the avenue passes, is said to have been inspired by the piazza of Saint Peter's in

Rome; it is flanked by colonnades of Bath Stone, honey in the sun, within one of which I noticed a man, beetroot-browed and barefoot, working his way through a few cans of Special Brew as the afternoon wore on. Beneath the colonnades are the catacombs. These are locked behind cast-iron gates marked with a forbidding emblem of snakes coiled around inverted torches. It is possible to peer through and see the coffins. I never do this without feeling a little ghoulish. Still, though, I look.

Brompton is owned by the Crown and managed as a Royal Park. 'This was Queen Victoria's favourite cemetery,' Sheldon said. 'She visited here in the 1860s. She didn't actually get out the carriage, mind. She just rode up and down and buggered off.' There are 200,000 or so people buried here, the best known of whom is Emmeline Pankhurst, the suffragette leader, who died in 1928 and whose grave is marked by a modernist take on a Celtic cross. Laid at its foot was a basket of purple and white flowers tied with purple, green and white ribbons, and a card: 'With love from your nieces and great-great-nieces.' As a fan of the films *Kes* and *An American Werewolf in London*, I was also pleased to find the grave of Brian Glover, a simple, flat, grey slab, his name and unusual path through life – 'Wrestler Actor Writer' – bright with fallen seeds.

There are some remarkable tombs. The most beautiful is that of Frederick Leyland, a shipping magnate and art collector who died in 1892. He was a patron of the Pre-Raphaelites, and his faux-medieval monument is by Edward Burne-Jones: a copper chest, oxidised to a bright green, decorated with scrolling flowers and leaves. Grade II-listed, it sits behind railings which are kept padlocked, presumably because it is so valuable and therefore vulnerable. Suitably for a patron of the arts, it is a monument which stimulates the imagination.

It looks as though it might reasonably contain the sword of Arthur or Cup of Christ.

Similarly tantalising is the grave of Hannah Courtoy, described in the Friends of Brompton map as a 'mysterious society woman with fabulous wealth'. She died in 1849. Her granite and marble mausoleum, the tallest in the cemetery, is in the Egyptian style so beloved of the Victorians, but there's something rather steampunky and H. G. Wells about it, too. It is believed that the tomb was designed by Joseph Bonomi, the Egyptologist who is buried nearby, and there is a legend – or theory, depending on how you look at it – that it is a time machine, a proto-Tardis which could be made to work if only someone could find the key to the great copper door. The writer and musician Stephen Coates has developed a counter-theory – or legend – that the tomb is a teleportation chamber, and that there are similar chambers, disguised as mausolea, in each of the Magnificent Seven cemeteries. As a way of getting around London, that beats the Tube, and so it would be more than a little disappointing to get inside the Courtoy mausoleum and find it contained nothing but coffins and bird bones and dust. Let us hope the key is never found.

But back to Queerly Departed. 'Thank you for coming,' said Sacha Coward, co-creator of the tour. 'What a bizarre thing to do on a Friday night. You're all weirdos.'

We laughed, the fifty or so of us gathered in the Anglican Chapel. The drag queen. The bearded dude in the Grateful Dead tee. The teenager with a rainbow painted Aladdin Sane-style across her face. Me with my notebook full of graves. Weirdo is no insult. We were all, I reckon, happy to own that term.

After a couple of stops by the resting places of music hall performers, and the *Bride of Frankenstein* actor Ernest Thesiger, Sheldon announced what, for me, was the highlight of the tour: 'The bisexual Marchesa Luisa Casati, who puts Lady Gaga to shame.' Her grave may be the only understated thing about her – a small stone urn, half hidden by overgrown grass. Nevertheless, it was clear that this is a shrine of sorts. Someone had left a few lilies, wilting now. A photograph, propped up, showed a striking woman with intense eyes. It was taken in 1912, but had the same steely androgynous power as Robert Mapplethorpe's celebrated photograph of Patti Smith on the cover of her album *Horses*.

The Marchesa was a socialite, bohemian and muse, an Italian heiress who came to live in London later in life: in debt and in decline. She had been famous for her outrageous life and clothes. One outfit, created by the costume designer of the Ballets Russes in 1922, was made of electric lightbulbs and came with its own generator. She swathed herself in fabulous rumours; it was whispered that she owned wax dummies in which she kept the cremated remains of former lovers. That would have meant a whole lot of ashes. She elevated hedonism to the level of poetry, putting the cadence into decadence, the verse into perverse. She was death-tinged, doom-fringed. 'Cadaverous' is the adjective most often used to describe her appearance. In Paris, she was known as the 'Venus of Père Lachaise'. She wore necklaces of live snakes. She wanted to be 'a living work of art'. She died of a stroke in the summer of 1957 at the age of seventy-six and was buried with a pair of false eyelashes and a taxidermied Pekinese. Among the mourners, arriving from Venice, was her personal gondolier.

'Why is she not buried beneath a Parthenon? Why not a giant silver phallus or something?' Sacha asked. The answer is that she spent so much on indulging her various eccentricities and desires that she simply ran out of money. 'She ended up in a very small flat in Primrose Hill. As she aged, she became fearful of the way she looked. She hated the idea of her own mortality and became a bit of a recluse. People would see her scurrying around at night, going through bins, finding feathers and bits of fabric and plastic bags which she would turn into dresses. She was quietly creating her own look. She was still out there, putting *RuPaul's Drag Race* to shame.'

Sacha smiled. 'It is a sad ending for a personality that was so big, but at least people seem to know about Luisa. They are coming here and leaving photos and flowers and costume jewellery, objects that she may have loved. So now, before we move on, can I have a volunteer?'

A young woman shot up a hand: 'Me!' This was Lynsey Walker. She loves the macabre, loves fashion, and spends a lot of time in cemeteries. She had on a navy jumpsuit, red heels, dark blue lipstick, black sunglasses and a raspberry beret. Maybe not quite Luisa Casati levels of glam, but not half bad for an evening stroll in a graveyard. Lynsey was given an honour: asked to place a white rose on the Marchesa's grave, a task she performed with great respect. Afterwards, she explained why she had volunteered: 'When Sacha said that she didn't want to be pretty, she wanted to be art, I was like, "Yes!" I see that, I *live* that, I needed to give my rose to her.'

Milanese socialites, militant suffragettes, millionaire time travellers: it is funny who ends up in Brompton. That's the beauty of a London cemetery: they draw their dead from every corner of the earth. Their living, too.

On my way out, I saw an old lady throwing handfuls of seeds and nuts. I had noticed her earlier. She must have been here for much of the day. Her name is Colette, but everyone calls her Cola. She is Swiss and a friend to the squirrels and pigeons. She speaks good English with a strong accent. 'Nothing escape their eyes,' she said, gesturing towards the birds. 'They are very affectionate when they know you. They land on your head, your shoulder, everywhere on your body. They have sharp claws and they pull your hair.'

I like the fact that there are squirrels here, I told her, because it's said that this is where Beatrix Potter got the name for Squirrel Nutkin. She lived locally until her forties, and is said to have taken inspiration from the Nutkins family plot.

'Oh yes,' Cola replied, but wasn't really interested. Too focused on her creatures. She comes two or three times a week with food and clean water. So she wasn't here to visit a particular grave?

'No,' she replied. 'Once you're dead, forget it, that's oblivion.'

I laughed, delighted at the way she drew out the word: *oh-blee-vee-on*.

'Is true! Us, the people who are left behind, if we need to remember somebody, a relative or a dear friend, we can do it any time. We don't need to come physically to a place like this. It means nothing. Well, at least not for me. I only come to feed the pigeon and the squirrel.'

The dead don't need your peanuts?

'No! The dead don't need anything.' She held out a palmful of seeds. 'Once you're dead, you're dead, and that's the truth, believe me!'

*

'Oh, yes,' said Dr Julian Litten. 'We know each other, Kensal Green and I.'

Dr Litten, author of *The English Way of Death*, is the UK's leading expert on the history of funeral customs. He has been described as 'a man who has sniffed the air in a hundred burial vaults' and I can well believe it. Yet, when we met, he did not seem sepulchral. Perhaps it was his orange jumper, orange tie, orange-and-white striped shirt, orange jumbo cords, and two-tone tan brogues which gave an impression of cheer. He is seventy-three. At ease in his home, a sixteenth-century cottage in King's Lynn, he sipped a glass of white wine while we talked.

'Do you mind if I record this?' I asked.

'If it gives you pleasure,' he replied, wafting a small cigar in blithe assent.

He was the founder, in 1991, of the Friends of Kensal Green, the oldest – and one might say most senior – of London's Magnificent Seven cemeteries. His fascination with graveyards goes back to a childhood in Wolverhampton, when he would take the bus to visit Merridale, a grand Victorian cemetery, a 'haunting place' where he enjoyed the feeling of solitude and the stories on the stones.

His interest in funerary aesthetics deepened – literally – in 1971, when he was exploring the ruins of St Mary's, a very old church in South Woodford, which had been burned by arsonists. 'I remember one Saturday morning, the floor opened beneath me and I was plummeted into a burial vault.' Unhurt, more curious than frightened, he stayed down there and had a good look around. Not only that, he measured the vault, made notes on its construction, and satisfied his taste for expensive craftsmanship: 'I was very pleased to see the high quality of the coffin furniture.'

At Dr Litten's age, it is not uncommon for one's thoughts to turn to the grave, but his have tended that way for many years. His own funeral has been planned in every detail, and it has given him immense pleasure to do so. Not for him a cremation – 'Barbaric!' – it will, of course, be a burial, and it will, of course, be Kensal Green.

Once his remains have been washed and his hair combed, he will be clothed in an original Edwardian shroud – 'Never used, I'm pleased to say' – and his body laid in an inner coffin of elm. That will be placed in a lead shell and the lead shell in an outer case of oak, a reproduction of a coffin made around 1900 – 'Ravishing thing. It will have six coats of beeswax, hand applied.'

An Anglican requiem mass (he, unlike Cola, believes in life after death) will take place at All Saints, King's Lynn, at eleven o'clock on a Wednesday morning – 'Wednesdays are always good days for funerals. If anyone wants to come up from London, they can catch the 9.44 and will be in good time.'

From the balcony of the church, a trumpet, trombone, kettle drum and choir will play the Prelude to Charpentier's *Te Deum* – and the funeral will begin. It will be done properly, soberly, tastefully, which is to say in accordance with tradition. This, after all, has been Dr Litten's area of expertise; he would be mortified, both as an academic and as the corpse in question, to have his big day tainted by any modern infringements upon propriety. 'There will be no eulogies,' he sneered. 'Nobody standing up and talking about me. No ghastly child reading a poem and bursting into tears. No member of the laity reading any of the lessons. I think it's tish. Rubbish. It's got nothing to do with the English funeral. Their role is to sit in the pew and watch it taking place.'

The coffin, with eight bearers, will be preceded into the church by his heraldic arms. One of the undertaker's men will carry the crest on a pole, and the other will carry the tabard. The crest is a black helmet made by the Royal Armouries, sitting atop which is a wooden model of a black cat with its right paw resting on a skull. These are kept in readiness high on a roof beam above Dr Litten's dining room table. He pointed up at them as we spoke.

During the service there will be hymns, a psalm and – he is certain – tears. Afterwards, his coffin will be loaded into a glass-sided Rolls-Royce Phantom VI and whizzed straight down the M11 to London, where he will be interred in a brick vault twelve feet beneath the surface of the cemetery he loves. One might consider it a kind of homecoming. The mourners are to remain in King's Lynn, at the Guildhall, enjoying canapés and champagne – 'and saying what a prat I was, and what a waste of money, ha ha ha!'

He intends to be buried alongside his partner, Father Anthony Couchman. The grave, at nine feet by four, will accommodate them comfortably. As to which will lie there first, Dr Litten has a clear preference: 'I hope I die before he does.'

Why?

'Couldn't imagine a life without him.'

Their headstone – of Broughton Moor green slate – has already been made and carved and set in place. It includes Dr Litten's coat of arms and his motto, 'Through Death to Life'. Patiently, it awaits the men to match the names.

All of this preparation and foresight is admirable, indeed remarkable. But what if it goes wrong? Not to tempt fate, but what if, say, Dr Litten is blown up while flying across the Atlantic? All his planning will have been for naught.

'Couldn't care less,' he laughed. 'It will not be my concern. I shall be eating pâté de foie gras to the sound of trumpets.'

Kensal Green – or the General Cemetery of All Souls, Kensal Green, to give it its proper name – was founded in 1833, and was such a success that it entered the wider culture. G. K. Chesterton, in his well-loved poem of 1913 'The Rolling English Road', saw it as a final staging post on the way to the afterlife, writing that 'there is good news yet to hear and fine things to be seen / Before we go to Paradise by way of Kensal Green'.

ANGELS

For my part, when I visited Kensal Green I went by way of the Harrow Road. Iranian grocers, Polish tyre dealers, Portuguese delis, a Galacian social club, Turkish barbers, a Brazilian hair salon, an old-fashioned caff offering a 'builder's breakfast', the ethnic origins of both the breakfast and the builders left unspecified – it felt like a very London angle of approach to one of London's great cemeteries. Entering through the West Gate, I noticed lots of new-ish stones carved with Greek and Italian names. A Manchester United flag flew upon one grave. A funeral was underway, the mourners film-noir sharp in dark suits and sunglasses.

I took the path east towards the Anglican Chapel. It looks like a Greek temple. This must once have been beautiful and very grand, but now had an air of neglect, a feeling that, unfortunately, was general in the older part of the cemetery. Someone had laid an orange rose on the stone breast of Georgina Clementson – a young woman whose effigy, sculpted by her father, lies atop her 1868 tomb in one of the loggias of the chapel. The flower felt like a kindness. It lent her a certain innocence which even the pigeon shit spattering her memorial could not befoul.

Kensal Green was intended from the start as London's answer to Paris's Père Lachaise. It is the only one of the Magnificent Seven cemeteries to remain within private ownership. Its reputation as what Julian Litten calls 'the Belgravia of Death' was established in 1843 when the Duke of Sussex, sixth son of George III, was laid to rest here, starting a fashion among high society. His tomb is remarkable – a brutal granite slab. If death could be rendered in stone, it would surely look more like this great blank weight, almost ostentatiously unadorned, if such a thing were possible, than any of the fussy angels and skulls so common on gravestones. One of the Duke's sisters, Princess Sophia, is buried nearby –

her lofty marble sarcophagus, bristling with brambles, would afford anyone climbing to pick them a splendid view of the gasometer.

Where royalty led, the establishment followed: viscounts and vice-admirals, masters and commanders. Kensal Green became a prestigious place to be buried, a signifier of status. 'It is England's Valhalla,' Dr Litten had said. 'The magic of the place is who is buried there. Why did they not choose their local country churchyard? Why did they decide not to stay in India? Why did they want to have their remains brought back from Bombay? Because Kensal Green was *the* place for the gentry to be buried. And on the last trump they would all stand up, probably knowing one another, and there would be quite a welcome.

'They wished to continue their elitism in death and that is what Kensal Green was able to offer. You could buy a plot of any size you desired, of any depth you desired, and you could put up any monument you desired. That would not have been possible in the London churchyards. So, for a premium, you could get yourself a very nice space with something that the Anglican church could not offer: burial space in perpetuity absolute. And *that* is what made Kensal Green. It attracted the gentlemen and the nobility of the time. It was considered to be their cemetery. It was open to all comers ... provided your purse was deep enough.'

The list of famous names is remarkable. You could read your way around its seventy-two acres (Wilkie Collins, Anthony Trollope, William Makepeace Thackeray) or curate your own science and engineering tour (Charles Babbage, Isambard Kingdom Brunel). Extraordinary to think that *Vanity Fair*, the Great Western Railway and the personal computer all began as visions within brains within skulls within this soil.

Seeking out the graves of such giants is one way to see Kensal Green. Better, though, I think, to put one's faith in serendipity. While examining a photogenic mausoleum with a cape of ivy and caved-in roof, I noticed next to it an unusual headstone – a bust of a man in a suit jacket, waistcoat, high-collared shirt and tie, his face a mossy green. The grave of Emidio Recchioni.

He was an Italian anarchist whose politics led to a number of spells in prison. In 1899, he left Italy for London, where he opened a delicatessen, King Bomba, at 37 Old Compton Street. This became a meeting place for other exiled activists, but it also introduced new sensations to British taste: pasta, Parmesan, salami, wine in straw-covered bottles. If you were anti-fascist, but pro-*fiaschi*, then King Bomba was the place for you. It was certainly the place for George Orwell, Emma Goldman and Sylvia Pankhurst, who are among those said to have hung out there. In 1932, the *Daily Telegraph* named Recchioni as a conspirator in the failed assassination of Mussolini; he sued the paper for libel. Two years later, he died during an operation on his vocal cords. 'Only a handful of earth and ashes,' his epitaph reads, 'but impregnated with the spirit of a man who lived, suffered, and deserved well of mankind.'

There are more than 250,000 people buried in Kensal Green, and there is a strong sense, in certain parts of the cemetery, of different eras, different sorts of lives rubbing up against one another. The democracy of death.

Crouching to examine some wonderful carved griffins holding up a Victorian tomb, I chanced upon the black slab of a sixteen-year-old schoolboy – Byron Upton – who died in 1982, killed by a train. He had taken magic mushrooms and lain down on the track at Pimlico station. He was 'reunited' with his mother, Ann, the gravestone explains, on her death in 2017. There is a lovely picture of the two of them together, by David Hockney – one of his Polaroid composites, made just a few months before the boy's death. Another of Hockney's subjects, the fashion designer Ossie Clark, attended Byron's funeral ('Reggae music and prayers,' he wrote in his diary. 'I threw earth on the coffin and walked away crying') and was, in turn, laid to rest here following his own death in 1996. He had been killed by a young Italian man with Caravaggio looks and Dionysian tastes. Clark was stabbed thirty-seven times. His former lover, in a psychotic episode thought to have been brought on by drugs, had taken him for the devil.

This is how it goes. You come to mourn and, later, to be mourned. The stones spread slowly across the earth, a coral reef of remembrance.

*

THE LONDON garden cemetery movement, of which Kensal Green was the first fruit, grew out of a crisis – the city's churchyards were full to overflowing – and a resulting change in the law: a series of Burial Acts passed during the 1850s which prohibited almost all further burials within the city itself.

London's population in 1801 was approximately 960,000. Forty years later, it had grown to two million. There were a great many more Londoners and a great many more London dead; cholera outbreaks kept the scythe sweeping sharp and swift. By 1840, the daily death rate was 125. In 1843, a government report declared that 50,000 people were being buried each year in 203 acres of ground. 'Within the period of existence of the present generation,' wrote Sir Edwin Chadwick, the report's author, 'upwards of a million of dead must have been interred in those same spaces.'

These statistics, and Chadwick's comment, do not quite convey what this meant in the churchyards themselves. For a vivid, sickening illustration of that, we have *Gatherings from Grave Yards*, a polemic written in 1839 by George Alfred Walker, a surgeon and apothecary who argued that stinking air emanating from overcrowded churchyards – 'the pestiferous exhalations of the dead' – was causing disease and death among those who lived, worked and walked nearby. He believed, incorrectly but not unreasonably, that the typhus fever which so often afflicted his patients was caused by their proximity to burial grounds saturated and engorged with rotting flesh.

'Burial places in the neighbourhood of the living are, in my opinion, a national evil,' Walker wrote, 'the harbingers, if not the originators of pestilence; the cause, direct or indirect, of inhumanity, immorality, and irreligion.'

Known as Graveyard Walker, he established the Society for the Abolition of Burials in Towns, arguing that the government should intervene, as the government in France had done, to close the churchyards and inner-city vaults of the capital, and that Londoners should instead be buried in new, large cemeteries, such as the pioneering Kensal Green, which were then at a safe distance from population areas. He reported, approvingly, the research of one Dr Haguenot, a Frenchman, who sought to establish the toxicity of church-yard odours by opening a grave in Montpelier and testing its effects on a few unfortunate animals. 'Cats and dogs thrown into this grave, were strongly convulsed,' Walker noted, 'and expired in two or three minutes, – birds, in some seconds.'

Charles Dickens gives us a flavour – or, rather, a whiff – of the London burial grounds in the mid-nineteenth century in his 1853 masterpiece *Bleak House.* When the law-writer Nemo dies from an opium overdose, he is buried in a shallow grave in 'a hemmed-in churchyard, pestiferous and obscene', the air so poisoned that it leaves a slimy coating – 'witch-ointment' – on the iron gate, and where the dead, in the form of disease, rise up as 'an avenging ghost at many a sick-bedside'. Indeed, three characters in *Bleak House* do sicken, one fatally, with what appears to be smallpox.

Dickens seems to have been both repelled and fascinated by these places. 'Such strange churchyards hide in the City of London,' he wrote in an essay called 'The City of the Absent'. 'As I stand peeping in through the iron gates and rails, I can peel the rusty metal off, like bark from an old tree. The illegible tombstones are all lop-sided, the grave-mounds lost their shape in the rains of a hundred years ago . . . In an angle of the walls, what was once the tool-house of the grave-digger rots away, encrusted with toadstools.'

Such a scene, and sentiment – the shivery pleasure of decay – will be familiar to any contemporary lover of ceme-teries. We all have our favourites. The churchyard which Dickens considered his 'best beloved' was one he called Saint Ghastly Grim. In fact, it was St Olave's, which is still there on Hart Street; it survived the Great Fire and is the burial place of Samuel Pepys. If you visit, take time to notice the three stone skulls on the gate. Dickens once felt compelled to venture out at midnight in order to admire these by the flash of a lightning storm.

The model for the churchyard in *Bleak House* was, it is thought, the burial ground at Russell Court, off Drury Lane. This would have been very familiar to George Walker, whose practice was at 101 Drury Lane. If Dickens only hinted at the horror, perhaps mindful of the feelings of his readers, Walker was much more blunt in the account he gave of the place, noting that the surface was level with the first-floor windows of the overlooking houses. 'A man who had committed suicide was buried here on the 20th May, 1832,' Walker wrote; 'the body was in the most offensive condition, and was placed within a very little distance of the surface.' Building work done on a house adjoining the burial ground, the surgeon noted, had revealed 'large quantities of human bones' beneath the floor, the consequence of body parts dragged there from shallow graves by 'vast numbers' of rats.

Had Dickens read *Gatherings from Grave Yards*? Or was it simply that he had witnessed the same obscenities? In *Bleak House*, Jo – a ragged orphan who makes a little money sweeping the filthy streets for those who want to cross – shows Lady Dedlock the grave of Nemo, who, years before, had been her lover. They come to the iron gate:

'He was put there,' says Jo, holding to the bars and looking in.

'Where? O, what a scene of horror!'

'There!' says Jo, pointing. 'Over yinder. Among them piles of bones, and close to that there kitchen winder! They put him wery nigh the top. They was obliged to stamp upon it to git it in. I could unkiver it for you, with my broom, if the gate was open. That's why they locks it, I'spose,' giving it a shake. 'It's always locked. Look at the rat!' cries Jo, excited. 'Hi! Look! There he goes! Ho! Into the ground!'

Burial in shallow graves, sometimes only two feet deep, was widespread. Space was at such a premium that it was quite usual for bodies to be exhumed before they had properly decomposed in order to make room for the next occupant. Coffins would be smashed up for firewood, the nails and fittings sold, the corpses chopped by axe and spade. John Eyles, a gravedigger for the churchyard of St Clement's in Portugal Street, recalled in 1842 recognising his own father's head when his coffin was broken open by workmates: 'I knew him by his teeth; one tooth was knocked out and the other splintered; I knew it was my father's head, and I told them to stop, and they laughed . . .'

Gatherings from Grave Yards, an extraordinary act of reportage populated by drunken gravediggers and rapacious undertakers, anatomises the visceral scandal of this. George Walker's book, intended to outrage, leads the reader through a chamber of horrors: a mourner attending a burial steps on a pile of earth – he is standing, it turns out, on the body of the grave's previous occupant, placed to one side and only lightly covered with soil. The skin slips off, like an overripe plum, and the mourner almost falls into the hole.

Worse even than that was Walker's account of Enon Chapel. It was founded on Clement's Lane in 1823 by Mr W. Howse, a Baptist minister, as a financial speculation. Its upper floor, used for worship, was separated from the burying place below by nothing more than wooden boards. Fear of body snatchers seems to have driven people to have their loved ones interred in this place, which undertakers referred to as the Dust Hole, at fifteen shillings a time. Coffins were buried at first; then, when the ground was full, piled up to the ceiling. Walker estimated that up to 12,000 bodies had been crammed into a space measuring around sixty feet by thirty over a period of sixteen years. How was this possible? It was rumoured that bodies were slipped into the open sewer which ran through the vault in order to make room for more.

The chink of money, and what people would do to get it, is almost audible when one reads the accounts of Enon Chapel and the whole sordid business of burial in Victorian London. Testifying before the 1842 Select Committee on the Improvement of Health in Towns, William Burn, a 'master carman', said that, during a period when building work was being done in the Enon vault, he had been employed to remove the earth dug up and had taken away around sixty cartloads. 'I have no doubt,' he said, 'that the greatest portion of what I removed was human bodies in a state of putrefaction.' Earning two shillings and sixpence per load, he drove this foul mulch over to the neighbourhood of Waterloo Bridge, where it was used as landfill in the construction of new roads. One day a human hand was observed among a cartload of soil. Burn considered that 'it did not appear to have been buried probably a month; it was as perfect as my hand'. Horrible though that recollection may be, it is perhaps not so sinister as the seven words with which the carman justifies the part he played: 'I got paid for what I did.'

Coffins laid in vaults were supposed to be lead-lined in order to prevent the leaking of fluid and gas, but the minister who owned Enon Chapel seems not to have been particular on this point. The consequences of such unsanitary practice were nightmarish, Walker writes: 'Soon after interments were made, a peculiarly long narrow black fly was observed to crawl out of many of the coffins; this insect, a product of the putrefaction of the bodies, was observed on the following season to be followed by another, which had the appearance of a common bug with wings. The children attending the Sunday School, held in this chapel, in which these insects were seen to be crawling and flying, in vast numbers, during the summer months, called them "body bugs" – the stench was frequently intolerable . . .'

Worshippers, murmuring prayers, found they had an odd taste in their mouths; it was common, during services, for four or five women to faint and be carried outside; they took the taint with them, bringing home bugs and odours in their clothes; locals were troubled by the smell and by rats; meat, exposed to the air, went bad. Walker writes:

> I have several times visited this Golgotha, I was struck with the total disregard of decency exhibited, – numbers of coffins were piled up in confusion – large quantities of bones were mixed with the earth, and lying upon the floor of this cellar (for vault it ought not be called), lids of coffins might be trodden upon at almost every step.
>
> My reflections upon leaving the masses of corruption here exposed, were painful in the extreme; I want language to express the intense feelings of pity, contempt, and abhorrence I experienced. Can it be, thought I, that in the nineteenth century, in the very centre of the most magnificent city of the universe, such sad, very sad mementos of ignorance, cupidity, and degraded morality, still exist?

Walker's revulsion is palpable. Of all the horrors he saw, he seems to have taken Enon Chapel personally. In 1847, he purchased the property. It had, by then, spent a few years under the ownership of a society of teetotallers, who held dances in the former chapel: 'one of the sixpenny hops of the day', according to a contemporary account, 'where the thoughtless and giddy went to foot it away over the mouldering remains of sad mortality, part of the bygone generation then turning to dust beneath the dancers' feet'.

On taking over the building, Walker set about removing the remains. The bones brought out into the light formed a pyramid so large that some 6,000 people came to view it. Walker had these taken to Norwood Cemetery and buried at his own expense in a single grave twelve feet square and twenty deep. One of the Magnificent Seven, Norwood was known as the 'Millionaires' Cemetery' on account of the many wealthy families who buried their loves ones there. It is pleasant to think that the poor, jumbled masses of Enon Chapel came to reside, at last, at a respectable address.

As for the chapel itself, it became a venue for concerts, gambling, boxing and theatre before, eventually, being demolished. Its site lies beneath the London School of Economics, a fitting foundation for an institution dedicated to study of the 'dismal science'; what, after all, could be more dismal than a place where the dead were seen as a mere commodity, disposable stock?

In the end, though, some good did come of it. Enon Chapel was one of the notorious cases inspiring changes in the law which saw the burial grounds of the inner cities of England and Wales closed and large new cemeteries opening in what were, at that time, areas of low population density.

Kensal Green, as the first cemetery of that type in London, was the model. It was, according to one commentator, a 'beautiful garden of death'. These were no stinking boneyards. The idea was that such places would be much more than mere conveniences for the disposal of remains; they would be elegant showcases of wealth and taste, triumphs of landscaping and architecture. Tree-lined paths and neoclassical chapels. The serenity of eternity. The sorrow of a graveside visit might be lightened by the pleasure of a promenade. You would come to grieve and to be seen grieving. 'Indeed,' write John Turpin and Derrick Knight in their book on the Magnificent Seven cemeteries, 'these were one of the few places where widows and single ladies might visit unaccompanied. There could even be matrimonial possibilities . . .'

It is difficult from a twenty-first-century perspective, given the run-down nature of so many once-grand burial grounds, to appreciate the creative vision, the sense of being at the cutting-edge, which surrounded cemeteries in the nineteenth century. Death was alive with possibilities. The architect Francis Goodwin planned a national cemetery for Primrose Hill. It would be grander than Père Lachaise, cost £400,000 to realise, and feature a temple modelled on the Parthenon. It was never built. Another architect, Thomas Wilson, had a plan for Primrose Hill on an even larger scale. Rather than Greece, he took ancient Egypt as his inspiration. He proposed a pyramid, faced in granite, its base the size of Russell Square. It would contain 215,296 catacombs on ninety-four levels, sufficient to provide eternal rest for five million dead. It, too, was never built. This was Ozymandias stuff, but it demonstrates the ambition that the Victorians had for their cemeteries. What they did get around to building was impressive enough.

To walk in Kensal Green now is to sense the vanity and economic power of the nineteenth century as an almost palpable force, its energy and industry rendered in stone. Just as Turner captured the rain, steam and speed of the Great Western Railway in his painting of that title, Kensal Green is a freeze-frame of a period of huge forward momentum. It is Victorian Britain, ossified.

This place and others like it were theatres of a sort. Here, performed daily, was England's eldritch pageant. Julian Litten sketches this spectacle in *The English Way of Death*: 'The 1890s witnessed the golden age of the Victorian funeral: the horse-drawn cortège, the flower-decked funeral car with its encased burden, and sable mourning coaches containing weeping ladies swathed in crêpe and black bombazine, supported in their grief by stiff-lipped husbands, brothers and uncles resembling the top-hatted beetles in contemporary caricatures by Griset. On the road, two dreadful mutes lead the way, harbingers of death itself, whilst the tramp, tramp, tramp of the attendants' measured paces re-echo the clop, clop, clop of the horses' hooves . . .'

The epic pomp and scale of Kensal Green meant that, even in its heyday, it had detractors. Isabella Holmes, a remarkable chronicler of London's burial grounds, wrote in 1896 that it was 'truly awful, with its catacombs, its huge mausoleums, family vaults, statues, broken pillars, weeping images, and oceans of tombstones, good, bad, and indifferent'. Certainly, its sheer size can be overwhelming. Try to focus on individual memorials, though, and it begins to seem extraordinary.

It is the grand monuments which catch the eye: Andrew Ducrow, the circus performer and proprietor known as the 'Colossus of Equestrians', whose mausoleum is a kind of psychedelic Graeco-Egyptian funhouse; the colonialist tomb of Major General Sir William Casement, which appears to be borne aloft by four grim figures in turbans; William Mulready, the celebrated Irish painter, who lies in effigy atop his own grave as if reclining upon a bed – the figure is extremely lifelike, cast from an artificial stone called Pulhamite, and it is difficult to resist reaching out a gentle hand to strum the laughter lines around his eyes. The natural response to all this faded grandeur is: 'They don't make 'em like that any more.'

But, just sometimes, they still do.

On a showery day in a hot summer, I walked into Kensal Green through the West Gate and followed one of the internal roads to a roundabout on its West Centre Avenue. A man stepped out of a black Mercedes and we shook hands. He was tall and slender with silver hair and wore an air of weary calm like cologne. 'We ought to get out of the rain,' he said, so we sat down to talk inside his son's mausoleum.

Mehdi Mehra, a 57-year-old Iranian businessman, owns a property company with his wife, Mary-Anne. In 2015, their eleven-year-old son Medi died in a riding accident. He was thrown from his horse and hit a tree. According to Islamic tradition, he was buried within twenty-four hours of his death. Sitting at the graveside, in the splintered days that followed, Mr Mehra had a vision: 'I could see this place, completely as it is now, in my mind.' Around his son's grave, he built a memorial on a scale the Victorians would recognise.

It is a half-circle, thirty metres long by fourteen deep and eight high. The twenty-one Corinthian columns give it a neoclassical look, but there are Islamic touches ('God is great' in Arabic) as well as Christian (angels at the corners and doorways, holding torches, books and flowers). It is tempting, when describing the monument, to lean hard on statistics (350 tonnes of granite! 200 of concrete! 150 tonnes of steel!) but the story of Medi's Island, as the place is known, cannot be told in vulgar numbers. The memorial is open to the elements. It has a crown of girders rather than a roof. However, a gazebo erected inside keeps the weather off those who come to sit, as many members of the public apparently do.

Mr Mehra's parents, Hosain and Pouran, are buried here, and he will be himself when his time comes.

The centrepiece, of course, is Medi's burial plot, but one could overlook this, mistake it for something else. It is, essentially, a flower bed, planted with roses and pelargoniums and lilies in whites, pinks and yellows. Butterflies glide past a life-size bronze statue of Medi sitting on a bench. The sculptor has depicted him wearing school uniform and carrying a football. One casual arm is draped over the back of the bench and his left leg is crossed over his right knee. Perhaps this is what Keats meant by easeful death: a young lad taking the air next to his own grave.

Mr Mehra had the memorial constructed in China, based on his sketches. It was shipped over in parts and rebuilt on site. He was hands-on throughout: pouring concrete, driving the lorry, overseeing every tiny detail. He says he is not a fanatical person, but it is clear that the project required a certain obsessive focus. 'The whole of that time is blank,' he said. 'Even though I remember it, I don't remember it. It was dark, it was morbid, it was hard, but this part' – the building of the memorial – 'was easy.' He felt some force driving the work.

When Medi died, Mr Mehra visited the grave every day, all day, for four years. 'I just didn't want to do anything else. The business, everything, I just couldn't deal with it. When I left this place, I would shake and want to come back.'

Was it, I asked, a kind of addiction?

'I don't know. My boy had gone and I knew that. It wasn't that I didn't want to leave him here on his own; *I* didn't want to be on my own.'

Medi Oliver Mehra seems to have been an old soul, at ease in adult company. 'From the day he was born, he wasn't a baby,' Mr Mehra recalled. 'He was a friend, rather than a son, to me and his mum.'

He was bright and caring. Took pleasure in helping others. He spoke English and Farsi, loved football, played Macbeth in the school play three months before his passing. His funeral was held in St James's Roman Catholic Church, Marylebone. It was a place of worship he had liked to visit; the family would go there to light candles. Although brought up as a Muslim, he had been taught that God was God, and that there was little difference between church, synagogue and mosque. That is why his memorial reflects different faiths and cultures. Medi's mother does not visit the place, Mr Mehra explained; she finds it upsetting. She honoured his memory in a different way, engaging with her son's school friends, and building a pipeline to bring water to 18,000 people in Ethiopia. 'The enormity of what has been built was my husband's initiative,' she told me. 'I think the beauty eases the pain.'

Mr Mehra's idea for the memorial was that it should attract others. It should be a place to work through one's problems. It is very common, he explained, to find people sitting on one of the stone benches amid the scent of flowers; people who have no connection with the family, but who are drawn to the place as a shelter in every sense. Just the week before, he met a man whose marriage had failed and who was not allowed to see his child. Together, they talked it through.

He himself no longer visits as much. He still comes every day, but perhaps only for an hour or two at a time. Something changed. Medi's bedroom had been kept exactly as it was. 'Then two years ago, about five in the morning, the alarm went off and smoke was coming out of his room. It was burned to absolutely nothing. It began beneath his bed, but the fire brigade could not find anything that had caused the fire.' Mr Mehra took this as a sign: 'He was telling me not to be here.'

The fire felt like the end of something. Soon there was a new beginning. 'We had a little boy. He is now fifteen months.' It is not quite true to say that the loss no longer hurts, but the sense of nothingness, of no purpose, no future has passed. 'The birth of Ollie brought an opportunity to see the world through a child's eyes once more, and learn alongside him to find beauty, life and hope, and to create new dreams.'

And what of his old dream? His vision of the memorial to his lost child? Mr Mehra's relationship with what he has created is ambivalent. He feels no regret about building on such a scale; feels, indeed, that it was out of his hands, fated. Yet there is a love/hate aspect to it all. 'Sometimes I wish this place didn't exist.' It only does so because his son died.

We talked about time; the way that a memorial like this carries the story of someone's past far into the future. 'I wanted something to last,' he said. 'Long after I've gone.' He was very familiar with Kensal Green and had seen how the Victorian monuments had aged, some not so well. He had seen the broken glass, the worn stone. He felt okay about that. After his own death, even if Medi's Island was not maintained, if the roses withered and the tent rotted, even if the interior all went back to grass, it could continue to be a place where people could come and sit and think. Those stone angels would still stand guard.

'Would you mind if I take your picture?' I asked.

He said no problem, and sat next to his boy. Next to his bronze likeness, that is; leaning on his shoulder, right leg pressed against the prayer beads strung around Medi's left arm. It was a sad sight, and strange. It spoke of closeness and distance. Here was love. Here was death. A father unfathered. The cosmic unfairness of that.

Why, though, did he want there to be a statue of his son?

'I don't know,' he replied. 'Some things you can't explain, even to yourself.'

CHERUBS

On one of those bright, cold Edinburgh days when the sky is by Yves Klein and the skyline, as ever, by Mervyn Peake, there is no better way to spend one's time than a turn in the city's graveyards.

But which? It can be a tricky choice. St Cuthbert's, where Agatha Christie was married and Thomas De Quincey is buried? Canongate, where the poet Robert Fergusson, who died penniless in Bedlam at twenty-three, lies beneath a stone paid for by Robert Burns? No. Fascinating though these places are, I would always choose to walk up the cobbled lane off Candlemaker Row and pass beneath the arch of elegant letters which spell out, in black iron, a single word: Greyfriars.

This is a kirkyard, to use the Scots word, with some life in it. Its atmosphere and appearance – a sort of luxuriant gothic – have long made it a popular spot to pass an idle hour. A set of portraits taken between 1843 and 1847 by the photography pioneers David Octavius Hill and Robert Adamson show Edinburgh's middle class at play: men in tailcoats, women in shawls and bonnets, posing by some of the more picturesque monuments. Greyfriars was old even then, the first burials having taken place in 1562, and those leisurely Victorians were drawn here, no doubt, by the same sights which attract modern visitors – the fanciful carvings of dancing skeletons, and cherubs dandling skulls on chubby knees.

As with much of the city, Greyfriars gives the impression of not being quite real, a set for some film as yet unmade. It brings to mind fictional graveyards of the most atmospheric sort: the tilted stones and glowering skies of James Whale's *Frankenstein*; the wind howling across the Kent marshes, giving churchyard trees a gallows creak, in David Lean's *Great Expectations*. A row of large and elaborate memorials are built – like eerie conservatories – into the back of some very old houses which adjoin Greyfriars. The people who live there have their rear aspects partly obscured by these monuments. One kitchen window is hemmed in between two huge vaults, a window box on the sill bright with geraniums – a tomb with a view.

I visited Greyfriars on an overcast morning in November, with Richard Usher, a tour guide. He was fine company: amiably waspish, he was in his thirties but seemed a later vintage, with an old-school manner and an old school tie. He is a member of the family which, in the nineteenth century, made millions in whisky distilling and gifted to Edinburgh the Usher Hall, the city's beautiful domed concert venue, on the steps of which Richard now starts his tours.

Earlier, he had pointed out the grave of John Knox, the religious reformer, who died in 1572 and was buried in the St Giles' burial ground. Alas, Edinburgh's sometimes questionable history of redevelopment is such that one of Scotland's most important historical figures now lies beneath parking bay 23 of the law courts. Unlike Richard III, there are no plans to restore him to some lofty tomb more befitting his status. Knox, at a push, might take comfort from the fact that on the day I visited there was a black F-type Jag parked above him, a suitably stern and funereal car. He might also be pleased that few people pause to observe his indignity. Knox hardly seems to be on the tourist trail at all.

Greyfriars, though, is likely busier than it has ever been, thanks to the Harry Potter tourism boom. J. K. Rowling wrote parts of her novels in the Elephant House café, the rear windows of which overlook the kirkyard. The Elephant House seems always to be busy with Potter pilgrims. Afterwards, some wander among the graves in search of the lair of Thomas Riddell Esquire, after whom it is said Rowling named her character Tom Riddle, the boy who became Voldemort. Thus, a nineteenth-century gentleman, who died in 1806 at the age of seventy-two, is experiencing a curious afterlife at the nexus of tombstone tourism and Pottermania.

The Harry Potter connection may be drawing a new generation of visitors to the kirkyard, but there is a particular story with which Greyfriars will be forever associated, and one needn't spend long in the place to hear about it.

'El pequeño y devoto Bobby . . .' A Spanish tour guide with dark curly hair was standing outside the front of the church, waving her arms with a degree of animation quite beyond native Edinburghers, a people who consider a furrowed brow ostentatious non-verbal communication. She was encircled by a large group of Spaniards, ooh-ing and aah-ing as the story unfolded: '. . . *durante catorce años durmió fielmente en la fría piedra de la tumba de su maestro . . .*' At this, there was a little gasp of admiration, and then, as she reached the climax – *'El perro más amado y célebrado de Escocia!'* – spontaneous applause.

The most famous and celebrated dog in Scotland. It could only be Greyfriars Bobby. His story sounded much more exciting in Spanish than it has ever seemed in its rather mawkish English-language telling. Here is how it goes. In 1856, a man called John Gray, aka Auld Jock – sometimes described as a shepherd and at other times a nightwatchman – bought a Skye terrier pup, which he named Bobby. The pair were not together long; Gray died in 1858. Bobby, bereft, spent every night for the next fourteen years sleeping by his master's grave until his own death in 1872. He became, in life, a local celebrity and, in death, a legend, the subject of several books and films. Bobby's grave, marked by a pink granite headstone, is a shrine. Instead of flowers, people leave sticks, the better for the dog to chase. Whimsy, of course, but there is something moving about that little pile of wood.

Given Bobby's devotion to his master, it is surprising that the dog's stone is some distance away from from John Gray's grave. Bobby's memorial stands on its own, directly in front of the church, separate from the rest of kirkyard. 'When Bobby died, the minister at that time would not allow the dog to be buried alongside John Gray,' Richard Usher explained. 'He said that it would be sacrilegious for a dog's body to be buried beside humans.'

Two women, listening in, weren't having this.

'*What?* What a jerk!' said the younger.

Usher smiled at this outburst. He'd heard it all before. 'The minister,' he replied with an air of mild irony, 'spoke on behalf of our Lord.'

'Listen,' said the young woman. 'The Lord *loves* dogs.'

Her name, she told me, is Adeana Calloway. She is an actress and model, and the owner of two poodles, Chester and Oliver, who were back home in Cambridge while she visited Edinburgh with her mother, Jayne, a professional medium.

'Not to interrupt your talk,' said Jayne, 'but where is the grave that's supposed to have the poltergeist attached to it?'

Usher, a sceptic on matters occult, waved a dismissive hand. 'Oh, it's that big mausoleum over there.'

Adeana and Jayne wandered off, ghostwards. They stopped outside the tomb of Sir George Mackenzie, a former Lord Advocate known as Bloody Mackenzie for his violent religious persecutions. The seventeenth-century mausoleum, which resembles a malevolent pepper pot, is reputed to be the most haunted place in Edinburgh; a great many people have reported unpleasant experiences in the vicinity.

'There have been four hundred and forty documentations of people being scratched and bitten here,' Jayne said, peering through a small window set into the double doors. She could sense 'bad energy', but was sceptical about the idea that a poltergeist was responsible for the attacks. 'Probably a demon,' she sniffed.

In any case, the Mackenzie haunting held only passing interest. Jayne was here on other business.

'I have come to see if Greyfriars Bobby is still out here, and free him if he is,' she explained. 'Some say they have heard him barking. I'm going to return tonight with some little doggy biscuits.'

Adeana elaborated: 'It would be sad if he is still attaching himself to his owner's body, and doesn't know he has moved on. He's trapped. He deserves to be at peace. So, we're here on Mission: Save Bobby.'

This, I think, is one of the excellent things about graveyards: the encounters one can have with the living. You turn up expecting to admire some interesting memorial carvings and somehow find yourself chatting with two perfectly lovely people who have travelled a few hundred miles with the sole intention of assisting a spectral hound.

One could mock them, of course. A cheap laugh could be had. Better, though, to take one's cue from the tone of these old stones, the words of love carved by careful hands – now bones themselves – into granite and marble so long ago. 'Rest in peace' has become a cliché, but its egalitarian message retains real power, especially at a time when tolerance and compassion seem, across the world, under threat. This is what graveyards can teach us: to extend to the living the kindness and respect we lavish on the dead.

'If he *is* out here,' Jayne said, 'it's time for little Bobby to go to the light.'

*

IT WAS JANUARY, and I was off to meet the man from Valhalla.

Bob Reinhardt, an art teacher, has for almost twenty years spent the school holidays visiting Scotland from his home in the United States, an annual pilgrimage made in order to explore Edinburgh's historic burial grounds. Today, he had promised to show me around the one he loves above all others: Warriston Cemetery, in the north of the city.

It was, perhaps, inevitable that Reinhardt, who is in his mid-sixties with a silver beard and affable manner, would have a taste for graveyards. He grew up in Valhalla, New York, a small town notable for being surrounded by no fewer than six major cemeteries, the best known of which, Kensico, is the last resting place of Billie Burke, who played Glinda, the Good Witch of the North, in *The Wizard of Oz*. Reinhardt cannot quite agree with Glinda's sentiment that 'there's no place like home'. He has discovered, amid the ivy and old stone of Warriston, a sort of spiritual homeland which has cast an unbreakable spell upon him.

'I feel a strange satisfaction coming here,' he said when we met, sweeping an arm around the cemetery with a proprietary air. 'When I'm home in Philadelphia, I close my eyes and I can see every bit of this place.'

The January sun was low and strong, melting the frost from the grass; yet, in the cold shade of crosses and obelisks, ice persisted unthawed in long streaks of white – bridal trains flowing behind stone-faced brides. Frost gleamed on fallen headstones, turning mossy memorials into illuminated manuscripts. Ladybirds, I shuddered to notice, were wintering in the eyes, nostrils and puckered lips of a fat stone cherub, part of a memorial to two infants – one called Janet, the other, a boy, unbaptised – who died in the 1890s.

Warriston opened in 1843, designed by the architect David Cousin, who also created Edinburgh's Dean, Newington,

Rosebank and Dalry cemeteries. It is a fourteen-acre site containing tens of thousands of graves and surrounded by a boundary wall which rather hides it from the street. To those few contemporary visitors who do venture inside, it will appear old-world and overgrown, but in its day it epitomised the modern way of death. It was a response to problems posed by Greyfriars and the city's other ancient burial grounds.

Something about Greyfriars which had struck me as remarkable, in a macabre sort of way, were the two remaining mortsafes: iron cages fitted above graves in order to deter body snatchers – or resurrectionists – intent on stealing corpses to supply the medical school. The 1832 Anatomy Act, which allowed licensed anatomists legal access to unclaimed corpses and to bodies donated to medical science, was intended to put an end to body-snatching; however, public fear of such defilement did not disappear overnight.

In Warriston, prospective purchasers of lairs were assured that they and their loved ones would not be disturbed. Bodies were to be buried at a standard depth – six feet – which would discourage human predators and prevent remains rising to the surface, where they might threaten the health and trouble the mind of the populace. It was often difficult, in chaotic old kirkyards, for new graves to be dug without disturbing previous burials, even those which had not been in the ground very long, and it was not uncommon for bones and body parts to be exposed. Warriston offered a guarantee: 'no remains of humanity will at any time unpleasantly meet the human eye'.

Prints from when Warriston was new show men in top hats and ladies in bonnets, holding parasols, strolling within its grounds and admiring the view of Edinburgh Castle. Jules Verne, visiting the city in 1859, found it an agreeable spot. 'In such a cemetery,' he wrote, 'death does not take on the funereal gloom of France's mausoleums and truncated columns; the tombs are like charming cottages where life flows past, leisurely and pleasant.'

His own tomb, in Amiens, features a sculpture of the author, in a death-shroud, bursting free of the grave. The French writer, should he ever rise up for real, would doubtless be saddened to see what became of Warriston.

In private ownership, it was neglected and allowed to decay, so that by the 1970s, '80s and '90s many of its stones were vandalised, knocked over, and swamped by ivy. The thick vegetation and lack of visitors made it an ideal spot for drug deals and cruising, and, as it became known for these activities, fewer and fewer people chose to set foot inside. It was even known for police to search there for murderers on the run. Little wonder that in *The Hanging Garden*, a novel by Ian Rankin, a man is found lynched in the cemetery. It became, in short, a no-go area for everyone except those for whom no-go areas are exactly where they want to go. In 1994, a compulsory purchase order by the council brought the cemetery into public ownership, but it remained in an awful state: a lawless jungle, Edinburgh's id.

It was this dismal scene which had greeted Bob Reinhardt on that first day, in 2002, when he discovered the place. He was in Edinburgh helping to run a school exchange programme. Crossing the old railway bridge that divides the cemetery, he happened to look down, and found himself intrigued enough to take a walk inside.

'I was very excited, but a little cautious,' he told me. 'What you're seeing now is not what I saw.' The weeds were, he estimated, six to eight feet high, and the narrow paths were more like tracks. It felt like walking through a tunnel. 'You could not see ten feet in front of your face.' Trees had grown up where none had been planned, hiding stones from view and even pushing them over. Occasionally, though, he would catch glimpses of what must have been, at one time, magnificent headstones. Eminent Victorians, their profiles rendered on bronze reliefs, would appear to be peering through the foliage. 'And that struggle between Mother Nature and the man-made sculptural pieces was really interesting. So I started taking pictures.'

He has not stopped since. Reinhardt has taken around 60,000 photographs of Warriston and other Edinburgh burial grounds. It has become an obsession. He has exhibited his work at the city's Central Library and his pictures were used by the Royal Commission of Ancient and Historical Monuments of Scotland, now part of Historic Environment Scotland, as a way of documenting the cemeteries. Should a headstone fall, should a stone angel be smashed by stoned devils, Reinhardt's photographs provide a record.

As we walked around, he took pictures on his phone. Leaf-litter obscuring names and dates; fallen stones, draped in moss. The artist in him is drawn to decay, but it saddens that part of him which sees Warriston as a historic resource and a place where people can come and seek out their ancestors. He wishes he had the strength to turn over all those stones which are lying flat on their faces. Here and there, dozens of old headstones were stacked together like dominoes. Unstable stones are often brought down in old cemeteries in case one should fall and kill a child, as happened in Glasgow in 2015.

Warriston is pretty, in its own way. In the absence of people, nature has flourished. A heron, more building than bird, a humpback bridge in flight, lifted from the Water of Leith – the river which runs along one side of the cemetery.

A few years ago, one Fourth of July, Reinhardt formed the Friends of Warriston Cemetery, a group dedicated to fighting back against the ivy and invasive weeds. Their sworn foes are Japanese knotweed and Himalayan balsam. They meet each Tuesday and Saturday with forks and shears. They have picked up tonnes of bottles and beer cans, planted thousands of daffodils. It is a huge area to cover for only a few volunteers, but, helped by the council, they have made an enormous difference. Paths have been re-established and a great many memorials rediscovered. The place has been opened up and is now popular with dog-walkers, joggers and all who appreciate elegiac beauty. It is not a miracle. It has taken sweat, blisters and an endless willingness to engage with bureaucracy.

'We make real discoveries,' Reinhardt said. 'Someone will shout, "Wow, look what I found!" and we all rush over and read who it is. And we've brought that person back. It's a treasure hunt.'

CHERUBS

He pointed out several memorials, now splendidly visible, which had been entirely hidden by ivy. Many had been crowned by thick green caps as deep as a man's arm; the volunteers, clipping stems, lifted these off like bells. Under one such cap they found Christ. The statue had once stood on a pedestal as part of a headstone. Now, he stands at the side of a tree, gazing up at its trunk, the arms of his cross broken, giving him the appearance of carrying a boombox. He is oddly comedic but does not lack dignity.

'We found him right there behind the tree, completely covered with ivy, two years ago,' Reinhardt explained. 'I swear every time I come here he's moved, like, four or five inches towards his pedestal. I'll often contact some of the other Friends and ask: "How far did Jesus get?"' He shook his head. 'I really wish we could put him back up there. Where he is just now, it's too easy for some wisecracker to come and push him over.'

There is still a huge amount of work to be done. The volunteers have no desire to bring the cemetery back to how it would have looked originally; even if such a thing could be done, the decay, like wrinkles on a face, is part of its charm. They would, however, like to uncover all the stones and make them accessible, a job which will take many years, not least because every spring and summer the greenery starts growing again.

I was curious as to why Reinhardt bothers. This is not his city. It's not even his country. Yet he has spent an enormous amount of time and probably money flying back and forth across the Atlantic. Why does he care?

'This place at one time was a beautiful work of art,' he replied. 'It had meaning. It was a reflective place. And it was just shut down and neglected. If we have the power and capacity to change that then we should.

'Cemeteries are about the eternal, so isn't it nice that we have reopened all these stones? It's about giving another voice to these people who have been forgotten. Their memories are coming back. All of a sudden, a few hundred years later, here they are again. I love that we're doing that. It's kind of cool.'

This was, perhaps, an indelicate question, but, having spent a few hours wandering around the cemetery with Reinhardt, it didn't feel inappropriate to ask: would he like to be buried here one day?

'I'd love for that to happen. Legally, I don't think it's possible. This is a closed cemetery. There are still burials, but only when families who already have graves reopen their plots.

'But . . .' he laughed, '. . . *if* my ashes just *happened* to fall out, and *if* the wind *happened* to carry them over to Section O, the middle section, not that I'm specific, then that would be good.'

The difficulty would be in getting his ashes from the United States to Scotland. 'But I've got colleagues who've said they'll help.'

'Wow,' I laughed, 'you've got it all planned.'

Reinhardt chuckled. 'Yeah, it's kind of in my will.'

A sudden bang disturbed the peace, causing crows to rise and circle. It was the one o'clock gun, Edinburgh's trusty timekeeper, which has been fired from the castle ramparts for almost as long as there have been graves here. Loud enough to wake the dead, one might say, but there was no sign of that. Alexander Smith, the poet and essayist, slept on beneath his great Celtic cross as he had since typhoid finished him off at the age of thirty-seven in 1867. Smith's friend, the landscape painter Horatio McCulloch, died a few months later; his grave, too, is marked by a Celtic cross, not quite so grand, but distinguished by a fine carving of his pet Skye terrier. This dog, I would like to think, knew Greyfriars Bobby, a brother of the same litter.

It was not to the resting place of either of these grand men of Scottish culture that Reinhardt led me last. He had a humbler grave in mind: 'Here she is! This is Nancy. This was one of the first things I found, and I felt there was an incredible innocence to it.'

The grave was that of Annie Paton Spence, known – the stone says – as Nancy, who died on 25 January 1933, at the age of three years and three months. She is buried beside a man and a woman, William and Margaret, whom I assume were her parents. They had to live for a long time without their little girl, dying in 1969 and 1975 respectively. One imagines them both coming to this spot, tending the grave, laying down roses and a few unspoken words, until that day when the mother had to start making the visits alone. Did anyone come here after Margaret's death? Perhaps not. A grave is like a flower in bloom. It has a season, a bright moment, beyond which visitors are no longer drawn.

This grave was topped by a small stone figure, a girl in a gown, eyes closed, hands clasped in prayer. Over her right shoulder, an arc of stone feathers, frozen mid-flutter. One might regard such a memorial as cheap sentiment, a Disney notion of death. I prefer to think that it was a comfort to the parents. There was a very similar stone on the grave of my own little brother, whom we lost at fourteen months. Nancy's parents, like mine, will have wanted to do their best for their child, to give her, as a last gift, something pretty.

I didn't say any of that to Bob Reinhardt. How could I? Nancy's headstone, for him, is symbolic of this whole cemetery: 'A cherub with a missing wing kind of represents what this place feels like.'

Damaged, he meant, but still beautiful.

LILIES

BELFAST, EASTER SUNDAY. It was high noon and the crowds had gathered for the parade.

Or, rather, parades. To avoid internecine tension and the possibility of violence, three separate republican marches were setting off at different times from different junctions on the Falls Road. In each case, the destination was the same: Milltown Cemetery, where the fallen would be honoured with speeches and silence, bowed heads and unbowed hearts. 'Families of the patriot dead,' a voice boomed from speakers, 'will you please assemble at Beechmount Avenue, thank you.'

These annual processions commemorate the Easter Rising of 1916, the armed rebellion aimed at overthrowing British rule. They honour, too, the so-called 'patriot dead', which includes not only the rebels of 1916 but also members of paramilitary groups who would more commonly be described as terrorists. Beechmount Avenue is known as RPG Avenue (there is a little home-made sign on the wall) after the rocket-propelled grenades which were often fired from the corner, by members of the Provisional IRA, at British army armoured vehicles during the 1980s.

If anyone was under the consoling illusion, however, that Ireland's political violence was over, that the deaths being remembered belonged to a dark history now past, the events of three nights before – Holy Thursday – would have provided a stinging corrective. A police search for firearms and explosives in homes on Derry's Creggan estate had led to a riot. Petrol bombs were thrown, vehicles hijacked and burned, and at 11 p.m. a masked gunman had opened fire on police lines. Lyra McKee, a young journalist observing the unrest, was shot. She was taken to Altnagelvin Hospital, where, anointed by a priest, she died. The New IRA, a dissident republican group, admitted responsibility. Here was yet another life lost before it had properly begun. All those callow ghosts. The Troubles too often recall Pozzo's bleak line in *Waiting for Godot*: 'They give birth astride of a grave, the light gleams an instant, then it's night once more.'

This was the hottest Easter weekend on record. The weather made for a festive atmosphere, more feast than wake. Sleeves were rolled up, displaying tattoos of Christ crucified, Che Guevara risen. Sunshine gleamed on the golden badge – in the form of an AK47 – pinned to the uniform of a member of one of the flute bands. From the dark entrance of the Beehive bar, a song came keening out: *Oh, do not stand at my grave and weep . . .*

'The Ballad of Mairéad Farrell' is a lament for an IRA member shot dead by the SAS in Gibraltar, in 1988, at the age of thirty-one, while planning a car bomb intended to explode during a parade of British soldiers. She, too, is buried in Milltown. So common a destination has it been for young paramilitaries that Anna Burns, in her novel *Milkman*, refers to it not by name but, sighingly, as 'the usual place'. Some of the Milltown dead are children killed in crossfire. Others died for their cause, or because they opposed one held dear by others. The inscriptions burn with anger and white-hot pride: 'Slain by apartheid guns in the hands of a British death squad'; 'He who dies for Ireland lives'. One phrase is so common it is almost the Milltown mantra: Murdered For His Faith; Murdered For His Faith; Murdered For His Faith.

On Beechmount Avenue, the families were gathering. They held photographs and lilies. Some names on the picture frames were familiar, and called to mind old news reports. This man starved himself to death in prison. This teenager died when the bomb he was transporting went off prematurely. These women, shot dead on the back seat of a family car, were sisters.

For me, having grown up on the UK mainland, following the Troubles through the lens of the BBC, there was something bewildering, even unsettling, about seeing armed rebels celebrated and mourned. What unsettles is the seduction. There is a dark romance to these ideas of sacrifice and martyrdom. They colour Belfast like some hidden pigment just outside the visible spectrum. It is in those murals – loyalist and republican – which brighten the gable ends of houses. It makes red redder, black blacker. It is in every drop of blood spilled on these streets.

Irish republicanism has been described as a death-cult, and whether or not that is fair, it is certain that the dead help keep the movement alive, and have done for a long time. In 1915, at the Dublin funeral of Jeremiah O'Donovan Rossa, a member of the Irish Republican Brotherhood, better known as the Fenians, the revolutionary leader Patrick Pearse gave a famous oration in which he argued: 'Life springs from death; and from the graves of patriot men and women spring living nations.' The speech is regarded as a key event on the road to the Easter Rising, galvanising support for armed rebellion. Pearse ended with an attack on the British state: 'They think they have foreseen everything, think they have provided against everything; but the fools, the fools, the fools! They have left us our Fenian dead, and while Ireland holds these graves, Ireland unfree will never be at peace.'

Those words are carved into granite at one end of the republican plot in Milltown Cemetery. This area, enclosed within a low wall, is the destination of the largest of the Easter parades and is regarded by some as a sacred site. The plot holds the remains of seventy-seven republicans, most of them members of the Provisional IRA, who were killed during 'active service' – in other words, while fighting the Brits with bomb or gun or by other means. Bobby Sands is one of three hunger strikers who died in the Maze prison in 1981 and are buried here. Within the movement and among those sympathetic to it, Sands is a star, icon, idol. His smiling, handsome face beams down from murals, out from T-shirts. Stalls on the Falls Road sell Bobby Sands photos and scarves.

Here in Milltown, he is not just admired but venerated. On my first visit to the cemetery, I had seen a young woman spot his grave – a simple black marble slab – and let out a noise somewhere between a groan of pleasure and a sob of pain. She had crossed herself then knelt to pray. Rising, she turned to her mother. 'Heartbreaking, isn't it, maw?' she said in a Glasgow accent. 'Those boys, they were so brave.' A few steps away, at the grave of another IRA volunteer, a little boy held his father's hand. 'Did you know him, Daddy?'

'I did, son.'

Here was the passing of something from one generation to the next. A torch? A disease? Pick your metaphor, choose your side.

Since 1869, almost 200,000 people have been buried in Milltown; among that multitude, just one Protestant. It is a striking place, rich in Catholic iconography. Entering through a grand sandstone arch carved with the words *Et expectio resurrectionem mortuorem et vitam venture saeculi* ('And I await the resurrection of the dead and the life of the world to come'), the visitor soon passes the wonderful marble monument above the grave of John Burke, a shipping magnate who died in 1922. It shows Our Lady and Mary Magdalene lamenting the Crucifixion. The dirt of almost a century has turned Christ and his mother a sooty grey, but Mary Magdalene has somehow remained white and pure. These figures are everywhere in Milltown, in renderings which veer from profund to kitsch. On one of the newer graves, someone had placed a statuette of the Virgin next to a bar of Fry's Chocolate Cream.

I had come to Milltown's republican plot on the day before the parades to speak with Joe Austin. He is chair of the National Graves Association, Belfast, the organisation which cares for the graves and monuments of those, including members of the IRA, who have died in the cause. Austin, who is sixty-seven, with round spectacles and an air of quiet authority, is a veteran republican activist and has been a member of Sinn Féin for, he told me, almost fifty years.

We sat on a granite bench on which were painted some words of Mairéad Farrell: 'I am a volunteer in the Irish Republican Army and a political prisoner in Armagh jail. I am prepared to fight to the death if necessary.' Her grave was just a few feet away.

It is sometimes said that a cemetery can tell the story of a city. For Austin, Milltown tells the story of a struggle. 'For republicans, the honouring of the dead is very, very important,' he had explained. They are, as he sees it, the cornerstone of the cause. He quoted Pearse's line about the Fenian dead, then added: 'Graveyards are an aspirational location. They reflect the memory of those who died, but they also reflect why they died, what they died *for*.

'The people buried here are not just names for us. There's seventy-seven buried in this particular plot; I would know every one of them. I would know their families. I would know the circumstances in which they died. These are people who I have come through struggle with.'

The Gibraltar Three – Mairéad Farrell, Sean Savage and Dan McCann – are buried together. 'Executed by SAS,' says a marker, '6th March 1988.' The deaths were controversial.

Although their intentions were murderous, they were unarmed when they were shot dead.

Farrell and McCann were killed on Winston Churchill Avenue, Savage around 150 yards away. Soldiers had kept them under observation from amid the tombstones of Trafalgar Cemetery. Farrell, the eldest of the three at thirty-one, died from shots fired at close range. These entered her back, exited her chest, and, according to the pathologist who performed the autopsy, 'pulped her heart and liver'. Father Raymond Murray, the priest who conducted Farrell's requiem mass in Belfast, said in his eulogy that she had 'a violent death like Jesus'. A headline in *The Sun* offered a counterpoint: 'WHY THE DOGS HAD TO DIE'.

In an atmosphere of huge tension and mutual suspicion, Joe Austin flew out to Gibraltar and – no easy task – brought the bodies back for burial. During the flight back to Dublin, alone in the back of the plane with the coffins, he spoke ceaselessly to the dead. 'I was exhausted,' he recalled when I asked about this. 'I was very emotional, I had achieved what I set out to do, despite all the difficulties, and so my conversation was, "We're going home. I'm bringing you home." It was a conversation that lasted for hours. There was defiance in it as well. I'm an Irish republican and these were people who had just been executed who were personal friends of mine, as well as comrades.'

What you have to understand, Austin insisted, is not only how Farrell, Savage and McCann died, but how they lived. 'They lived as active, committed, *accomplished* IRA volunteers. I'm not disguising the fact. They knew what they were doing, they knew how to do what they were doing, and they done it.'

Would they be seen, then, as fallen heroes? 'Everybody who lies in these plots is a fallen hero to the community they come from . . . There's no equivocation about it. That's what they are.'

Austin had told me that the republican plots in Milltown are, for those who share that political outlook, akin to the British military cemeteries in Flanders. Asked whether the huge death toll of the Troubles was worth it, he replied, 'Well, that's like asking someone who was involved in the D-Day landing if it was worth it.'

Many would find those comparisons repulsive. Similarly, most people outside West Belfast – and sympathetic communities in Glasgow and elsewhere – would probably find it hard to accept the description of IRA members as heroes.

'I understand that,' he nodded. 'As a republican, you have to live with the fact that you are responsible for hurt and pain and death, as well as being on the receiving end. Anybody who doesn't take the responsibility for that, and the part they played in that, do themselves and the cause a disservice. My life, part of it, has been to be fully committed to a struggle that hurt people, that killed people, that took their lives. Republicans should not look for exemption from that. But equally the prospectus that only republicans hurt people, only republicans took lives, only republicans done the unpleasant things is, in many ways, a disservice to those who died.

'There's a well-worn phrase: one man's freedom fighter is another man's terrorist. Well, one man's hero is another man's killer.'

The first burials in the republican plot took place in the summer of 1972 and the last in 1996. These might be regarded as warriors' graves. To be laid to rest there, it is necessary to have died as a result of some form of violence in the cause, whether that be in a shoot-out or through the slow suicide of hunger strike. The dead lie on either side of a central path around forty feet long. No funerals have taken place since the Good Friday Agreement established an imperfect peace. The flowers and flags and headstones, at a certain point, run out. 'Our greatest ambition,' Austin said, 'is that no one else is ever buried here.'

Nevertheless, the space for future burials remains; unchancy soil for a bitter crop. It is perhaps the most toxic fifteen feet of land in the whole of Northern Ireland: gunmen's graves as yet unfilled.

*

The oldest burial ground in Belfast, Friar's Bush, is hidden behind a high wall and open only by appointment. It is a peaceful two acres, a little overgrown, with a number of interesting stones. A great carved harp wreathed in shamrocks marks the grave of Kevin T. Buggy, who died in 1843, one of several prominent newspapermen buried here. Not far away is the ivy-draped wall tomb of Bernard Hughes, known as Barney, the baking magnate and philanthropist, creator of the much-loved Belfast bap. He died in 1878.

You could walk along Stranmills Road and never know Friar's Bush was here. There are very few visitors. An unofficial tour guide, Gerry Ward, lives in the gothic gate lodge, which is known as the coffin arch. He seems glad on behalf of his neighbours, the dead, on the rare occasion when someone shows an interest. Many of the stones are so eroded their inscriptions cannot be read, and that is how this graveyard, as a whole, feels – a place being worn away from memory, scoured blank by time.

Friar's Bush first appears in the historic record in 1570, but is likely much older. This is where Belfast's Catholics were buried before Milltown was built. Indeed, the whole reason for Milltown's existence was because Friar's Bush became full to overflowing. The population of the city had grown from 70,447 in 1841 to 121,602 by 1871. As in life, so in death. A plaque records that eight hundred victims of the Irish Famine are buried in Friar's Bush, within a weed-choked patch of ground, near the entrance. This area is known as 'Plaguey Hill' because it also served as a cholera pit.

Although Friar's Bush is on a busy road, and right next to the Ulster Museum, this was once countryside, part of the old Cromac Wood. A painting of 1782 shows an Irish Volunteer – a militiaman in scarlet uniform – taking his ease in the graveyard, his rifle on the ground beside him, with Georgian Belfast in the distance beyond the fields.

The graveyard's secluded location made it suitable for the secret celebration of mass during the Penal Era of the late seventeenth and eighteenth centuries, when Catholics were discriminated against and persecuted. A little way into the graveyard, at the end of a grassy track known as the Paupers' Path, is the old hawthorn from which this place gets its name. According to one version of the story, at this spot a monk – a white-haired old man – was wont to say mass, having rowed across the River Lagan in his little boat, or *curach*. One Sunday in winter, a day of heavy snow, he was shot through the heart just as he was about to give the last blessing. He fell at the altar, an oak table, and was buried where he lay. The ground, when I visited, was carpeted with tiny flowers – white as a blizzard, white as hair.

It is unlikely that Friar's Bush was used as a mass station after 1769 as, in that year, a house was found for clandestine worship. However, the graveyard remained a target of anti-Catholic bigotry. Funerals were heckled, and a wooden Celtic cross, erected inside the gates, was often attacked and defaced. On one occasion, in 1864, the caretaker saw off a mob with a shotgun.

This, though, was in the graveyard's final years. It had become known as an unhealthy, unpleasant place. An 1863 report in the *Belfast News Letter* linked overcrowding to the spread of fever: 'The dead have been huddled indecently into reeking graves. They have been denied the cheap covering of a little earth, and the natural consequences follow. The living neglect the dead, and the dead come back in the form of noxious vapours and foul disease to plague, and it may be, destroy the living.'

In 1869, with the opening of Milltown, Friar's Bush closed. From that point, only families who already had burial rights were allowed to be interred in the graveyard. The painter Paul Henry, who grew up in the area, recalled in his memoir *Further Reminiscences* that, by the 1880s, it was a rarity to see a funeral, although every now and then the gates would creak open to admit mourners. He found the place both fascinating and repellent, recalling his childhood impressions with a Dickensian eye.

'I often saw,' he wrote, 'the old caretaker of the burial ground, a hunchback with a face deeply marked with small-pox, and his son, a morose man with scowling face and high cheekbones. I never saw a woman in the neighbourhood who might be wife or daughter, and I imagined that these two men lived alone in the tiny house which stood beside a little dark door. Sometimes on a dark night I would hear the rusty old gate clanging in the wind but would see not one going in or out. And after night fall, when no light shone from the tiny window, it was the house of the dead.'

In response to the poor condition of the graveyards, including Friar's Bush, the corporation built a garden cemetery, Belfast City, on the Falls Road. Designed by the surveyor and landscape gardener William Gay, its paths are laid out in a shape of a bell, perhaps a pun on the city's name, and since 1869 it has tolled for more than a quarter of a million citizens.

On the morning of my visit, City Cemetery was pleasantly warm. Rats scurried through the forget-me-nots and a police helicopter hovered above the trees. A woman sat with her back against the headstone of her mother and sister, taking in the sun. She used to play in the cemetery as a child, she explained, back in the sixties and seventies, and now here she was, visiting the grave of her playmate and the woman who called them in for tea.

I was there with Tom Hartley. A former Lord Mayor, Hartley is an authority on Belfast's graveyards, and has written books on Milltown, City and Balmoral (the Presbyterian burial ground). As Hartley is a Catholic, his family, including his parents and younger brother, are buried in Milltown. For a long time, City did not seem the place for him. It was understood, among the kids of his 1950s neighbourhood, that the cemetery was where the devil lurked. Children would not tarry on their way to the Falls Park. 'We'd get to the gate there and all run like hell . . .' More recently, however, he has come to appreciate City for its stories and the beauty of its stones. 'This is my cemetery and my history, too,' he said. 'In all its complexity, this is me. I feel a very strong connection with this place.' Indeed, he will be buried there himself, when his time comes, at the top of the cemetery, 'in the shadow of the mountain', with a grand view of the hills to the north-west where, at hard moments in his life, he has taken comfort in walking alone.

Hartley, who is seventy-four, has an interesting take on death and the rituals we have developed to formalise it. 'For tens of thousands of years, human beings have been burying our dead. We are part of an experience that is ancient, and it's so obvious that we fail to see it.' We have come to regard burial and funerals as mundane, he believes; we don't appreciate the importance of these acts to our civilisation. 'Somewhere, tens of thousands of years ago, somebody, some-where decided they would bury their dead and, in doing that, they unfolded a whole series of human changes.' Our ideas of history and art, our sense of place, even the development of emotions such as grief have emerged, he feels, from how we treat our dead.

His thinking on all of this was formed, I suspect, when he was still a boy, not yet five. When someone in the neigh-bourhood died, word would go around. It would be observed that a black bow had been tied on the front door, and this was a sign of a wake house. Hartley and his pals would gather outside until one of them worked up the courage to knock. 'Missus,' they would ask, 'can we see the dead?' Invited in, they would troop up the stairs. The corpse would be laid out on the bed. He remembers, with a child's-eye view, that you would see the feet first.

There was a sense of stopped clocks, stilled air. 'The room would be heavy with that aroma of candles.' A circle of children around the bed, still so near the beginning of their lives, witnesses to the end. A gabbled prayer, the sign of the cross, and then back outside to the streets. They weren't being morbid. This was common. 'It was a very important mechanism in the community. Even though you might be frightened, and pushed up the stairs by the ten kids behind, you saw a dead person. I think it's fundamental to coming to terms with the idea that some day you die.'

We hadn't walked far through City when we came to a broad grassy track sloping downhill towards the Falls Road. 'This looks like a path, but is in fact the site of an underground wall,' Hartley said. 'You know the story?' It was around nine feet deep, he explained, and had been built at the time of the cemetery's construction. It's still there. If we were to dig down, we'd see it. In 1869, Bishop Patrick Dorrian had negotiated with Belfast Corporation that the city's Catholic population should have their own fifteen-acre section. He would not bless the site unless he had full control over who was to be buried there; unbaptised infants, suicides, someone who had bought a grave as a Catholic but then converted to Protestantism – none of these people could lie in consecrated ground. The wall was intended to maintain the purity of the Catholic area, protecting that soil and those souls from being contaminated, as it were, by the rest of the cemetery.

I found that a depressing thought: the sectarian division that choked Irish lives not loosening with death, but continuing to tighten within the earth's embrace.

Hartley, though, had a positive take. For him, that wall is a bridge. It is a linking device which can be used to tell a tale of Belfast's people as a whole. By telling the story of the wall, he is able to talk about the two communities, Catholic and Protestant, and the burial grounds which serve them.

In the end, you see, the wall was unnecessary. Bishop Dorrian, unable to reach an agreement with the corporation over who had the final say on who could be buried in the Catholic section, used his £4,000 compensation to purchase land nearby and open a cemetery for the sole use of his flock: Milltown.

Between them, for Hartley, what do the two cemeteries represent? 'The very complex, layered and often difficult history of this city. Human lives don't go in parallel lines. In life, there's not them and us.'

What, even in Belfast? 'Anything but.'

Hartley enjoys a complicated yarn. He likes to wade into muddy waters, and never yet found a narrative arc he couldn't sink. Storytelling, for him, is an extreme sport. He will point out the grave of the Reverend David Mitchell – 'Who Entered Into Rest On The 14th Of March, 1914, In His 90th Year' – and a minute later will have made the jump from this cemetery in West Belfast to the battlefields of the American Civil War, where the clergyman's relations fought for the South. He will point out the grave of the Reverend Richard Rutledge Kane, saying, 'He was the senior Orangeman in Belfast and yet he was an Irish speaker. He was one of the sponsors of the Gaelic League.'

To spend a morning walking around this cemetery with Hartley was to make the acquaintance, if briefly, of shipbuilders, tobacco kings, footballers, journalists, gunrunners and those killed by the gun. C. S. Lewis's mother. The man who photographed the *Titanic*. The grave of a woman called Annie, who was born in 1870 and died in 1973, her life spanning *Die Walküre* and *Dark Side of the Moon*.

'You never quite know where a headstone's going to take you,' he said. 'There's so much that you can take from a cemetery, and really what you need is imagination. Sometimes it's the little detail. Look at this here.'

He pointed out a tiny lizard carved into the side of the grand 1913 headstone of George McMullin and his family. How on earth, I asked, did you spot that?

'Ach, you have to notice everything.'

This might well be the taphophile's credo. Notice everything. Regard each stone as a story waiting to be told. Accept that to walk in a cemetery is both a privilege and a lesson in humility. We are here now to read the memorials and walk on, but one day it may be our names with moss growing in the letters. Will anyone find our tales worth the telling? Will anyone, descendant or stranger, sit on our graves in the sun and think with fondness or curiosity about who we were?'

'See this?' Hartley said, laying a hand on a large Celtic cross, intricately carved with birds and animals. 'If ever you're feeling precious, come and touch this stone. This is Irish limestone. The sediment was laid down three hundred million years ago, and you can still see the fossils. See those?' I could. The thought was dizzying. A palaeontologist would regard this gravestone as a mass grave. 'And the design is so beautiful. It's not just a piece of funerary architecture but also a work of art.'

So this is where Hartley comes when he needs some perspective? 'Yes, because it will remind you that we're only here' – he clicked his fingers – 'like that.'

*

THE EASTER PARADE was outside City Cemetery now, working its way up the hill to Milltown beneath bunting in green, white and orange. Some marchers were dressed in the uniforms of 1916 and carried replica rifles. The flute bands were going strong. Earlier, outside the Royal Belfast Hospital for Sick Children, a little girl had come out on to the pavement attached to a drip, banging gleefully on the top of her dialysis machine to the rhythm of the drums.

Pavements on both sides of the Falls Road were packed with onlookers. At the head of the parade was Mary Lou McDonald, the leader of Sinn Féin, bright in emerald green. The marchers passed armoured vehicles and ice-cream vans, and, at the top of Hugo Street, a large poster put up by the political party Saoradh – the organisation often said to reflect New IRA thinking – showing a bloody hand, lying limp, a syringe loose in its grasp. 'Drug dealers not welcome in our communities!' it declared. Next to the poster was a

black plaque commemorating, in gold letters, the death of Pearse Jordan, an IRA member shot dead by police, aged twenty-two, in 1992.

West Belfast has an extraordinary number of these memorials; a through-the-looking-glass version of the blue plaques which signpost the former homes of celebrated Londoners. Instead of famous lives, Belfast's plaques mark infamous deaths. I had seen a lot of them the day before while out walking with Danny Morrison.

A republican activist turned writer, Morrison was director of publicity for Sinn Féin throughout the 1980s. He is well known for a phrase used during a speech at the party's conference in 1981: 'Who here really believes we can win the war through the ballot box? But will anyone here object if, with a ballot box in one hand and the Armalite in the other, we take power in Ireland?' The Armalite was a type of rifle much used by the IRA.

Morrison was in Long Kesh Detention Centre in 1972 and 1973, suspected of IRA membership, his captivity the result of the British government's controversial policy of internment – imprisonment without trial. He is the author of several books, including a memoir, *All the Dead Voices*, which muses upon those he has lost. These include his uncle, Harry White, a senior figure within the IRA who worked for a time as a bomb-making instructor in Dublin, where his students included the teenage Brendan Behan. Another hard loss was his best friend, Jimmy Quigley, who died at the age of eighteen in 1972 while trying to ambush a British army patrol; he is buried in the republican plot in Milltown.

Was Morrison himself ever a member of the IRA? In his youth (he is now well into his sixties) he helped them: selling raffle tickets to raise funds, taking his turn on the street barricades, hiding guns and grenades beneath his bed. Throughout his life, too, he has been a defender of the idea of the armed struggle. But beyond that? It is a question he chooses not to answer.

We had met at the foot of the Divis flats. Fifty-five metres tall, bricks the colour of scabbed blood, the tower block is a landmark in West Belfast. In the rising heat of the morning sun, tricolours and the odd Palestinian flag hung from open windows.

To me it was a sunny morning, summer on the breeze, but to Morrison, as he led the way through the streets, it must have looked something like Bruegel's *The Triumph of Death*: a city of skulls and fire. His intimate acquaintance with the Troubles meant that he remembered the bodies vividly; in the immediacy of his telling, it was as if they lay there still.

Here, on the corner of Linden Street and the Falls Road, in July 1981, his friend Nora McCabe was shot in the head with a plastic bullet fired by a police officer. The last time he had seen her was New Year's Eve; they had linked arms and sung 'Auld Lang Syne'.

There, on Iveagh Drive, in September 1971, seventeen-month-old Angela Gallagher was killed in her pram by a ricocheting bullet – from the gun of an IRA sniper shooting at an army patrol – as her eight-year-old sister wheeled her along to a sweet shop. Morrison had been in his bedroom, writing an essay for his A-levels, when he heard the shot and ran out to see what had happened. He arrived in time to see the child being carried in the arms of a neighbour. Nora McCabe and Angela Gallagher are both buried in Milltown Cemetery.

In the two hours or so I spent with Morrison, the body count kept rising: 'A fifteen-year-old boy in that newsagent over there was shot dead . . . the newsagent on this side of the road was shot dead for selling *An Phoblacht*, the republican news . . . the guy above the barber shop was shot dead by the loyalists . . . a butcher was shot dead in the shop further up . . . young lad, IRA man, shot dead by the RUC here.'

It's astonishing, I said to him, the way he sees the city. Through his eyes, it's just bodies.

'Well, that's the price of struggle. I can't help but view Belfast that way. The dead are always with us, and sometimes more powerful after death than they were in life.'

It is striking the extent to which, in this part of Belfast, martyrdom is built into the very bricks. Those black plaques are everywhere, commemorating members of the IRA and other paramilitary groups, often at the place where they fell; murals depict the fallen as heroic figures; gardens of remembrance soothe the memory of violent ends with well-tended flowers.

What you won't see is the poppy. That symbol of sacrifice and remembrance, ubiquitous – almost sacred – in England, is absent from West Belfast. As we walked, Morrison had pointed out where British soldiers had been killed. He did so without any sense of triumph or relish, or sorrow or regret. They were just another part of his necrology. It seems to me, an outsider, a pity that the deaths of British soldiers are invisible. No plaques for them. No golden letters to mark where their blood was spilled, where lives leaked away. This seems, if nothing else, poor storytelling. In the fifty years between 1969 and 2019, there were approximately 3,600 deaths in the Troubles; according to the Ministry of Defence, more than 1,400 members of the UK armed forces were among the dead. For those deaths not to be marked on the walls of Belfast means that the narrative is incomplete. The streets are like a book with every third page ripped out.

Is there no chance, I had asked Morrison, of those soldiers being memorialised here in some way? He shook his head. It was all still too raw and recent and personal; the history of the Troubles is disputed territory, heavily mined with grudges. 'You could commemorate a soldier who had maybe killed your brother.'

And then he said the one thing which, during our time together, truly gave me pause. The families of English soldiers, he seemed to suggest, are almost blasé about losing their sons overseas. What he meant was that the long history of Empire has normalised the idea of death in service; Johnny joins up and is killed in India or Cyprus or Belfast, and that's the end of it. 'Well, that's not the end of it for us,' he said. 'Our dead are precious.' I was surprised by this. Morrison is a very intelligent and reflective person, yet here he seemed unable to see the world through the eyes of others. No side of any war has a monopoly on tears.

We had, by this time, arrived in Milltown. Morrison was a witness to the most infamous episode in the cemetery's history. It was 16 March 1988, the day of the funeral of the Gibraltar Three. Mairéad Farrell's coffin had been the first to be lowered into the grave in the republican plot, and bearers were about to lower Dan McCann's, when the ceremony was attacked by the loyalist paramilitary Michael Stone, using hand grenades and a pistol. Three people died and sixty were wounded. Stone claimed to have been targeting the republican leadership. As he later stated in a memoir, 'I had three men in my sights and I knew that, if everything went according to my detailed plans, then this time tomorrow Gerry Adams, Martin McGuinness and Danny Morrison would be dead.'

But Morrison was not by the grave when Stone attacked. He was standing beside the hearses. 'Next thing,' he recalled, 'an explosion. Dirt comes flying over our faces and we dive down underneath the cars. I was convinced we were being mortar attacked from a loyalist area across the motorway. There was a couple of explosions, and screaming, and then shooting.'

News footage shows the chaos and terror of the scene. Grenades throw up clouds of graveyard clods. Uncertain of the direction of fire, mourners – children among them – huddle behind headstones in fear for their lives. Gerry Adams, the then-leader of Sinn Féin, takes the microphone and appeals for calm. Stone is spotted and some of the crowd chase him in the direction of the motorway. He turns back and fires.

Among the pursuers was Kevin Brady, a member of the IRA, who worked as Danny Morrison's driver. He was shot in the stomach. Busy putting the wounded into taxis and ambulances, and then dealing with the media, Morrison did not realise that Brady had been hit. He was in the press centre on the Falls Road when word came through from the morgue.

One might assume that republicans such as Morrison would become inured to sudden death; that, through frequent small doses, they build an immunity to grief. Not in this case. He loved Kevin Brady. 'Oh boy,' he told me. 'Awful. Awful. I wept for him the way I wept for Jimmy.'

This being Belfast, where blood begets blood, the matter did not rest. At Brady's funeral, three days later, a silver Volkswagen Passat carrying British army corporals David Wood and Derek Howes – both wearing civilian clothes – drove towards the cortège, which had left St Agnes's chapel following the requiem mass. Danny Morrison was among the coffin-bearers: 'We were approaching the junction of Andersonstown Road and Slemish Way when we heard people begin to scream and saw the car speed towards us.'

Some of the mourners, thinking this was another loyalist attack, ran towards the car. The driver, Corporal Wood, tried to reverse, but the vehicle was surrounded, and the soldiers dragged out. They were beaten and stripped, before being driven in a black taxi to a patch of waste ground and executed.

The cortège, meanwhile, continued on its way to the usual place. There is a tradition at IRA funerals for a rifle salute to be fired above the coffin. On this occasion, however, gunfire came before anyone had reached the graveside.

'We could hear,' Morrison recalled, 'the shots that killed them.'

*

THE EASTER PARADE at last arrived in Milltown. In fierce afternoon heat, dignitaries gathered at the republican plot.

Wreaths were laid, Hail Marys said. The Last Post sounded. Gerry Adams was among the onlookers. He was unmistakeable, a figure from history. He lifted a little boy – a figure from the future – and swung him up on to the wall of the plot for a better view.

Joe Austin said a few words and introduced Mary Lou McDonald. The politics of this moment were tricky. Two days earlier, the Sinn Féin leader had condemned the murder of Lyra McKee. Now she was standing by the graves of seventy-seven people who believed in the politics of the gun and bomb. How to hammer one and honour the other?

'There is no more fitting place for a republican to be on Easter Sunday,' she began, 'than at the graveside of our patriot dead.'

Applause. Flags flew: the red hand, the three crowns, the tricolour, the harp, the eagle and sword.

The days of armed struggle should be in the past, McDonald said: 'The war is over.' There is a democratic pathway to the united Ireland republicans crave. That should be the legacy, she suggested, of the sacrifices of previous generations; it would be a nation worthy of Bobby Sands and all his fallen comrades.

'There are some who object to us remembering our dead,' she said. 'To them I say, no one has the right to censor or deny grief.'

The message was clear: we weep for whom we wish, and we wish for a land worth the weeping.

*

BELFAST, Easter Wednesday. It was high noon and crowds had gathered outside St Anne's for the funeral of Lyra McKee.

The Church of Ireland cathedral was consecrated in 1904. Romanesque arches make it seem much older. In 2007, the so-called 'Spire of Hope' was added – a forty-metre stainless-steel needle rising up into the Belfast sky, intended as a symbol of the promise of the Good Friday Agreement. On a pillar behind the pulpit is carved the word 'Justice'.

That's what everyone here wanted. A reward of up to £10,000 had been offered for information leading to the conviction of those responsible for the killing. But today wasn't about justice, or its coarse cousin revenge; the people had come to celebrate and mourn.

Inside, the chairs were filling up. One of McKee's friends laid out yellow scarves with black stripes. Mourners had been invited to wear clothes which reflected her love of Harry Potter. Yellow and black, the Hufflepuff colours, represent wheat and soil.

Across the aisle from me, a young man wore an 'I Stand With Lyra' T-shirt. A little to my right was Father Joseph Gormley, the priest who had anointed McKee in hospital. I had seen him on the news, calling for the Easter parade through Derry to be cancelled: 'They are just adding pain upon pain. Who do they think they are?' I shook his hand, but asked no questions. I wasn't there as a reporter, not quite.

McKee's family and her partner, Sara, were at the front. When the British Prime Minister entered the church, she went over to the family and crouched down to speak to Lyra's mother, Joan, who was in a wheelchair. Grief confers status. A loss, if it is great enough, can raise you above world leaders. But who would choose such monstrous elevation?

The cathedral doors opened and a cold air blew. People turned with pale faces. The coffin was beautiful, as these things go, carved with Celtic knotwork and a cross. But there was no masking the horror, the brute physical fact of it.

McKee was twenty-nine when she died. No age at all. She had been a late developer – in her early school days, she struggled with reading, and required extra support – who became precocious. There were journalism awards and a book deal. A bright future, everyone said. Robbed, everyone said. There was a sense, listening to the service, that what had happened was not only murder, but also theft; a thing of value had been stolen from the world. One could not help but think, as her story was told, of all the stories she'd now never tell.

This service would become known for the electrifying moment when Father Martin Magill, a Belfast priest, asked of the assembled political leaders, 'Why in God's name does it take the death of a twenty-nine-year-old woman with her whole life in front of her to get to this point?' He meant the coming together of ideological enemies, united in their condemnation of what had happened, and he received a standing ovation for that. But what went unreported – and what will stay with me, I think – were the words of Nichola Corner, McKee's elder sister: 'As Spiritualists, Lyra and I do not believe in an afterlife.' Note the present tense. 'We know beyond any doubt that the human soul is eternal, that death is not the end of life, and that we are all welcomed into a spiritual existence after the physical death.'

The coffin was borne out of the cathedral and applauded by the hundreds gathered on Writers' Square as it was placed into the hearse and driven away.

She was buried at a quarter to four on a hazy afternoon. The great crag of Cave Hill was a dark silhouette; gorse, coming into bloom, gave the landscape a Hufflepuff look. McKee had climbed the hill the year before, searching for the body of a young man thought to have killed himself. 'For those in the north of the city,' she wrote, 'Cave Hill was becoming a bit like Aokigahara, the forest in Japan where lost souls went when they couldn't take any more.'

Once the gravediggers had done their work, and the mourners gone, the only sound was birdsong. The grave was covered in floral tributes: 'Team Lyra' in the rainbow colours of the gay pride flag.

LILIES

One card read, 'Words fail me.' That felt about right. We carve words on stone to remember our dead – their names and dates and some blandly appropriate text. The formality and finality of headstone convention takes all the mess of grief and loss and reduces it to something that can be said with hammer and chisel. Beloved wife of. Sadly missed by. But that wee card with its admission of the limits of language felt real. Perhaps these are the truths we should engrave in straight lines and elegant fonts: Words fail me. I don't know how I'm going to get through this. I will never be the same again.

Lyra McKee lies in a corner of Carnmoney Cemetery, north of Belfast. She is wearing a flower in her hair.

PHOEBE

IT WAS SUNDAY MORNING and the bells of St Nicholas were ringing out. The door to the tower had been left open, and the ringers could be seen, pulling on sallies in red, white and green. The church, which is thought to have been here in some form since before the Norman conquest, is high on a hill overlooking town and coast. The English Channel, dull as a tarnished mirror, appeared silver between rooftops and steeples.

I was here with Louise Peskett, who conducts a tour called Notorious Women of Brighton. Some years ago, while working as a guide at the Royal Pavilion, she realised she was spending most of her time talking about the achievements of men. What, she wondered, have all the women being doing while these men were building palaces and fighting wars?

'Brighton and Hove is a real treasure trove of women's history,' she told me. 'Margaret Damer Dawson, who many think was the first policewoman, was born here. Some of the first women doctors to practise in Britain came to Brighton to open hospitals. The first British woman to swim the Channel was born in Brighton. We've also got the first woman to ever get a blue plaque for services to witchcraft. She was called Doreen Valiente. She was known as the "Mother of Modern Witchcraft". She only died in the late 1990s, and a lot of people who I take round on tours remember seeing her when she worked in Boots.

'And then of course, there's the incredible Phoebe Hessel. Hers isn't a spectacular headstone, but what's written on it is remarkable. Shall we have a look?'

The stone, though plain, is prominent. Quite large, with a rounded top, it is close to the front of the church and surrounded by a small fence. Lichen and dirt meant it was difficult to make out the inscription, but Peskett knew it well, and read aloud:

In Memory of
PHOEBE HESSEL
who was born at Stepney in the Year 1713
She served for many Years
as a private Soldier in the 5th. Regt. of foot
in different parts of Europe
and in the year 1745 fought under the command
of the DUKE of CUMBERLAND
at the Battle of Fontenoy
where she received a Bayonet wound in her Arm
Her long life which commenced in the time of
QUEEN ANNE
extended to the reign of
GEORGE IV
by whose munificence she received comfort
and support in her latter Years
she died at Brighton where she had long resided
December 12th 1821 Aged 108 Years

The life, and much-deferred death, of Phoebe Hessel is a BBC drama waiting to happen. It even has a ready-made title: 'The Stepney Amazon', a nickname based on her birthplace and warrior nature. Two London streets – Amazon Street and Hessel Street – are named after her, as is a Brighton bus that serves the route between Steyning and Rottingdean. The various accounts of her life are in slight conflict. Not everything adds up. There is a mythical air about her. She straddles centuries, addles certainties. She was an Orlando, a Zelig, a marvel.

She was born Phoebe Smith. When she was fifteen, her sweetheart, Samuel Golding, a soldier, was sent with his regiment to serve in the West Indies. Rather than be separated, she decided to go with him, disguising herself as a man and joining up. Other accounts vary on this point. Some say that it was her father, a military drummer, who began the pretence; on the death of Phoebe's mother, he disguised his daughter as a boy and enlisted her in the army so she could accompany him on the fife. Either way, it is said that she served first in Montserrat and then Gibraltar.

How her true identity was discovered is unclear. One version goes that, with her lover being wounded and discharged, she unburdened herself to the wife of the general and was sent back to England to marry. Another story has it that, being found guilty of some army misdemeanour, she was ordered to be whipped; on the baring of her upper body, the game was up. 'Strike and be damned!' she cried, unrepentant and unashamed. A third take, one which Louise Peskett considered the most likely, suggests that the moment of truth came with that bayonet wound: 'I imagine her lying on the battlefield, and the army doctor running over, taking off her clothes and getting the shock of his life.'

Phoebe had kept her own confidence well. Her voice, apparently, had always been strong and masculine – she took pride in that. Asked many years later about her deception, she explained that she had confided in no one: 'But I told my secret to the ground. I dug a hole that would hold a gallon, and whispered it there.'

She and Golding settled in Plymouth; on his death, she moved to Brighton and remarried – to a fisherman, William Hessel – living, at times, in poverty, or close to it. She travelled with a donkey, selling fish; later, she sold apples and gingerbread from a stall, and became a well-known character at a time when the town was becoming a fashionable resort. The churchyard of St Nicholas also holds the graves of other figures from Brighton's golden years. Martha Gunn, so-called Queen of the Dippers, was the most celebrated of those who made a living from helping wealthy women to bathe in the sea. She was big and strong; if Phoebe was an Amazon, Martha was a sort of Siren. A satirical cartoon from 1794 shows the French, having made the mistake of invading England via Brighton, being seen off the beach by Gunn, who has hoisted an enemy officer into the air and is poised to thump him round the chops. She and Hessel were contemporaries; it would be delicious to think they were cronies.

In the year before the cartoon of Martha was drawn, Hessel was involved in one of the curious incidents which demonstrated her talent for cameo appearances in history. She was a crucial witness in the capture of James Rook, a highwayman, whom she had overheard talking about his part in a mail robbery while drinking in the Red Lion at Shoreham (she herself liked a drink, a habit from her soldiering days, perhaps). Rook and his accomplice, Edward Howell, were tried, found guilty and sentenced to death. Their bodies were hung from a gibbet in Hove, and, as they decayed, Rook's mother took to collecting her son's remains as they fell to the ground. She would venture out most often in bad weather, hoping that wind and rain would cause more body parts to fall; once she had gathered his entire skeleton, she buried it under cover of night in Old Shoreham churchyard. This terrible manifestation of maternal love inspired Tennyson to write a poem, 'Rizpah', which imagines a mother kissing the very bones which had been strengthened by her milk.

'I was just thinking,' Peskett said, standing by Hessel's stone, 'that it's actually quite thrilling to be in such proximity to her, even though a couple of centuries separate us and she is long gone.'

Such is the false intimacy of the grave. To stand where someone lies brings us so close to them. Near and yet far. It was easy, in that spot, to imagine Hessel in life: in her brown serge dress, her white apron, her black cloak and bonnet. She would have a tale to tell.

Her longevity is in itself fascinating. She was a witness to history in a way few were. There can't be many who lived in the reigns of five monarchs. She fought for one King George and was kept in old age by his great-grandson. George IV, as Prince Regent, met her in Brighton, called her 'a jolly old fellow', and gave her a pension of eighteen pounds a year, saving her from the workhouse. She was invited, as the town's oldest resident, to be guest of honour at a banquet for his coronation. She had rolled the dice and put herself in a situation – fighting in Britain's wars – where she might have expected an early death; instead, she came up double-sixes and lived a remarkably long life. Yet that, too, had its sorrows. She survived two husbands and all nine of her children. She grew blind and lost the use of her legs. Unable to see, unable to walk, unable to forget, she lived on.

'Other people die,' she said, in 1821, 'and I cannot.' What sadness and defiance in those words. The end came within three months. All her life had lacked was death and now she lacked for nothing.

CEDAR

VIEW OF LONDON FROM HIGHGATE CEMETERY.

'LET US ENTER,' said Peter Mills, 'the land of the dead.'

The tour guide léd the way through the colonnade and up the steps. A path curved uphill, out of sight. This had been a great garden of death; now it was a living wood. Birds sang. Wild garlic exhaled its morning breath. Stone angels peeped, like fawns, from between the trees.

London felt, in one sense, very far away. Yet what could be more London than Highgate Cemetery? George Eliot, who wrote *Middlemarch*, perhaps the finest English novel, is buried here; fans push pens into the soil of her plot. Karl Marx, expelled from France, moved to London in 1849 and wrote *Das Kapital* in the Reading Room of the British Museum; busloads of Chinese tourists troop into the cemetery, pose by his iconic tomb, and troop back on to the bus without having visited any other grave. Highgate is, too, the last home of Adam Worth – 'The Napoleon of Crime,' according to his stone – who is thought to have inspired Conan Doyle to create Professor Moriarty; Joseph Bell, the inspiration for Sherlock Holmes, is buried in Edinburgh's Dean Cemetery, at a reasonably safe distance.

Here lies George Wombwell, the Victorian menagerist, whose grave is topped by an effigy of his favourite lion, Nero. Here lies Tom Sayers, the bare-knuckle boxer, beneath a mournful marble sculpture of his pet mastiff, Lion. Here lies Malcolm McLaren, leonine punk impresario; in *The Great Rock 'n' Roll Swindle* he emerges from a Highgate tomb wearing a tartan suit and singing the Max Bygraves song 'You Need Hands'. Here lies Michael Faraday, whose discovery of electromagnetic induction means we have electricity today.

Here lies, in a lead-lined coffin, Alexander Litvinenko, the former spy, who was assassinated by Russian agents using green tea poisoned with radioactive polonium. Here lies poor Lizzie Siddal, the artist and model whom Millais painted as the drowned Ophelia, and who died, aged thirty-two, having sunk beneath a laudanum tide; when she was exhumed seven years later, so that her husband, Dante Gabriel Rossetti, could retrieve a book of poems he wished to publish, the coffin was, it is said, full of her hair – it had continued to grow after death and now glowed, in copper coils, by the light of a graveside fire.

Britain's best-known and best-loved cemetery is, in short, a place of legends in both meanings of that word. Some of the city's greatest and most terrible stories have their full stop here. It is where London's live-wire narrative energy is earthed.

'The place is alive,' Martin Adeney, the chair of the trustees, told me. 'It's an oxymoron, a living cemetery, but that's what Highgate is. This is a place to celebrate as well as to come and mourn.'

In the summer of 1839, Highgate became the third of the city's 'Magnificent Seven' cemeteries to open, following Kensal Green and West Norwood. Its founder and architect, Stephen Geary, intended it to be deeply theatrical and theatrically deep. Both intentions found their perfect expression in the cemetery's centrepiece, the Circle of Lebanon – a great dry moat, enclosing an island of twenty vaults, created by digging down from ground level. This island was, and still is, reached through the Egyptian Avenue, described in 1865 as 'a cold stony death-palace' – a tunnel through the hillside, lined with solemn iron doors, each decorated with an inverted torch, symbolising the everlasting life of the dead within. At the centre of the island was a grand tree, a

CEDAR

Cedar of Lebanon, perhaps a hundred years older than the cemetery itself. It had been part of the Ashurst estate, the seventeenth-century home of a former Lord Mayor, but now the tree became a symbol of Highgate, appearing in stained glass in the Anglican chapel. Photography arrived in London in the year the cemetery opened, and the Cedar has always been a popular subject, emblematic of Highgate's sepulchral flash, but also hinting at Eden.

During my first visit, an oppressively hot day in July, I had walked around the Cedar with the head gardener, Frank Cano. A warm, amiable man in his forties, he's into motorbikes, stone circles and gold-panning. He has been known to hug a tree. Looking across from the outer edge of the moat, he spoke about the Cedar with paternal anxiety. It was struggling, he said.

At some point during its long life it had lost a high limb, and, as a result, the trunk had become sunburned. The snow, when it fell, did not suit it either, causing branches to bend and break. Weakened by sun, worn down by snow, scorched by lightning, getting on for three hundred years old, it was frail, vulnerable to pests and fungi. It was also in the unique position of being the largest pot plant in the world, its roots bunched behind the vaults. No one quite knew what effect this restriction might have, but the tree – though still hugely impressive at around twenty metres tall – was visibly ailing. Some of its limbs were being supported by braces which brought to mind those weird crutches Dalí used in his paintings to hold up melting faces.

An enormous amount of money had been spent on injecting special feed into the ground around its roots, and once a year compressed air was blasted into the soil. The point of all this was to keep it alive. In this land of the dead, the Cedar of Lebanon could not be allowed to die. Its historic and symbolic importance was too great. Would the Beefeaters allow the ravens to leave the Tower of London? No. And so it was with this tree. Some 170,000 Londoners had been buried in the Highgate earth with the promise of immortality; alone among them, the Cedar was expected to attain that state without dying first.

For Frank, it was personal: 'Not in my time as head gardener do I want that tree to die. If I had to dance around every tree in London to get extra money to keep this one alive, I would do that. It just can't die while I'm here.'

At thirty-six acres, Highgate is around half the size of Kensal Green, though clever landscaping gives the impression of a much greater area. An early guidebook offers a glimpse of the cemetery at the height of its magnificence, when it was hosting more than thirty funerals a day: 'In the genial summer time, when the birds are singing blithely in their leafy recesses, and the well-cared-for graves are dazzling with the varied hues of beautiful flowers, there is a holy loveliness upon this place of death, as though kind angels hovered about it, and quickened fair Nature with their presence, in love for the good souls whose tenantless bodies repose there.'

It could not last. The growing popularity of cremation (legally sanctioned since 1902) and the death toll of the First World War were two blows which, together, proved fatal to the great garden cemeteries. With so many lying dead and unrecovered in Belgium and France, the idea of ostentatious individual mourning began to seem absurd. If a soldier son whose body had never been found could be remembered with nothing more than a picture on the mantelpiece and a name on the local memorial, what use was a grand vault? If, at a fraction of the price, the deceased could be burned and scattered, or kept in an urn, why bother with the expense and fuss of a grave? Behind all this, too, was growing religious doubt. Resurrection was no longer a sure and certain hope; no need, then, to keep intact the body in expectation of its eventual rise. Judgement Day had itself been judged, and found wanting.

From the 1930s, the great cemeteries went into a death spiral. With ever-decreasing income, the private companies which owned them were unable, or unwilling, to spend money on their upkeep. Maintenance at Highgate became minimal. The place became overgrown and much vandalised. It developed a haunted, hag-ridden air. The architecture critic Ian Nairn, writing in 1966, called Highgate 'the creepiest place in London; no Dickensian stretch of the river can match this calculated exercise in stucco horror, now itself decomposing'. The Egyptian Avenue, he noted, was a 'blood-curdling scream' rendered in stone. 'The cemetery closes well before dark, and a good job, too.'

Photographs from the 1960s to the 1980s show Highgate in poor repair, its great monuments crumbling. It remains badly overgrown, full of trees that were never supposed to be there. Some 99 per cent of the tree stock is reckoned to be self-seeded ash. Life flourishes within this accidental wood. The cemetery is home to nine species of bat, and several bird species, including the linnet, cuckoo, skylark and fieldfare. Foxes have been spotted carrying mouthfuls of hot cross buns, and, in 2013, two wallabies were unexpected visitors. Highgate's most exotic creatures are, sadly, never seen: around a hundred rare orb-weaver spiders living in the Egyptian Avenue vaults, whose presence was discovered a few years ago during a bat survey carried out by the London Wildlife Trust. Thought to have been in residence for more than 150 years, they require complete darkness, and there is a desire on the part of management that they should not be unsettled by human activity; the spiders, however, are perfectly free to unsettle us. Peter Mills tells his tour groups: 'They're watching.'

From the 1970s, the policy in Highgate was one of 'managed neglect' – romantic decay being conveniently to British taste – but a new conservation plan has laid out a different approach. A huge amount of the vegetation obscuring the ground has already been removed, with much more yet to go. It isn't a question of taking out every bit of ivy, if that were even possible, as ivy is part of what one expects to see in an old graveyard, but the plant is shrouding and slowly destroying a lot of the headstones, so it must be managed much more effectively. The tree situation, too, must be brought under control. The plan is to remove those which are damaging, or at risk of damaging graves, and obscuring historic views. It used to be possible to admire St Paul's Cathedral from Highgate, and one day it will be again. The cemetery is home to six very old yews; younger trees around these, competing for light, will be removed, creating a halo effect, prolonging the lives of the ancients. This is all a huge amount of work, and must be done with care. One can't just take an axe to a Highgate tree; they must be brought down bit by bit in order that they don't fall and damage tombs; roots are poisoned or left to rot rather than being dug out, lest they bring up bones.

'This cemetery is our history,' Frank Cano had told me. 'We need to maintain it for people in the future. It could be a family member, ten generations on, coming to look for their ancestor's grave. It would be nice if, when they get here, there's something left.'

In the days of Highgate's decline, as visitor numbers dropped, rumour rushed in to fill the vacuum. This was a period of pop occultism, when bright Swinging London gave way to darker pleasures: an interest in the supernatural and mysticism expressed in film, books, music and, eventually, the media. The cemetery duly became the focus of a paranormal panic. Eyewitness reports of a tall, dark figure with red eyes and a top hat, dubbed the Highgate Vampire, began to appear in first the local and then the national press. The resulting hysteria climaxed on the evening of Friday, 13 March 1970, following a television news report, when around a hundred people, some the worse for drink, climbed the cemetery walls in hope of seeing the creature for themselves.

John Lydon, the Sex Pistols frontman, recalled in his memoir being a teen swept up in this craze: '. . . we'd break into the crypts where the bodies were on shelves, open up the coffins and have a look. We'd see which bodies hadn't deteriorated. Was the vampire thing real? So many people were doing it, it was almost like a social club down there. You'd meet so many people, loonies mostly, running around with wooden stakes, crucifixes and cloves of garlic.'

One might be tempted to consider this rock-star hyperbole were it not that the cemetery still bears the scars of that time. When Peter Mills, the Highgate guide, showed me inside the brick-lined catacombs, he explained that the reason some seals were broken on the recesses, and coffins exposed, was as a result of intruders searching for the vampire. He shone a torch over the caskets; in many cases the wood had come away and the lead lining was visible. He didn't think that they would ever be covered back up; this vandalism was part of the cemetery's history. In every sense, perhaps, its darkest moment.

On Easter Sunday, 1975, the West Cemetery closed its gates. Highgate was dying. But there was still hope. In the October of that year, following a protest against the closure, a Friends group formed – the first in Britain to look after a graveyard – and by 1981 they had taken ownership.

Work began on restoring the most important monuments. There was, in the air, the beginning of a new appreciation of the world of the nineteenth century; a feeling that long-neglected public spaces could be a way of understanding the values and aesthetics of that earlier age. The same spirit of visionary nostalgia which revolted against the proposed demolition of St Pancras station now animated the digging out of decades' worth of pigeon shit from the marble interior of the Beer Mausoleum.

Sir John Betjeman, writing in 1978, described Highgate as a 'Victorian Valhalla'. The poet had a knack for marketing, and his nickname has stuck. This is the only graveyard in Britain that can be said to be a brand. As one staff member put it to me, with a sincerity that brooked no bathos, 'We are the cemetery equivalent of a Mars Bar.'

*

APPROACHING Highgate after climbing Swains Lane, where the poet Shelley burst into tears at the view over London, one has a choice.

A right turn takes you through the gates of the East Cemetery; pay a small entrance fee and you can wander at will, following a visitor map to the graves of Marx and Eliot and the rest. A left turn takes you beneath the great stone entrance of the West Cemetery, the older and grander part, which can only be accessed by guided tour. This policy, which is under review, was developed with an eye to helping to preserve the grand monuments on the west side, and with a care for the privacy needs of those visiting loved ones.

The balancing of private and public, already tricky when a famous person is alive, becomes even more delicate when they pass away and can no longer police their own boundaries. Family members will want a place to grieve; those who knew the star but not the person may treat the grave as a shrine. Take George Michael, who died on Christmas Day, 2016. His grave is not on the tours, but people do sneak off to find and photograph it; every day, members of the public call up, asking if they can visit, and are told no. On the star's most recent birthday, fans held a candlelit vigil outside the gates, and went on the tours wearing George Michael T-shirts. 'It's an ongoing battle to stop people going there,' one Highgate staff member told me. 'If you're a real big fan of somebody, why would you not be respectful towards the wishes of the family?'

I turned left. I had an appointment with Ian Dungavell, Highgate's chief executive. The cemetery was itself at a crossroads, and he had promised to explain about the path they planned to take.

Dungavell is an architectural historian and a former director of the Victorian Society. He has been CEO since 2012. Although the cemetery is owned by the Friends of Highgate Trust, he is responsible for its day-to-day running and for enacting policy decisions made by the Friends. Sometimes tasks come out of nowhere, such as the Saturday not so long ago when he found himself spending several hours scrubbing red paint from the tomb of Karl Marx, which had been vandalised with political graffiti. Dungavell, Australian-born and in his fifties, has a slightly formal demeanour which leads one to expect academic blandness in his speech; in fact, he reaches, often, for poetic imagery. Of cleaning Marx's tomb, he said: 'That felt a really nurturing thing to do. It was almost like washing a corpse for burial.'

We met in his office, and soon came to that crossroads: his most pressing ongoing concern was making sure that Highgate is able to continue to function as a working cemetery; more simply, how to find room to bury people. 'That wonderful idea – the Victorian cemetery – had built into it the seeds of its own destruction,' he said. 'The Victorians shirked the question of what was going to happen to these places when they filled up.'

To counter the horror of the London churchyards, of all those corpses being dug up, half rotten, in order to make room for more, the garden cemeteries offered burial in perpetuity. One's body could rest with dignity until the resurrection. But the eyes of the Victorians were so fixed on paradise that they looked past a nearer future – a century or so hence, when their cemeteries would be full, or close to it. When, on 26 May 1839, Elizabeth Jackson of Golden Square, Soho, became the first person to be buried in Highgate (having died at thirty-six from tuberculosis), she would have been alone in a great empty space. Not for long, though. Highgate today is close to capacity. It is estimated that fewer than fifty graves remain for coffin burials, although more space could be created in the short term through landscaping; ashes burials take up much less room, and are therefore available in greater numbers. Still, the internal thinking, when I visited in the summer of 2019, was that the cemetery had only seven years left before it would have to close to new interments.

The consequences of this would be twofold: one financial, the other philosophical. Highgate gets around half of its income from burial. It is the most expensive cemetery in Britain, the price determined by pressure of demand and the kudos of the name. An ashes grave will cost from around £4,000, a coffin burial around £22,000, including the fee for digging. The cemetery needs to raise £1,500 a day in order to meet its running costs. Clearly, if it becomes impossible to bury people then that will have a huge impact on Highgate's viability.

Money aside, though, what happens when a cemetery no longer welcomes the newly dead? It dies. Recent grief is the pulse of a graveyard, the beat below one's feet. Without that, a cemetery is little more than a park, or, at best, a tourist attraction that the public will pay to enter. 'This is a spiritual landscape, and that relies on a connection with the current generation,' Dungavell said. 'That link between the present and the past is absolutely crucial.' If people no longer have a personal impulse to visit, if they no longer have a reason to care, then a cemetery will, over time, diminish in significance. Old and insignificant graveyards, especially in London, are always threatened. Land is sold, stones are taken up, graves built upon. Look at the bodies dug up beside Euston Station to make way for the HS2 rail network.

Even Highgate, Dungavell believes, is at risk from future development. The West Cemetery, with its world-class landscape design, might be safe, yes, but the East? 'Fast forward two hundred years, with the demand for affordable housing, and much less survival of memorial stones than there is now, and developers might be going, "Well, who are all these people?" There's Karl Marx, but he'd be moved across to the West Cemetery. George Eliot might be moved. But it would be relatively easy to see where they might just cover the rest over. History shows us that you can't be complacent at all, so I'm really worried about that, and that's why I think the most important thing is to be able to keep burying.'

He has a plan: grave renewal. The idea is that the cemetery would take back ownership of long-abandoned graves, and the memorials on top of them, in cases where it was judged that they were no longer wanted by the families who had bought the rights. Only plots last used or, if empty, sold more than seventy-five years ago would be used for new burials.

There are a few hundred empty graves in Highgate, purchased in the nineteenth century, but never used. Of the occupied graves, those which are unmarked, or on which the marker is so deteriorated as to be unreadable, would be especially favoured – if records show that there is space for further coffins to be placed on top of those already within. A damaged headstone of this sort would be removed and replaced by one carved only with the name of the newcomer, although records would be kept of the earlier occupants.

It is thought that it might very occasionally be necessary to 'lift and deepen' old graves; in other words, to remove whatever is left of a coffin or coffins, dig down further, place the remains back in at the lower depth, then lay a new burial on top.

Council-run cemeteries in London can already do all of this, but Highgate requires a change in the law to give it the authority and has thus put forward a Private Bill to Parliament.

These pressures are not unique to Highgate. Analysis by the *Telegraph* newspaper of 1,300 cemeteries around the UK has revealed that two in every five have less than a decade of space remaining. The situation in London is particularly acute, and the price of a plot has risen steeply. It is akin to the property crisis; those who can afford to bury in the city, or who are lucky enough to inherit space in a grave, will do so – most, however, will either cremate or be forced to seek a cemetery further out.

Highgate, though, because it is so well known, is in the unique situation of having to work out where to draw the line between being a visitor attraction – a place of public pleasure – and a working cemetery, a place of private mourning. Some of the reporting around the lack of burial space has suggested that, if the cemetery gets to the point where it can no longer take new interments, it will be forced to increase footfall by opening a café, an exhibition centre and so forth. The truth is not quite that straightforward. It is possible that these developments will happen anyway, as there is a desire to improve facilities, but there is very little space on which to build, say, a museum and shop. Even if it could be done, should it? And how far should one go in making money from the exploitation of the illustrious dead?

One of the top-selling items in Highgate's small gift shop is a cookie-cutter in the shape of Karl Marx. 'Before we had the cookie-cutter, we sold loads of *The Communist Manifesto*,' Nick Powell, the visitor experience manager, told me. 'The sales of those have dropped off dramatically.'

'Did you have to think carefully,' I asked, 'whether it was right to stock the cookie-cutters?'

'Do you mean are we dishonouring Marx by selling these things?'

'Yes,' I said. 'By bringing capitalism to bear upon his image.'

Powell laughed. He seemed to think the question absurdly po-faced, and perhaps it was. So I tried another: 'Have you ever made any Marx cookies yourself?'

'I have,' he said, nodding. 'With icing for his beard. They were fantastic.'

*

A WALK IN Highgate's East Cemetery begins, if one is fortunate, with Joseph Burt. The volunteer's domain is the little hut just inside the gates, from where he takes the entrance fee, hands out visitor maps, and keeps an eye on dogs while people daunder among the dead. He is in his late fifties and looks a bit like David Hockney. He was wearing, on the day we spoke, a pair of shorts with toucans on them ('Primark –

five quid'), Gucci-ish loafers ('A little place in Maida Vale – twenty-five quid'), and a blue shirt with enough buttons undone to reveal a golden crucifix. Heavy gold rings completed the look. I liked him before he started talking. As soon as he did, it was love.

'I've known George thirty years,' he said, meaning George Michael. 'A very good friend of mine. He used to sing things to me before he recorded them. I was the first to hear "Careless Whisper". I said, "George, record this. It's going to be a big hit." He was a lovely friend, a lovely guy.'

A young man and older woman came into the hut. 'Two adults, please,' said the man. 'Thank you very much. I come from Transylvania and this is my mother.'

Joseph said his pleased-to-meet-yous and then returned to the matter in hand: his relationship with Highgate. He had been a volunteer for fifteen years, he said. He loves the history and architecture, finds it beautiful. Eighteen months before, his partner had died; his grave is here, very close to the hut. 'He's going to be on the map. He's very well known.' Paul Annett was a producer and director, best remembered for his work in the 1970s and '80s. He made episodes of *Poldark*, *Widows*, the Jeremy Brett *Sherlock Holmes* and – a favourite horror film of mine – 1974's *The Beast Must Die*.

The two men were together for twenty-two years, but Joseph himself does not intend to be buried in Highgate. He plans to leave his body to science. 'I've chosen three songs for my memorial service. One is "Send In the Clowns". Then Leo Sayer's "The Show Must Go On".' He couldn't, offhand, remember the third.

I wondered whether he had considered not returning to volunteer at Highgate after his partner's death. Didn't he worry it would be too upsetting? 'No,' he replied. 'Paul wanted to be here, which really surprised me. So I visit him every time I come. I make sure the grave is doing okay, that it's watered and so on. I'm pleased he's here. We had a great life.'

After saying goodbye to Joseph, I took a turn among the graves. There are so many famous people buried in Highgate, they can catch you by surprise. You can be walking along a path, thinking about nothing in particular, and all of a sudden there's Beryl Bainbridge. It was odd – and oddly touching – to notice the headstone of Bert Jansch, the great folk singer and guitarist; it didn't seem so long since we were sitting in his flat in Kilburn, having a cup of tea.

One of the most striking graves near the entrance to the East Cemetery is that of Philip Gould, the political strategist. He died of cancer in 2011. His memorial, *The Prodigal Daughter*, is the work of the artist and writer Charlie Mackesy. It shows two bronze figures, a man and a child, embracing beneath a simple stone arch. The keystone is carved with three Gs – for Gould's wife Gail and daughters Georgia and Grace; the thumbprints of all four are pressed into the back of the statue. In his remarkable memoir *When I Die: Lessons from the Death Zone*, Gould recalled visiting Highgate with Gail to choose where he would be buried. He liked the idea that people would be looking at his grave, that the dead and the living could meet on that spot, in that moment of attention. 'It gives me great comfort to know that I will be there,' he wrote. 'This morning I stood at my grave and I thought: God, I do feel very, very happy to be going to this place.'

The man who showed Gould to his grave was Victor Herman, the sexton. In *When I Die*, he is described as a 'six-foot-six giant with a shovel over one shoulder'. When I met Victor, he lacked the shovel, but was in every other respect exactly as you would expect, and desire, a gravedigger to be. A big man, made bigger – physically and emotionally – by years of work. 'Grave-digging's in the blood,' he said. 'I dug my first grave when I was about thirteen years old. By hand. I did my first funeral on my own at sixteen.' He was now fifty-eight. His father, Bill, was a gravedigger and Victor learned the craft of it from him, and from other older men who had worked in Highgate for a long time. He knew one of the gravediggers who had, one oil-lit midnight in 1954, exhumed Karl Marx for reburial in the more prominent spot where he now lies. Victor's philosophy on how best to dig a grave? 'My way or don't bovver.'

I mentioned Philip Gould, how happy he had felt to have found his grave, and Victor's face brightened at the memory. 'I do lots of funerals like that. I get guys who are terminally ill, they have literally just been told by the hospital across the road that they've got six months to live, and they come here, the nearest cemetery, realising that they have to work this out for themselves, that perhaps no one else is going to do it, or wants to do it.'

It is very common for him to meet men and women who he will, before long, bury. 'They go to the extent of lying down on the plot and looking up at the sky. It's amazing. You get them up, and they shake your hand and hug you. I think they are the strongest people in the world. Not only have they just been told they've got six months to live, they've taken a humungous burden off the whole of their family. They've come here, they've chosen a plot, they've paid for it, they've gone to the undertakers; all they've got to do now is go and die.'

That is the opposite of denial, isn't it? To go and meet the fellow who is going to dig your grave is confronting death head-on. 'Absolutely,' he said. 'I don't believe too much in The Big Man' – he raised his eyes heavenwards – 'but I believe in making sure that people's minds are at rest.'

Those who come to see him are, naturally, often upset. It cannot be easy, even after so many years, to talk about burial with a mother who has lost a baby. 'For me, it's the hardest thing you can do, the saddest thing you can do, but the proudest thing, too. You've helped them on a journey that they don't want to be on.'

I can see how his pragmatic compassion could be a comfort. To discuss your own end, or the life and death of a person you love, with the man who wields the spade would, I think, have a certain intensity that might be healing. There is no false sentiment with Victor. He knows the weight of a clod, the finality of the sod.

'If you don't mind me asking,' I said, 'did you bury your own father?'

'Yeah,' he nodded, 'I buried Dad. My dad's wishes was, "Don't bury me in that fucking cemetery, I've been there long enough." We knew he was going to die. He had cancer. He said, "Just throw me in the skip, that'll do me."

'I said to my mum, "Come on, let's get him a plot at Highgate. Me and my sisters will pay for it." She looked at me and shook her head: "No, no, no. He will haunt me, he will haunt you, he will haunt your fucking sisters." But I done it. He's just outside the door there.'

Bill Herman died in 2005. He was cremated and his ashes were interred close to the entrance to the West Cemetery. Victor must walk past the spot a dozen times a day. He leaves a can of beer by the grave on the old man's birthday. Strange, though, that he should ignore his father's wish not to be laid to rest in Highgate. Except, he didn't. Not entirely.

'I buried ninety-nine per cent of him,' the gravedigger said. 'The other one per cent I did throw in a skip.'

*

H. G. WELLS, walking in Highgate one sunny morning in the last years of the nineteenth century, found himself dismayed by the uniformity and poor workmanship of the memorials, all those obelisks and urns and angels. 'One may go from end to end of this cemetery and find scarcely anything beautiful, appropriate, or tender,' he wrote. He cared little, even, for Wombwell's lion, and was himself cremated at Golders Green, in 1946, his ashes scattered at sea.

Were Wells to walk in Highgate now, Neil Luxton believes he would find more to please him.

Highgate's in-house stonemason is in his late fifties with a slightly piratical beard. He seems uneasy with the word artist, preferring to think of himself as a craftsman, but has an artist's way of talking about his work. 'The right way to do it is the old way,' he said. Tools and hand and eye. 'When you work stone, there's nothing like getting a rapport with it, getting the feel of it. Corin Redgrave there, you see,' he said, pointing across the path at the actor's memorial, a simple stone of Westmoreland slate. 'I drew that by hand. You could do that with a computer, but you don't get the same empathy, the same deep feeling.'

We were sitting on a bench in the East Cemetery, where most of the notable modern memorials are located. His stones express something – in their shape and the quality of the lettering – about the person they memorialise, in the same way as the best painted portraits are not mere likenesses but capture some inner spirit, too. He likes to have a proper conversation with whoever is commissioning the stone: the bereaved partner or family members, or sometimes the person who is going to die. 'I try to have a headful of the person. They can tell me deeply personal things. You'd be surprised how intimate someone gets in grief.'

He wants to understand them. He's looking for the seed of an idea, something that will sprout. He carries in his mind 'a little montage of their life' and tries to convey that through his eloquent hands. 'A monument should be a statement of their life: how it stood, the things they've done, their achievements possibly. Some people have just been a really good person and you can portray that on a stone. Sometimes I get a tiny little hint and it all clicks. The classic one is *Dead*. Have you seen *Dead*?'

We got up and strolled down the path to look at *Dead*. It is one of his showstoppers. Probably the most photographed stone in the cemetery after Marx. The headstone of the artist Patrick Caulfield, who died in 2005, is a long, upright slab of grey granite, a tonne in weight, cut into four steps ascending from right to left, with the letters D E A D punched through the block in brute art deco holes. Based on a sketch by Caulfield, it took three or four months of sweat and bleeding hands to make. The stone is funny, but it's Beckett laughter: a dank echo in the dark.

Luxton reckons he has made around 2,000 memorials in Highgate. One might think of the cemetery as a gallery showing his life's work. Jeremy Beadle, that's one of his: carved to look like a shelf of the huge antiquarian books the TV presenter loved. Stones Luxton made years ago are beginning to show their age. 'I kind of like to see them look old.' Clients sometimes ask for headstones in materials that won't wear or weather, that will always look new. 'But I don't think that's the point of a monument. It should last with your grief.' As a human has a lifespan, a stone should have a deathspan. It shouldn't last for ever. What's the point of an unvisited memorial still standing and legible generations after the person has died? 'It becomes empty. It's just a piece of stone with someone's name on it.' Better that it should fade and sink and crack.

He recalled the wisdom of a joiner he knew who had made a wooden memorial, from a piece of oak, for his father. 'By the time this thing rots away,' the man had said. 'I really hope that I won't be of a mind to keep going to the grave. I'll remember Dad for what he was, and when this headstone goes, it'll go with the bad memories of losing him.'

Leaving the stonemason to his work, I walked over to the grave of Malcolm McLaren. The Sex Pistols manager had died in 2010. His funeral was a spectacular. The coffin, in a hearse pulled by four black-plumed horses, was spray-painted with the words 'TOO FAST TO LIVE TOO YOUNG TO DIE'. McLaren was sixty-four. Mourners in a green double-decker, following the carriage, sang along to the Sid Vicious version of 'My Way'.

The headstone is very dark granite, with the initials MM set into a shield, a spoof of the Warner Brothers logo. Punk pilgrims, I noticed, had left offerings of safety pins on the ledge beneath the bronze death-mask. Although Neil Luxton had worked the stone, the mask was the creation of another man, and is one of three death-masks this artist has in Highgate.

Nick Reynolds is an artist and musician in his fifties. He plays harmonica with the band Alabama 3. When we met for a drink in a pub near Highgate, he stood out: a rangy lupine presence, a wolf in sunglasses and sandals.

I asked about Malcolm McLaren. He had died in Switzerland, and Nick first saw the body four days later. 'He had that sneer in life, he had that sneer in death,' he recalled. 'He was a good-looking corpse, if there's such a thing. He looked fucking great, considering.'

To make a death-mask, Nick first applies a thin layer of moisturising cream, and then coats the face in sloppy, jelly-like alginate. Once this has set, a layer of bandages soaked in plaster of Paris goes on top, creating a solid mould. Into this mould, he pours wax. After he has resculpted the fine details of the features to his satisfaction, the cast is taken to a foundry and converted into bronze.

While I had been glad to speak about McLaren, what I really wanted to hear about was another of his Highgate death-masks: that of his own father, one of the Great Train Robbers. Bruce Reynolds died, at the age of eighty-one, in 2013. Fifty years before, he had been part of the gang who robbed the mail coach of the Glasgow–London night express, stealing almost three million pounds. He went on the run, along with his young son, first to Mexico, and eventually back to England. He was arrested in 1968 and sentenced to twenty-five years.

His grave is near the entrance to the East Cemetery, part of the way up a small, steep bank. You could miss it easily. The death-mask, like that of Malcolm McLaren, seems at once to attract and repel. You reach out a hand and draw it back. You want to touch and not to touch. It is a human face and one is drawn to it; yet it is a dead face and taboo. The mask is set inside a stone arch, suggesting a railway tunnel, and there are words carved on either side. To the mask's right: 'This is it!' – the words Reynolds said into his walkie-talkie as the train approached. To the left: 'C'est la vie!' – his stoic response when arrested. In a graveyard full of marble-smooth declarations of piety, the stone is sharply unrepentant.

Nick Reynolds had been staying with his father, in his flat, as the older man wasn't well. 'I woke up in the morning and he was dead,' he recalled. 'So it was just a natural instinct for me to do him there and then.' He called a friend for help with the death-mask, and started the process with the body lying on the couch. It wasn't an emotional experience. This flesh was not his father. He regarded the situation as an important opportunity. 'If I had waited till he'd had an autopsy and gone down the morgue, he'd have looked like shit. Ideally, you should make a death-mask within two to three hours of them dying. Unfortunately, most have been dead a week before I get to them.'

He visits Highgate on his father's birthday and the anniversary of the train robbery. How, I wondered, would he characterise his relationship with the mask?

'Oh, I talk to it,' he replied. 'I've got one in my flat as well, so I talk to him all the time. It's kind of like having him in the room. The Greeks and the Romans believed in animism. You would make a statue, and you believed that through wishful thinking, incantation, prayers, rites, mumbo-jumbo or whatever that you could actually summon the spirit to reside within that shape.

'This is why I really got into doing the death-masks in the first place: they're tremendous cathartic tools. When somebody dies, you're missing the space that they occupied. I'm not saying that a death-mask is a good replacement, but to have that perfect image that you can touch and talk to has great healing powers. There's a woman I know, she sleeps with her husband's head. She said to me, "Thanks to you, I wake up in the morning and he's there with the sun shining on his face."'

There would be some, no doubt, who would find this creepy. But not Nick. 'It's touching,' he said, finishing his drink. 'Everyone's face is the seat of the soul. It's how you identify people, it's their uniqueness. To just burn it, or let worms eat it, is a terrible waste. I think everyone should get a death-mask done . . . and I'd make a lot more money.'

*

THE NEWEST PART of Highgate, in which most burial space remains, is known as the Mound. It is an area of raised ground, not far from Karl Marx, accessed by a short winding path. It has a peaceful atmosphere; because it has more recent burials, there are a lot of flowers, and bees drowse through the air. Residents of the Mound include the actor Tim Pigott-Smith ('Goodnight sweet prince,' says his stone, quoting Hamlet) and the graphic designer Storm Thorgerson, known for his wonderful album covers for Pink Floyd among others.

At the back of this section, two graves lay side by side, covered in flowers and flags and photographs. A young man and woman were sitting on the grass beside them, smoking and listening to music, visibly upset. 'These two were friends,' said the man in heavily accented English. 'We were all friends together. Same community.' He pointed to the grave on the left. 'He was killed in Syria, by Isis.' He nodded to the grave on the right. 'Someone stab him last month. Just off Seven Sisters Road.'

Now the woman spoke. 'We had his funeral ten days ago.'

Mehmet Aksoy, also known as Fîraz Dağ, was a filmmaker and activist, a Kurd who had moved to London with his family as a child. In September 2017 he was working as a press officer for the YPG, a group of Kurdish fighters, when their base, near Raqqa, was attacked by Islamic State jihadis. He was shot dead, aged thirty-two. His burial, two months later, was attended by three thousand mourners, the coffin draped in the yellow flag and red star of the YPG, and cries of 'Şehîd namirin' – martyrs never die – disturbed the tranquil air.

'It was extraordinary to feel the great outpouring of grief,' Ian Dungavell recalled when I asked about the occasion. 'Highgate was back to being what a cemetery should be.'

Barış Küçük, who now lies next to Aksoy, was among the mourners that day. The young Kurd came to the end of his own short life on 3 June 2019, slashed behind his left knee by a man who stole his phone and a bottle of beer. He was thirty-three, worked as a chef, and had lived in London since he was a child. It was more than sad, it was shocking to see these graves next to one another; two friends, one killed for his beliefs, the other for his possessions; a martyr and a murder victim – one in a war zone, the other in Zone 3. The Küçük family, speaking after the trial, noted that their son's name means 'peace' in Turkish. 'It feels,' they said, 'as if we too are now covered in the same soil that covers our Barış in his grave.'

I was about to leave the Mound, and Highgate, when I noticed a grave very different from the rest. Sonny Anderson's headstone, made by Neil Luxton, is grey slate, gives his dates – the winter of 1999 to the summer of 2011 – and informs all visitors that this boy had been 'DESTINED FOR GREATNESS'. The genius of the stone, though, the detail which catches the eye and snags the heart, is the top-left corner. Here the slate has been broken off, and, built in its place, is a new corner – made of bright Lego bricks.

Sonny Anderson was diagnosed with cancer when he was nine. Two years of hospitals and treatments followed, but the day came when his parents, Zoe and Gavin, found themselves in the incomprehensible situation of having to work out how to mark their son's grave.

'He was so young,' Zoe said when we spoke on the phone. 'I just didn't know what to do, because we were expecting, all the time, that he was going to survive. Choosing to bury him was our way of keeping him as close to us as we possibly could.' Sonny's sister, Ruby, picked Highgate, and they settled upon that particular spot because they could hear kids playing football on the neighbouring estate; Sonny had been a massive Arsenal fan. 'But then we were struck by this horror that everything in the cemetery looks so old. So we felt that we wanted to do something that was more representative of a child.'

They arrived at the idea of using Lego. They contacted the company to ask which adhesive they used to keep their models together at Legoland, and used it to build the corner of the headstone from bricks Sonny had owned and played with. 'And at his funeral,' Zoe said, 'all the children were given his Lego instead of earth to throw into the grave.'

He had loved Lego. In hospital for a bone marrow transplant, in the isolation ward, he passed the hours building sets. Although the bricks that form the headstone are glued together, the little Lego figures on top are not stuck down. These rotate seasonally: Santa's sleigh at Christmas, a chick or bunny at Easter, and so on. His mum had been up to Highgate the day before we spoke, changing the scene to *Star Wars*. 'If it's his birthday, we'll sit around the table and make a Lego and take it up to the cemetery with us,' she said. 'We get some comfort from doing it.'

Stuff goes missing, of course. That upset Zoe at first, but she has learned to let it go. She knows it's just kids being kids. Also: stuff comes back. Some youngsters from the estate had sneaked into the cemetery and taken figures, but older children, realising where the Lego had come from, took the little ones back to return it to the grave. There was a recognition that these toys were special; a feeling of solidarity, perhaps, with the boy who had gone on ahead where, one day, they would follow.

'Victor tells me often that when funerals are happening, Sonny's grave is a distraction for kids,' Zoe said. 'Sometimes children are burying their mums, which is pretty vile, and playing with the Lego makes it a little easier for them.'

She and her family feel that Sonny is buried in their hearts. But the grave is somewhere to go, and the Lego a ritual of remembrance. It is one of Highgate's 170,000 stories, another brick in the wall.

*

IT WAS LATE January. Snowdrops bent their wimples towards the damp earth. Seven months had passed since I had last been in Highgate. A blink of eternity's eye, but a lot had changed in the cemetery. Frank Cano, the gardener, was leading the way up through the Egyptian Avenue. I was nervous about what we would see on the other side of the tunnel. There had been some bad news.

The Cedar of Lebanon was dead.

It had happened like this. Frank noticed a fungus – Chicken of the Woods – about two metres up the trunk. Concerned, he asked a tree surgeon for tests. The findings were stark: the tree was rotten inside; if not felled, it would fall. Had the Cedar been in a woodland or a park, it might have been possible to fence it off, post notices warning of the danger, and let it come down in its own time. But in Highgate, 25,000 people passed underneath it every year on the tours, and it sat on top of a Grade I-listed catacomb full of people in coffins. The 'nightmare scenario' was that it would crash to the ground, killing and injuring the public, destroying the vaults beneath, and exposing the long dead. Ian Dungavell, sorrowful, gave the order to bring it down. 'It felt premature in the way that switching off a life-support system might do,' he told me.

CEDAR

That Sunday, several of the volunteers and staff had come to say goodbye. Frank Cano was not among them. 'I had a black cloud of guilt over me,' he explained. Had he done the right thing? Could he have done more to save the tree? Had he doomed it before its time?

On the following day, the Cedar was dismembered – limb by limb, the trunk sawn down to near the roots; and those, too, were eventually dug up. The absence was extraordinary. This tree was born a Georgian and died an Elizabethan. In its youth, it had enjoyed long views over a country estate. When it had grown a little older, they built a graveyard around it, laid coffins by its roots. It had been watered by tears, admired by poets and punks. It had known the sound of hooves and carriage wheels, and Luftwaffe bombers overhead. It had scoffed at the vampire-hunters, hearkened to the sound of the martyr on the Mound. It drank from the earth that had embraced so many, and grew in the sun that they missed.

At the far end of the Egyptian Avenue, Frank turned right, led the way along the Circle of Lebanon, and up some steps. We were on the edge of the moat looking across to where the tree had been. What was it like for him, I asked, to see it come down?

'Heartbreaking,' he replied. 'The tree was under my protection. I feel responsible for every living thing here.'

He had begun to feel better, though, as soon as they started to dig down to the roots. This was a revelation. 'I could see that the tree was condemned when the place was built.' During the construction of the Circle of Lebanon, the level of the ground had been raised, which meant that the trunk had been buried in a metre of soil. This smothering earth was what had caused it to rot. 'When we started uncovering this, I could see there was nothing I could have done to prevent the tree from dying.'

So . . . the cemetery killed the tree?

Frank nodded. 'It was given a death sentence a hundred and eighty years ago.'

He pointed over at the Circle. A young tree had been planted in the centre of the grass, where the old tree had been. Only three metres tall, it was dwarfed by its surroundings. Yet this new Cedar of Lebanon had a certain forlorn dignity; like a child at a parent's funeral, it provoked pity, but also admiration for the strength one could already see building within. It might, with luck and care, grow to thirty-five metres and live for a thousand years.

Frank regarded it, cheerfully. He could imagine it centuries hence, a veteran sentinel of the graveyard, shading tombs and sheltering birds, casting its long shadow on some future gardener, just like him, scratching his head and puzzling over how to prolong its life.

'You and I won't see that being an adult tree,' he smiled. 'But others will.'

UNMARKED

THE VERY REVEREND Andrew Nunn, Dean of Southwark Cathedral, waved, without breaking stride, to the driver of an orange Lamborghini who had slowed to watch the procession go by. Even supercars brake for God, and no wonder – it was quite a sight. Six priests and servers in white hooded albs, led by a verger in black and red robes, walked London's busy streets; a cross was held high, and clouds of incense from a thurible mingled with smells of fried onions and fatted calves from the stalls of Borough Market. We were on our way to say sorry to the dead.

There were around twenty of us processing behind the priests. We left the cathedral just after noon. Vapour trails criss-crossed the blue air. A St George's Cross, flying from the ancient tower, hung in a Saltire sky. Earlier, during mass, the Dean – an eloquent and sometimes wry man in his early sixties – had invited his congregation along. We would be going to Crossbones Graveyard, he said, resting place of the medieval sex workers who had been licensed by the Church but were not considered worthy of burial in consecrated ground. There would be a service in which he would express regret for the Church's complicity in historical injustice. 'It's not as heavy as it sounds,' he had added. 'There is some singing and some dancing. But not by me.'

Behind him as he spoke was a sixteenth-century altar screen – a wall of statues of biblical figures. All of them looked out towards the congregation, with one exception: Mary Magdalene, identifiable by her long hair, whose eyes were fixed upon the central statue of Christ. Saint Mary was present at the crucifixion. In the gospels of Mark, Matthew and John she is the first to witness the resurrection. Yet for hundreds of years of Christian tradition, art history and popular culture, she has been identified – some would say defamed and maligned – as a penitent prostitute, a woman within whom sensuality and spirituality interweave. The cathedral, in the medieval period, had a chapel dedicated to her – which might be because Southwark was, back then, a red-light district of sorts.

From the twelfth century, the area was part of the 'Liberty of the Clink' – not subject to the laws that governed the rest of the city. What happened in Southwark stayed in Southwark. Take a ferry there from across the Thames and you would find entertainments of the racier sort. Bull and bear-baiting? Step right up. Want to see the hot new plays: *Doctor Faustus*, *Volpone*, *Macbeth*? Step this way. The Liberty was under the control – if that is the word – of the Bishop of Winchester; the many brothels, known as 'stews', were licensed by him, and the women who worked there were thus known as Winchester Geese.

'How can the Church on one hand license these women and on the other bury them and their babies in unconsecrated ground, saying we don't want to know them?' Andrew Nunn had asked when we spoke before mass. 'That is what I regret. That is what we have to say sorry for.'

Crossbones is only a short walk from the cathedral. As the procession approached along Redcross Way, a woman in her late sixties was standing at the gate. She had tears in her eyes and goose feathers in her hair, her hands clasped as if in prayer. Around her neck: a crow's foot. This was Jennifer Cooper, a pagan – and retired bus driver – who is one of the Crossbones wardens, the volunteers who act as gatekeepers. 'Oh, this is one of the best days in the year,' she would tell me later. 'I start crying when I see the clergy coming round the corner with all their white and their gold on. It undoes me completely. Southwark Cathedral coming here! To say sorry to our girls! It's a bit late for them, you know, but the healing feeling is there. Marvellous!'

There are an estimated 15,000 people buried in Crossbones, but it does not look much like a graveyard. For one thing, there are no headstones, and probably never were. More than that, though, Crossbones has become a garden of remembrance to what one might call the outcast dead, their lives memorialised and celebrated by a community of people who see themselves as outsiders, margin-walkers, freaks. Their icon is Redcross Mary, the name given to a small statue of the Virgin, her blue mantle weather-bleached, her serene face chipped. She dandles in her arms not the Christ child but a small ceramic goose. She is the spiritual heart of Crossbones, a shrine to the homeless, abandoned babies, suicides and so on – a place to reflect upon and value those who, perhaps, were not loved and accepted in life. One young man, visiting recently, sat in the graveyard for two hours and then, on his way out the gate, turned back to say, 'Thank you for allowing me to be here.' His mother, a prostitute, had been killed by one of her clients. Crossbones was a place to remember her, too.

The procession from the cathedral passed beneath a long wooden canopy in the shape of a goose wing and into the graveyard proper. A young woman called Kirsten, in a black dress and floral headscarf, sang a Handel aria by way of welcome: *Sweet bird, that shun'st the noise of folly / Most musical, most melancholy . . .* Crossbones would already have been old when, in 1740, the work had its premiere just across the Thames.

John Stow, the sixteenth-century antiquarian, wrote in his 1598 *Survey of London* that the women working in the brothels of Southwark – the Boar's Head, the Cross Keys, the Cardinal's Hat and so on – 'were excluded from christian buriall, if they were not reconciled before their death. And therefore there was a plot of ground, called the single womans churchyeard, appoynted for them'. This is thought to be Crossbones. By the eighteenth century it had become a general burial ground for paupers; in *Gatherings from Grave Yards*, George Walker reported that it had been closed for around two years due to overcrowding – 'many of the poor Irish are buried in it' – but was being considered for reopening. It did so. In 1852, a group of local residents, fearful of cholera, wrote to the Home Secretary, Spencer Walpole, that it was a daily occurrence to see the gravedigger removing coffins in order to make room for new burials: 'When each of these exhumations have taken place, there have been seen in such human remains a number of skulls too numerous to mention, lying like half-devoured turnips about a sheepfold and cared for as little.'

We learn from Isabella Holmes in *The London Burial Grounds* that 'the famous Cross Bones' – she might have written *infamous* – closed finally in 1853. Other sources suggest that the last burials, a woman and a child, took place on Hallowe'en. Holmes quoted the inspection report that led to the closure: '"... it is crowded with dead, and many fragments of undecayed bones, some even entire, are mixed up with the earth of the mounds over the graves"'. As unconsecrated ground, it was sold at auction in 1886 and, according to a complaint raised by the local MP in the House of Commons, was used for 'penny circuses, switchback railways, waxworks and ghost shows, steam roundabouts etc, accompanied by steam and other organs, rattles, drums, bells and steam shriekers'. So much for the peace of the grave.

In 1992, work to extend the Jubilee Line of the Underground required a partial excavation of the site; archaeologists removed 148 skeletons from the mid-nineteenth century, around a third of which were those of children; of the adults, almost two-thirds were female. These people had it hard; cheap coffins, bent bones, lives lived in smog and slums. The Victorian social reformer Charles Booth, in his colour-coded poverty map of London, shows the streets around the grave-yard in shades of blue – meaning 'poor' and 'very poor' – and black: 'Lowest class. Vicious, semi-criminal.' George H. Duckworth, a researcher working for Booth, visited Redcross Way in March 1902 and wrote in his notebook that the street contained a 'notorious women's lodging house' at its north-east end, and that a constable had advised him against walking there alone. 'Police don't go down here unless they have to,' Duckworth writes, 'and never singly.'

One of the skeletons excavated for the Jubilee Line extension was a young woman who died in her mid- to late teens some time in the early 1850s. She has become known as the Crossbones Girl. There was a BBC documentary of that name. She was four foot seven and suffered terribly from syphilis, her bones pocked and pitted and scarred. Those who rest in unmarked graves are often those on whom life has left its cruellest marks.

Forensic anthropologists from the Centre for Anatomy and Human Identification at the University of Dundee have suggested that the Crossbones Girl was a prostitute, and – grim detail – caught the disease as a child. It disfigured her, but does not seem to have killed her. It has been speculated that her name was Elizabeth Mitchell and that she died in St Thomas's, a charity hospital, of pneumonia. If this is Elizabeth, then she died in the Magdalen ward – the part of the hospital where venereal diseases were treated. Her skull is kept in a cardboard box in a vault below the Museum of London, one of 20,000 Londoners from the Roman occupa-tion onwards who now rest there.

Crossbones is around thirty by forty metres. It had, when I visited, what I thought of as a post-apocalyptic look: rubble, cracked concrete, wildflowers everywhere. Buddleia with lolling purple tongues. Towers of hollyhocks seemed to mock and mirror the Shard, that great dagger stabbing the Southwark sky. Set into one wall was a cluster of wooden pipes used as nests by so-called solitary bees. 'Even the bees are outcasts here,' said one of the Crossbones regulars. 'But they are very happy, like many outcasts, actually, if they are allowed a chance to be themselves and walk their own path.'

Since 2014, the graveyard has been tended by volunteer gardeners from Bankside Open Spaces Trust, an environmental charity which also manages the site. The garden was created with raised beds and fresh soil so as not to disturb the dead. Any bones found were reburied. Prior to BOST's involvement, the space was known as 'The Invisible Garden', the creation of Andy Hulme – the so-called 'Invisible Gardener' – a security guard who lived in a caravan on-site. He also did gardening work for the fashion designer Vivienne Westwood and had inspired her menswear collection. Security was needed because the old graveyard was being used by heroin addicts as a place to shoot up. That's Crossbones: a place linking catwalk and shooting gallery.

Part of its charm, one might even say its importance, is as a weird liminal space right in the heart of corporate London: punky, DIY, 'haun-knitted' as we say in Scotland. Over the wall are building-site cranes, office blocks of glass and steel. Who knows how much this ground must be worth? Its value, though, is something different, deeper, not to be counted in pounds, dollars, euros, square feet. This is a place of skulls, stories, sadnesses; an oddball Golgotha. Those weeds pushing up through the cracks in the concrete – the crack gardens, they call them – seem important. There is a flaw in the ground, and a seed gets in, the light gets in; soon you have shoots, a stem, a driven flower. Everyday miracles are not for sale.

The Dean and the rest of the clergy took up position at the far end of the site. The service was about to begin. Drawn on the wooden hoarding behind them was a diagram of the old Liberty, including the Tabard inn, where Chaucer's pilgrims set off for Canterbury, and the Marshalsea Prison, where Little Dorrit was born. Chalked on another wall were the words:

> *and well we know*
> *how the carrion crow*
> *doth feast in our*
> *Cross Bones*
> *Graveyard*

'Tomorrow is the Feast of St Mary Magdalene . . .' the Dean began. 'This land on which we stand has received the bodies of women of our community and their born and unborn children, who served the needs of men, but whose own needs were ignored; who were paid a price for love but were refused the gift of real love; who were used to line the coffers of the Church but rejected by the Church; whose sins excluded them even though Jesus would have included them.

'My friends, we cannot undo the sins of yesterday but we can do right today, and that is why we are here, with regret, in remembrance and to continue what we began on this day some years ago: to pray for the restoration of this land, of these memories, and of the eternal souls of our sisters and their children. So let us pray.'

We prayed. There was poetry, chanting, a reading from the gospels. The Dean asked us to consider Mary Magdalene in Gethsemane: 'As she stood in a garden that had become a graveyard, we stand in a graveyard that has become a garden.'

He used an aspergillum – a silver ball on a stick, a kind of holy ice-cream scoop – to sprinkle water around Crossbones, an act of cleansing. Some of it landed on a rather startled black lab. 'Oh,' said the Dean, deadpan. 'That woke the dog up.'

The Christian part of the ceremony over, the clergy returned, job done, to the cathedral. Had the soul of Elizabeth Mitchell, and thousands like her, risen a little closer to heaven as a result of his efforts? It would be nice to think that she had no need for priestly intervention. Her life itself must have been a kind of hell, and death an end to pain. It would not be right to romanticise that life, or to make a cult of the misery of selling sex, historical or otherwise. But it felt like an honour to be part of honouring those women.

A man stepped forward holding a guitar by its rainbow strap. He had short white hair, and a bright blue Paisley shirt with a chunky string of beads in place of a tie. His blue jacket had a spine and ribcage painted on the back. This was John Constable, sometimes known as John Crow. He's a playwright, a poet, a shamanic street preacher. We'll be hearing more from him.

'Welcome to Crossbones!' he said.

*

Just a little past hole three of Ballycastle Golf Club is where you'll find it. You may not be looking for it, may not understand what it is when you first see it, and then, once you do know, you may wish you didn't. But still, that's where it is, the *cillín*.

'This,' said Toni Maguire, 'is where all the babies are buried.'

Maguire, who is in her mid-sixties, is an archaeologist and anthropologist. We were standing by a grassy mound at

the side of a narrow path leading to the ruins of the fifteenth-century Bonamargy Friary. It would look like a patch of waste ground were it not for a boulder, placed on the site recently by the local historical society. 'Cillín,' it read, in golden letters below a Celtic cross.

I knelt to push aside the long grass at the foot of the stone, revealing two lines in English:

> *In Memory Of All Those Buried*
> *Here In Unmarked Graves*

This is a cillín – a 'little church' – one of more than 1,400 across the island of Ireland as a whole. It is pronounced 'killeen' and you sometimes see it written that way. This one was in use until at least the 1950s, and the people buried here are, almost certainly, infants who died before they could be baptised.

Without that ritual to cleanse them of Original Sin, the taint passed down from Adam and Eve, infants were not permitted to be buried in consecrated ground; they would, it was thought, pollute the soil – and the souls of all those buried in it. Denied the solace and safe harbour of churchyard or cemetery, parents had to make their own arrangements. *Cillíní* were an answer to two urgent questions: one spiritual, the other practical. How to give your child a chance of getting into heaven when Roman Catholic theology and canon law – the Church's rule book – say it is impossible? And how, in the absence of a headstone or even an official name to put on it, to bury them so you can find them again?

Some places where you will find cillíní: inside or near very old ruined churches which have fallen out of use; on the boundaries of churchyards which are still in use; within stone circles; within *ráths* (ancient ring forts, often interpreted as being gateways to fairyland); on clifftops; near townland boundaries; on small islands accessible by causeway; at the side of holy wells; at the foot of hawthorn trees. Toni Maguire calls them a 'furtive presence' in the Irish landscape. These were clandestine spots with their own funerary culture. There would have been variation from place to place, no doubt, but there seems to have been an understanding that the child ought to be buried between sundown on the day it died and sunrise the following morning. We might picture a man setting out in the gloaming, a box beneath his arm, and returning in darkness unburdened – physically, at least. The instinct was to see your son or daughter well buried, despite the religious restrictions.

'Parents had to find a way to deal with this issue that didn't bring them into conflict with the Church, but at the same time allowed them to do what was morally right,' Maguire told me. 'It's about inclusion, but on a very secret level. They would never tell the priest, "I go up to the cillín, my baby's buried there," – but they'll do it quietly on their own.'

There is archaeological and historical evidence that cillíní have existed in Ireland since the early seventeenth century, although it has been suggested that they were used long before that and may even have their roots in pagan burial customs. Anecdotal evidence suggests that there was a continued culture of use until the 1980s and perhaps even beyond.

In a journal article of 1879, the Irish archaeologist William Wakeman observed that 'in many districts of Ireland, in fact all over the face of the country, are ancient cemeteries, usually of small dimensions, which time out of mind have not been used for the purposes of Christian burial. They were, and numbers of them are to this day, the depositories only of the remains of still-born or unbaptised children and suicides.' They are, he wrote, 'dreary and unhallowed places' and 'looked upon with horror by the modern Celt who in no case will approach them after dark'.

As that quote suggests, the use of cillíní was not restricted to those who had not received the sacrament of baptism. Others who could be denied burial in consecrated ground included women who died in childbirth, unknown bodies washed ashore, murderers, the excommunicated and those who had taken their own lives. Families who could not afford a formal burial would also lay children there.

The poet and Irish-language scholar Robin Flower, writing in *The Western Island*, his 1944 memoir of life on Great Blasket, off the coast of County Kerry, gives a solemn, vivid account of a cillíní funeral. A newborn has died, its father has made a coffin of 'raw, unhallowed wood', which he now carries at the head of a procession through the village. It is raining heavily – 'long veils drifting over the dead calm of the sea' – as they approach the cillín:

> We turned into a little promontory of the cliff beyond
> the houses, and stopped in an unkempt space of dank,

clinging grass, with stones scattered over it here and there. A man with a spade had dug a shallow grave, and there, amid the sobs of women and the muttered prayers of the whole assembly, the father with a weary gesture laid away his child. The earth was shovelled back, closing with hardly a sound about the little box, a few prayers were said, and then we all turned list- lessly away, leaving the lonely, unfledged soul to its eternity . . .

Flower, feeling oppressed by the occasion, stops in at the house of the island storyteller, Tomás, who explains the pur- pose and history of the cillín:

He took his seat on the settle and began to talk of the place we had just left. There, he said, the islanders had been accustomed to bury suicides and unbaptized children; a sad association, I thought, of those who had known nothing and those who had known too much of life.

Toni Maguire, when we had earlier discussed the meaning and atmosphere of such places, had a much more positive take. Those scattered stones spoke, she felt, of a certain tender dissent. 'If you take your baby and choose a really nice spot in the landscape that's important to you, that's taking control back from the Church,' she said. 'It's reassuring to me, as an Irish woman, that people stood up to them and were not prepared to accept, en masse, what their priest said. There's very much a defiance in that.'

She is an expert on the cillíní of County Antrim. For her master's thesis, she travelled around the region, armed with wellies and old maps and nineteenth-century books, seek- ing cillíní and plotting them out. In this way, she identified almost a hundred. But she didn't just look, she listened. She spoke to gravediggers and the elderly, picking up stories like pebbles of quartz, following the light darkwards.

As we drove over the high peatlands from Ballycastle to Cushendall, she recalled one of those conversations: 'This is where I saw the wee old man cutting turf.'

This would have been around 2005 and he was then in his eighties. She had pulled over to greet him, explained what she was about. They had spoken, at first, in generalities. Yes, he knew about cillíní; yes, there were a lot around here. Soon, though, he began to his own tale. He and his wife, in the early years of their marriage, lost a number of babies. They had their pick of cillíní, of course, but his wife worried that one day, when she was old, she would be unable to walk out to the moors and headlands to visit the children she had lost. What to do instead? Together, they made a plan.

At the time of the first miscarriage, the man dug a grave at the back door of the farmhouse, straddling the entrance, one half in the hall, one half in the yard. He lined it with old stones that he had taken from a disused cemetery, and laid the body inside. 'Then,' Maguire recalled, 'they put a flagstone over the top, so that every day, when they walked out that door, they would remember them.' They had a pact, the man and his wife: whichever of them died first, the other would make sure that the remains of their children went into the grave with them. That way, when the other passed away they would, finally, be all together.

I find that story moving, but also shivery and discomforting. It's the idea of having your dead so close. Walking across the grave of your children every time you go out to peg some washing – there is, for me, a horror in that.

Maguire nodded when I told her this, but couldn't agree. 'Sometimes,' she said, 'it's about your point of view. As a woman, I can see how the mother would think, "I've got them close with me. They're still here. I'm protecting them."'

When Maguire talks about cillíní, she does not do so in the dispassionate manner of a historian. Her strong emotional connection to these places is rooted, at least in part, in her own life experience. She and her husband have two adult children, but it was a hard road to get there. Before her successful pregnancies, she miscarried three children, including twins. 'So I have a real empathy with the babies and the mothers who lost them. I couldn't get past eighteen to twenty weeks. And I had nothing to bury. Then here's these women who maybe went full term, had a baby, the baby dies, and it has to be buried in the middle of the night. At some point they must have seen or held that baby, and then it's gone.

'Sometimes I think, "Was this particular research laid at my door? Did I have to have that experience of miscarriage in order to take this on and relate to it?" I feel these women and babies have nobody to speak for them. But I will bloody speak for them.'

If the souls of unbaptised infants didn't go to heaven, where did they go? The answer was limbo; specifically Limbus Infantum, the limbo of the infants, a place between heaven and hell. There is nothing in the Bible about this, but the concept developed over centuries of Church thinking. For the families whose child died, this would mean suffering what Toni Maguire calls a 'double death' – the child is lost to them not only physically but spiritually.

Archaeologists talk about cillíní sites as 'liminal' spaces, meaning that they are often on thresholds or boundaries of some kind. The entrance to a farmhouse, say, or – as in the case of Oileán na Marbh, the Isle of the Dead, off the coast of Donegal – an island accessible at low tide. The transitional status of such places reflects limbo itself: neither one thing nor another, a borderland between within and without, land and sea, divine light and infernal fire.

From the archaeologist Emer Dennehy, I learned the Irish expression '*dorchadas gan phian*' – darkness without pain – a horribly lyrical description of what these infant souls were believed to experience in the afterlife. Denied the presence of God for eternity, separated from their families for ever, they were being held responsible for the disobedience of Eden. Having not lived long enough to commit sins of their own, they were at least spared the hellish torments. There was, of course, plenty of pain for those left behind – the parents whose loss could not be soothed by any thought that they would be reunited in death.

Dennehy is an authority on the cillíní of County Kerry. 'The emotional side of it is what I'm drawn to,' she told me. 'What was going through the mind of the parent – the father or uncle – who was having to put the child in there? They would knowingly or unknowingly seek out a place that would reflect its marginalised status but also keep it safe. I'm caught by the emotions of what they, and the poor wife at home, would have gone through; not being able to mourn the child, not being able to mark its grave, and living with this quiet grief that they can't express. They were trying to do a kindness for the children using the means they had available to them.'

And the children themselves? 'They are the unknown dead.'

When, in the course of her work, Dennehy uncovers the remains of infants in unconsecrated ground, she performs a type of baptism over their bodies. She is a rational and intelligent professional in the twenty-first century, yet does this out of respect and sympathy for the beliefs of the men and women who, denied a churchyard, placed these children in the unblessed dirt. 'If I can bring solace to the soul of that child, or to the souls of the parents, I'll do it.'

Here is how it works. She recites – often just in her head – these words: 'If you be of Adam, I name thee John; if you be of Eve, I name thee Jane.' There are, she says, an awful lot of Janes and Johns out there now.

It is important that they have names, she feels. It is part of remembering. Without a headstone, without a name, they are forgotten. It's that old idea: you die twice; once when your heart stops beating, and again on the last occasion someone mentions your name. There's also a risk of cultural forgetting. Outside of archaeological circles, how well known are cillíní now? At one time, everyone in a community would have known where these places were and what they were for. But as they have fallen out of use, so too are they falling out of memory.

'A lot of these graves are unmarked, they are in field corners, and farmers, unwittingly, are going to plough up what's left,' Dennehy said. 'If that happened to a normal grave there would be an outcry. So why isn't it the same for these? No, we can't forget them. Sometimes I feel like I'm the only one crying for them. Who's grieving for these children now?'

It would be tempting, and perhaps even comforting, to think that the unbaptised were buried in this way only in rural areas, where religion and superstition were at their most powerful. Not so. In Belfast's Milltown Cemetery, resting place of the city's Catholics since 1869, a large area was set aside for such burials.

The bottom-left-hand corner of Milltown is marked on the cemetery map as 'poor ground'. It takes me around ten minutes to walk its perimeter. These were mass graves. Originally, there would have been no gravestones, but in recent years, as families discover and rediscover where their lost children and other relatives were buried, markers have gone up. These vary from proper marble headstones to simple wooden crosses to a fading painted cherub lolling in the grass, its wings clarted with strimmer cuttings. The dates of death range from 1937 to 1980. Although only a hundred or so graves are marked, it is thought that the remains of around 11,000 are interred here.

It is notable that almost all of these stones bear names. Even if a baby was not named by a priest, it would have been named by its parents and that name passed down through the family. One small wooden cross, though, has the words 'Unknown Child' written across it, and a date in the summer of 1969. This likely means that he or she was found abandoned, but there is something about the anonymity – no name, no gender – that gives this grave a symbolic quality: one standing for all. The cross may be falling apart, held together by ribbon, and the teddy bear which someone has placed at its foot may be dirty and damp, but this square foot of earth has, I think, as much poignant dignity as the Tomb of the Unknown Warrior in Westminster Abbey. Infant or infantryman, the lord knoweth them that are his.

This part of Milltown came to prominence in 2008 when it emerged that the Trustees, who operate the cemetery on behalf of its owners, the Diocese of Down and Connor, had leased the land to the Ulster Wildlife Trust; it became part of a larger nature reserve in that area, the Bog Meadows. The deal prompted an outcry – and soon a campaign, in which the archaeologist Toni Maguire was prominent – from those who had relatives buried there. The Church undertook a number of detailed surveys of the land, apologised for its mistake, and paid to take ownership once again. In 2009, Bishop Noel Treanor consecrated the ground.

I had come to Milltown to meet Siubhainin Ni Chutn-neagam. She is in her sixties and works as an ambulance controller. She has a relation here – her mother's youngest sister, Susan, after whom she is named. Susan Griffin was born in January 1938 and died in November 1940. She would have been baptised, so why was she buried in this part of the cemetery? Family legend had it that the little girl had choked on the bone of a fish, but the death certificate said diarrhoea, so now the best guess is that some sort of fear of infection caused her body to be laid here in an unmarked grave. A photograph thought to have been taken on her first birthday shows a little girl in a patterned gown propped up on a cushion and laughing at someone just to the left of the camera. A sibling perhaps. She was the youngest of twelve. 'My mum and her sisters remember her being in the coffin on the table in the house,' Siubhainin said.

It was a drizzly morning and we sat in the car to talk. The radio played Fauré. Rosary beads hung from the rear-view mirror.

We peered out through the rain. An elderly lady, standing by the grave of her baby brother, sloshed holy water from a bottle on to the ground. The stream looked like a skipping rope, but this was no child's game. It was deadly serious – an attempt to make up for all the years when this earth was unhallowed.

The figure reminded Siubhainin of an occasion, a few years ago, when she visited Milltown. This area of the cemetery was still overgrown and none of the graves were marked. Siubhainin had not yet found the grave of her mother's sister, and had come down, by moonlight, in the hope that she might somehow sense her presence.

'It was about five o'clock in the morning, and I saw an old woman – I would say in her eighties – just walking up and down, calling out and calling out. So I went over and asked, could I help. She told me she had walked this path every day for years, looking for her child.

'She was your old Irish lady, in the black. I know it wasn't a ghost because I held her hand. That day I said to her, "If your child is down in this land, I will find her." And we did. We found the child.'

Siubhainin and Toni Maguire began to search the public records, helping families to locate their loved ones. Often, the exact location had been lost to family memory. The graves were unmarked, the ground overgrown, and the burial – decades in the past – may have been witnessed only by the father of the child and the gravedigger, it being a convention in the old days that women did not attend. 'We were absolutely inundated with people,' Siubhainin recalled. 'Can you help me find my baby? Can you help me find my brothers? Can you help me find my sister? So many sad stories. So many people carried that loss with them through their whole lives.'

I asked Siubhainin how she feels about this ground. Protective, she said. There is anger, too. 'How many babies are buried down here because women weren't allowed birth control?' She seems to be a person of deep faith, but seeing the cruel consequences of theology has shaken her belief in the institutions of the Church. 'Now it's just me and my God. I don't have any in-betweeners.'

Limbo itself is now in an uneasy marginal place, theologically speaking; it is on the tideline of faith, somewhere between belief and disbelief.

From the early 1970s, the Catholic Church began moving away from the idea that the unbaptised should not be buried in consecrated ground, and the practice has now ended. Although a dead child cannot receive the sacrament of baptism, a priest will name that child as part of the funeral rite. In 2007, the Vatican published a document, *The Hope of Salvation for Infants Who Die Without Being Baptised*, the fruit of lengthy deliberation by Church scholars. The study concluded 'that there are theological and liturgical reasons to hope that infants who die without baptism may be saved and brought into eternal happiness', but that this remains only a hope, and therefore children, whenever possible, should still receive the sacrament without delay.

So does limbo exist? Is there a realm of darkness without pain in which reside the souls of those buried in cillíní and in the mass graves of Milltown? The Church cannot say for sure.

Still, the belief persists. 'I have a wee grandson who was born with a really serious heart defect,' Siubhainin told me. 'As soon as he was born, they rushed him straight to the Royal' – the Royal Belfast Hospital for Sick Children – 'and he was going on the air ambulance to Birmingham within hours for emergency surgery.

'Well, *I* baptised the baby. I had holy water, and they moved him towards me in the incubator, and I touched him with my fingers and baptised him. If he had died during the journey, I would know that he would be in heaven and he wouldn't be in this limbo. Then, as soon as he arrived in Birmingham, my daughter-in-law sent for the local priest and he came and did it officially.'

What she did is a 'baptism of desire'. It is also known as lay baptism or baptism on the floor – the idea being that if the child is in imminent danger of death, the faith of the person administering the sacrament, although not a priest, cleanses them of sin.

Siubhainin had told me earlier that although she had grown up believing in limbo, she had come to believe it was a nonsense. Yet, in that moment of crisis, she was taking no chances. No grandson of hers was going there, not if she could help it. Clearly, the belief goes deep.

She nodded. 'It's about fear.'

The rain had stopped. We got out of the car and walked over to the graves. I had one last question. The old lady in black whom she encountered that morning: what did she say when Siubhainin told her that she had found the place where, all these years, her child had lain?

'She just cried. Just cried and cried and cried.'

*

'WELCOME TO CROSSBONES!' said John Crow.

Four months had passed since the Feast of Mary Magdalene. It was November. The 23rd of November. That detail is important. Crossbones vigils are always held on the 23rd of the month, and this was the twenty-third anniversary of the night when the writer John Constable (sometimes known as John Crow) had a vision of what he calls 'The Goose' – part Mary Magdalene, part medieval prostitute, part muse – who dictated to him a long verse poem called *The Southwark Mysteries*. He was, back then, in a kind of trance, having taken the biggest dose of LSD he had ever risked, before or since.

It wasn't a hedonistic act. He had been seeking revelation, and found himself wandering the streets of Southwark in the small hours, visiting its ancient sites – the ruins of Winchester Palace, the cathedral and so on – before fetching up at the heavy gate to what, at that time, was a patch of waste ground covered in rubbish. The name Crossbones came to him in his vision, he says, and it was only later that he realised that this was the historic site of the graveyard. In that moment, he sensed that there was something special here; it seemed a sacred place that ought to be reclaimed.

That reclamation has been the great work of his life. In 2000, *The Southwark Mysteries* was performed at the Globe Theatre and at the cathedral. 'It's quite a challenging piece, let us say,' the Dean had told me. 'We had never had a devil with a huge phallus walking into the cathedral before. That raised a few eyebrows.'

More important, perhaps, than that acceptance by the religious and arts establishments is the way in which the grave-yard itself has become the focus of ceremony. Beginning in 1998, each Hallowe'en has been marked by a so-called 'vigil' at Crossbones; and from 23 June 2004 these became monthly. Led by Constable, in his John Crow 'urban magician' persona, these have a curious ambience – part utterly sincere magical rite, part playful bohemian happening, part performance art knees-up. David Bowie, in death, was named 'Angel of the Outcast' at a vigil; this was appropriate, as his misfit grace, his blurring of gender and sexuality, is very Crossbones. But it also gave everyone the chance to have a jolly good singalong to 'Starman'.

Constable, though, was now sixty-seven, and had not, of late, been in good health. More than that, he felt that his particular vision of Crossbones is 'a magical work' and it was time to bring it to a close. This, then, would be his final vigil, which was why, at 7 p.m., around three hundred of us were standing on the street outside the graveyard. The long, tall metal gate was locked. It was a barrier, a threshold; the living on one side, the dead on the other. One day, of course, we would all be on the other side of such a gate. For now, we looked in, and wondered.

The gate was covered in beads and photos and dolls and shoes and flowers, but mostly in ribbons, on which were written the names of the departed. John Onion, Glassmaker, 1725. Jason Fisher, pirate radio DJ, 2011. Lindsay Kemp, dancer, 2018. A crocheted pink hoop bore the names Tania, Gemma, Anneli, Paula and Netty. 'We remember the murdered women of Ipswich,' it read, 'as daughters, friends, lovers, mothers, and above all as women. For all they were and could have been.'

Through the gate, I could see Redcross Mary, lit by candles arranged in a crossbones pattern. Nearby were eight knee-high concrete figures of what looked like Buddhist monks. Some of them wore bright red knitted balaclavas. These Jizo statues are associated with miscarried, stillborn and aborted children, the Japanese word for which is *mizuko* or water child. 'One of the traditions connected with Jizo is that he's the protector of children who would not be able otherwise to enter paradise,' a Crossbones regular had told me during my previous visit. 'Just as in Christianity there are complicated traditions around unbaptised children, so in Buddhism it was believed that children who hadn't been through the initial rituals wouldn't be able to get over the river into the afterlife. But Jizo, being compassionate, smuggled them through in the folds of his kimono.' The statues had been placed in the graveyard by women who had lost children and wanted some kind of ritual through which they could express their grief.

Jennifer Cooper, the lady with the crow's foot necklace, was here, of course. If, once again, she had goose feathers in her hair, they were hidden by a sensible woolly hat. She had been coming to Crossbones for fifteen years, and is part of the collective which would go on to lead the vigils following John Constable's retirement. Her late husband, Chris, and eldest son, Gary, are remembered on the gate with ribbons and photographs, she explained, as are Chris's parents and brother. There was a time in her life when Cooper suffered from depression, and for two years could not even speak. 'But I would come every month to Crossbones and just stand. And this energy just accepted and held me. What can I say? This is my soul place. We're all here together.'

The air smelled of incense and gin, and a little dope. The Shard gleamed hard and bright in the London night. I wondered what the people up there would make of us down here? And, for that matter, what the skeletons below our feet would make of us up here, flesh-clad and expectant?

'Spirits of the dead, spirits of the living, kindred,' said John Crow, 'welcome to this, the 186th Crossbones vigil.' He was wearing a black velvet coat and a broad smile. 'We come here to remember the outcast dead, to remember our own lost loved ones, and to remember the living – all the outcasts, the street people, those with drug and alcohol issues, the sex workers, whether they are the victims of exploitation or choose what they do freely. We honour all of these people from the edges of society.'

What followed was extraordinary. Poetry, music, readings from *The Southwark Mysteries*. Morris dancers in top hats, face paint, and black and purple coats roared and strutted and clashed staffs to the sound of pipes and drums. The folk-punk musician Frank Turner performed 'The Graveyard of the Outcast Dead', a song inspired by this place. Raga Woods, an environmental activist in her late seventies, wearing a headdress of scarves and ivy, called out: 'We're connecting with the people whose bones were unearthed and who led us to be in this place. Hallelujah!' Someone else brought news from Liverpool: 'Tonight in Toxteth a pyramid is being made out of the ashes of dead loved ones.' Jules Allen, a mild-looking chap with a taste for serendipity, riffed on the significance of the number so important to Crossbones.

'The number of years that Yorick's skull lay buried before it was discovered by Hamlet?' he asked the crowd.

'Twenty-three!' came the reply.

'The number of hundred thousand stones in the Great Pyramid of Giza?'

'Twenty-three!'

'The height in feet that the tidal Thames rises and falls in central London every twelve hours?'

'Twenty-three!'

And so on. To be in the midst of this felt, at times, like participating in some sort of benign hippy death-cult. It was fun. But never frivolous. At a previous vigil, someone had read out their sister's suicide note, and that was as much in keeping with the spirit of Crossbones as the songs and laughter and chanting. This is a place of healing and tolerance. Where the poor were once dumped is now rich with meaning. It feels important, in the midst of London wealth, that there should be such experiences that money can't buy.

The ground is owned by Transport for London, and leased to Bankside Open Spaces Trust, which hopes to secure a long-term lease, guaranteeing its protection in perpetuity. There are plans to develop the immediate area for housing, office space, restaurants: the usual stuff for which London always hungers. While TfL has said that the graveyard will be safeguarded, BOST and the Friends of Crossbones wish to ensure that it retains its character and integrity, its wildness and weirdness – that it doesn't become a thoroughfare or a nice little park. Neither should it be a place where the comfortable middle classes come to feel sorry for the historical poor; it is for the poor *now*, for those who are hurting *now*. It is alive. 'Will Crossbones last for ever?' is a question you'll ask in vain. 'Will London last for ever?' comes the reply. The guardians of this place are not prophets. The city is full of old burial grounds concreted beneath playgrounds, car parks, and the courtyards of blocks of flats. Even the graveyards have graves.

With his wife Katy Kaos at his side, and a raven-headed staff in hand, John Constable, John Crow, brought his time as ringmaster of this skull circus to a close. He had told me earlier that he felt some sadness at letting go. Part of him wondered what, without the vigils, would keep him alive? But as the ritual drew to an end, he seemed joyful and without regret. He encouraged us all to press forward and touch the gates, wishing for health, peace and love. To call for these things on a dim street outside an old boneyard in an old city in the dying weeks of a dark year may well be daft. But it felt good to ask.

I thought of what Constable had told me when I visited on the Feast of Mary Magdalene.

'This is what Crossbones is about,' he had said. 'It's about seeing the beauty in brokenness. Which is why when people say sometimes, "When will the garden be finished?" I tend to reply, "We hope never." Because, like all of us, it's work in progress.'

ANCHOR

IT IS KNOWN AS the Green Isle, but as the boat approached over Loch Shiel, I could see that it was fringed with red: encircled, around its edge, by rowans, berries bright in the late-summer sun.

The farmer put in at the stone jetty and we walked up on to the island. This is the way the coffins come. Footsteps up the hill and into the interior must sink deeper, beneath their burden, than those heading back off. Could one analyse a footprint and identify grief in its tread? St Finnan's Isle, or Eilean Fhionnan – to give this place its formal names – would be the place to do it. The climb to the graves is short but steep. It must surely be hard on the bearers, trying not to slip or buckle under the weight.

We were fortunate; our business was not the solemn duty of a burial, and the heaviest thing to carry was a large drum of water – for cleaning headstones.

I was accompanying Robert Ross from the Common-wealth War Graves Commission as he went about his work. The CWGC looks after 170,000 graves in the UK, of which 21,000 or so are found in Scotland. A few locations have large numbers of burials – the Lyness Royal Naval Cemetery on Orkney has seven hundred – but most cemeteries in Scotland have fewer than ten war graves, and many are in far-flung locations. In a 339-mile round trip over the next five days, Robert Ross would visit, clean and maintain just twenty-seven graves – covering Moidart, the isolated Ardnamurchan pen-insula, and the Hebridean island of Eigg. To do this, he would have to make five crossings by ferry, plus the short hops in a wee boat to and from this island in the western Highlands.

It's his job. But is it also a sort of pilgrimage? 'Yeah,' he smiled. 'There's the word. It can be like a pilgrimage. Going to the place and seeing the grave and taking the time to do the work is a gesture. The people who are in the graves will never know, but *you* know that you've done it, and that matters.

'I'm a gardener, and to be able to create a space where people can come and feel able to be themselves and have that moment of grief and peace and remembrance – that's really important. It feels like the right thing to do.'

He is thirty-two and cheery company, taking the job seriously but wearing it lightly. As he spoke, he consulted a hand-drawn map and we headed up the hill.

One of the reasons war graves are so scattered in Scotland is as a result of air crashes and ships being sunk. Casualties were buried as close as possible to where they washed ashore. That could mean a tiny graveyard on a tiny island. Aircrew whose plane came down in the mountains or on a clifftop might be buried at the crash site if it was judged too difficult to recover them. Death strikes in its random way. Your ship is torpedoed and that eternal bier, the tide, carries your body to a remote part of the Western Isles. Your plane falls out of the sky on to a Highland peak, the consequence of which is that, decades later, the Commonwealth War Graves Commission has to plan how to visit and mark and then maintain that site. It is chaos colliding with order, loss with logistics. You are drowned, or killed on impact, or blown apart, yet you, in common with your fallen comrades, will have your grave marked by a headstone rising precisely 813 mm from the level of the soil. The grass, if you are buried in a CWGC cemetery, will be maintained at no less than 3.5 cm and no more than 6 cm in height. In this way, bureaucracy soothes brutality.

Two examples stand for all.

ANCHOR

The Monachs, a group of islands six miles west of North Uist in the Hebrides, have been uninhabited since 1942, except by the 10,000 grey seals that heave themselves ashore in autumn to mate and have pups. Since January 1917, one of those islands – Ceann Iar – has provided a home of sorts for Lieutenant William McNeill, whose ship, HMS *Laurentic*, struck two mines laid by a U-boat off the coast of County Donegal and went down with the loss of 354 souls. McNeill, an Orcadian, was carried 150 miles north to the Monachs, where he is said to have been found by fishermen. He was buried near the shore, the spot marked by a stone cairn and metal plaque. In what feels like a kind of cosmic balancing, the island of Ceann Ear – to which Ceann Iar is linked at low tide – holds the grave of Otto Schatt, a mechanic on the German submarine U-110, which was sunk by British destroyers on 15 March 1918. To visit the Monachs, CWGC workers must take a private boat from North Uist, and landing is highly weather-dependent. Still, they get out there around every five years to check McNeill's grave and clean his plaque, and do the same – even though it is not their responsibility – for Otto Schatt. The naval officer and the Unterseebootmann: enemies in life, neighbours in death.

Consider, too, the aircrew who, on 13 April 1941, crashed in wild snowy weather during a training flight near the summit of Ben More Assynt, in the far north-west of Scotland. The six bodies were discovered weeks after the crash, on 25 May. Robert Lowe, the shepherd who found them, buried them where they had died, using parts of the plane to create a makeshift cross. The site has been described as the most remote war grave in the UK. It is on a plateau high in the wilderness, about five miles from the nearest road, and getting to it means a challenging two- to three-hour walk. Thanks to the considerable efforts of the veteran rescue worker and guide

David 'Heavy' Whalley, and local mountain rescue teams, a 600 kg memorial stone was airlifted into place in 2013 by a Chinook helicopter and is now maintained by the CWGC.

'We have to go where they are buried,' Robert Ross had told me. 'That's what it's all about: being able to say, "This is where these people are. Don't forget them. We know where they are and we're going to look after them." That's how it's been from the start, when Fabian Ware was going around the battlefields of France.'

The CWGC was established by Fabian Ware during the First World War and until 1960 was called the Imperial War Graves Commission. Ware was a former editor of the *Morning Post*. Too old for active service at forty-five, he had led a volunteer ambulance unit in France. It was in October 1914, while inspecting wooden crosses in a makeshift cemetery, that he was struck by the thought of finding a better, more lasting way to mark the graves of the fallen. His two central ideas were that the dead should be treated equally, regardless of rank or station in life, and that the headstones should be permanent. Crucial, too, was his belief that bodies should not be repatriated to the countries from which they had come; they should remain buried where they fell, beside the men with whom they had fought. This was controversial – understandably, families very often wanted their loved ones brought home when possible – but there was a certain poetry in it. It was a policy encapsulated by the soldier-poet Rupert Brooke's famous lines:

> *If I should die, think only this of me:*
> *That there's some corner of a foreign field*
> *That is for ever England.*

For ever Scotland, too, of course, and Wales and Australia and India and the rest. There are almost 1.7 million

Commonwealth war graves and memorials at 23,000 locations in 153 countries, and in every continent except Antarctica.

There are two on the Green Isle: Private Mary MacDonald who died in 1944 at the age of twenty-three, and Dugald Grant, a deckhand, who died in 1916 aged twenty-six. They were both local to the area, from families with roots deep in Moidart, so it would have been thought right and proper that they were buried here.

It is an ancient Christian site, said to have been the base from which Finnan, an Irish monk arriving via Iona, spread the faith in the seventh century. He was followed by further missionaries from Iona Abbey, and, as a result of these associations, the island itself became a holy place. Clan chiefs were buried here, and the ordinary folk, too. Penitents would do penance on the island; if weather prevented their crossing, they would kneel on the shore and pray. There were annual pilgrimages on the feast day of St Finnan. A roofless church dates from the thirteenth or fourteenth century, and the oldest gravestones are thought to be early medieval.

The island is very small. You could walk its perimeter in fifteen minutes, but you would never do that; it's too rough and boggy. The ground grows firmer as you climb towards the centre and all the time there is the feeling of uneven stone underfoot – graves invisible beneath the grass. Deer swim out to the island and keep the worst of the vegetation down, but it is still quite overgrown. Here and there, a remarkable stone is exposed. A slab carved with a skeleton is said, by tradition, to be that of the Reverend Alexander Macdonald, who once lived in the turreted farmhouse now home to John Macaulay, the farmer who brought us here, although there is some doubt that the grave is his. That skeleton grave is from the seventeenth century, but others are much more recent. One, a boy – his name was Roman – who died at the age of nine months in the 1980s, is at the foot of a rosehip bush; next to Roman's grave, a candle decorated with a picture of the Virgin Mary made me think of the cillíní of Ireland. St Finnan's Isle, though consecrated, is certainly a liminal space: out there between the sky and the loch, tangled up in blue.

In his 1934 book *Scotland's Road of Romance*, Augustus Muir recalled travelling by steamer on Loch Shiel from Dalilea to Glenfinnan. As the boat passed St Finnan's Isle, the captain told him a tale: 'They say that the soul of the dead keeps watch over the island until the next burial, and then it is free to leave. I don't think I'm believing it, though some have seen a light on the island after it is dark.'

I like that story. Who doesn't like a ghost story? But the truth is that the island, at least during daylight hours, did not feel eerie. It felt serene. More, it felt like 'a thin place', as the Reverend George Macleod once described Iona, meaning that the material and spiritual realms seem close together. I sensed that most strongly in the ruined church. It is just a shell, with low walls and a carpet of grass, but no one who steps inside could doubt that it remains holy.

There is an altar at one end – a large stone slab on top of which someone had placed a piece of wood, roughly carved into the shape of a boat; a candle in the centre of this boat had melted down to a stubby mast. Set into the wall behind the altar is a stone cross, about two feet high, with the figure of Christ carved into it. Time and weather have worn away his features, if he ever had any, but I found this crucifix incredibly powerful and the overall effect of the church and altar was enchanting and disorientating. It was as though entirely different periods of history had come together, like clasped hands. If the Neolithic village of Skara Brae in Orkney had been a Christian settlement, it might look something like this.

Until recently, the altar had been graced by another object: a bronze handbell. Charles MacDonald, who was for many years priest in the area and is buried beneath the island's most prominent cross, wrote about this bell in his 1889 book *Moidart among the Clanranalds*:

> Its notes are remarkably sweet, and when rung out on a calm day during those moments when the loch is undisturbed by a passing breath of wind, they waken within the breast of the listener a feeling of sadness, which is not inappropriate in a spot where so many generations are quietly sleeping around. It has been left exposed on the altar for more than two hundred years, nothing saving it from desecration or being carried away except that deep feeling of reverence which Catholics and Presbyterians alike entertain for the place with which it has been so long associated.

If only. The bell, which is now thought to date from around AD 900, was stolen at some point during the summer of 2019. The thief, or thieves, must have used bolt cutters to cut through the chain which attached it to the altar. This, I think, was a truly wicked act. Also pointless. Whoever has this bell in a display cabinet or safe in their home can surely derive no pleasure from it. The object's sacred force comes from its long association with that island, the solemn tolling amid hills and water. Think of the priestly hands that have held it, the grieving ears that have heard it. Without the great dark wave of Ben Resipol looming above the island, without ravens grunting as they row through the air, what power or purpose can that bell have? Ring it as the thief might, it will be tongueless and silent until – God willing – it is returned to that stone altar and Highland sky.

'Ah, here's the first one already,' Robert Ross said. He had spotted Private Mary MacDonald's grave. A dragonfly, enjoying the heat of the sun-baked slab, rose as we approached. The headstone is modern pink granite, replacing an earlier wooden cross. I had passed MacDonald's former home on the drive here: a fairy tale-looking cottage called Kinacarra, with smoke coming from the chimney and pieces of driftwood woven into the fence. It was sad to think of her leaving that pretty house, never to return. She joined the Auxiliary Territorial Service, the women's branch of the army, the most famous member of which was Princess Elizabeth, later the Queen.

Most members of the armed forces who died during the world wars and are buried in the UK tend to have either succumbed to their wounds after being invalided back to Britain, or else died from illness or accident while stationed here. Mary MacDonald died in hospital in Lincoln on 26 April 1944. The cause of death is listed on her casualty card as tubercular meningitis. It must have been a great blow to the family. She was the youngest of five siblings. A Gaelic-speaker and Catholic, with black hair and hazel eyes, she was reputedly a great beauty. Her parents and brother John, all of whom she predeceased, share the same grave.

'There used to be a large population here, and a huge number of people have been interred on the island,' Kenneth MacDonald had told me when we met the previous evening. He is a local house-builder. His father and Mary were cousins. 'Members of my family have gone to that island for nine hundred years. It was common to dig up a skull or two of your ancestors when you were burying your relatives. When a friend and I dug the grave for my aunt, Marjorie MacDonald, we came across two skulls which we very carefully replanted by creating a hollow and putting them back in. Her funeral was the next day. All the boys wore their kilts and we had a piper. Back in the 1970s, it would only be men who went out to the Green Isle, but more recently everybody goes.'

ANCHOR

The desire to be laid to rest on the island is not simply because it is beautiful, but because it links you, body and soul, to an ancient past. To be buried here is often an expression of faith and belonging – to the church, to family, to the wider Highland culture. This place may have been made holy by its association with a saint, but it is, in our time, sanctified by stories. Each new burial adds another few new lines. It is an island, but it is also a manuscript, a palimpsest, which will never be completed.

Angus Peter MacLean, who lives in Mary MacDonald's former home, told me that he had been attending burials on the Green Isle for sixty years, since he was in his early teens. Traditional Highland funerals, he feels, are often positive occasions, psychologically and emotionally, as a result of the active role mourners play in the ceremony. There's something about the labour – carrying a coffin, working a spade – that creates a sense of proper conclusion and farewell. 'Everything is done by the people,' he said. 'The grave is dug and then filled in by relatives and friends. You don't see a council man waiting with his digger.'

You dig the earth that will, one day, be dug for you?

'Yes, exactly,' he replied. 'It feels absolutely right, the way we do it here.'

Robert and I walked up over the top of the island and found the second grave. Dugald Grant lies almost directly beneath a rowan. No poppies for him, but a scattering of scarlet berries. His stone, unlike Mary MacDonald's, is the standard Commonwealth War Graves Commission type. It is modest, made of granite, with a rounded top. Between carvings of an anchor and a cross, there is his name, age and date of death – 23 May 1916.

He was a deckhand with the Royal Naval Reserve, assigned to HMS *Vernon*, the collective name given to a group of static ships, or hulks, anchored at Portsmouth, where men were trained in the use of torpedoes and mines. He had joined the navy in February 1916, following three years in the Lovat Scouts, a Highland regiment of the army, but his service was to be all too short. He died in Haslar naval hospital, near Portsmouth, from measles and pneumonia. An obituary in the *Oban Times* headlined 'Patriotic Moidart Family' shows a handsome young man with a moustache and naval uniform, looking a little to the right of the camera, as if something slightly amusing has caught his eye. The article notes that 'In civil life, he was rural postman between Dalilea and Kinlochmoidart, and was very popular in the district.'

The previous afternoon I had visited Grant's nephew, at his home not far from the island. Duggie Cameron was named after his late uncle. Hanging by a short black leather strap on the wall above his fireplace was Dugald Grant's whistle, which he would have used, while walking his postal route, to let people know they had letters. It was returned to the family after his death. The Post Office he joined in 1912 was the largest single employer in the world, but it was at the end of its golden age. By December of 1914, 28,000 PO workers had enlisted in the armed forces. By the end of the war, 75,000 staff had joined, and it was never quite the same again.

Cameron is eighty-two and, like many Highlanders of his generation, does not seem an emotionally demonstrative person, nor did he ever meet his uncle, but that whistle on the wall seemed to sound a long note of sorrow. He keeps it on display, he explained, because it meant a lot to his mother, Margaret, Dugald's sister. A lungless whistle, a tongueless bell – in those silences, loss.

Dugald Grant's body would have made its long journey home by train from Portsmouth to Glenfinnan, where the coffin was loaded on to the SS *Clanranald*, a little steamer, and carried up Loch Shiel to the pier at Dalilea. A horse and cart would have taken this sad burden to the church for the funeral, and then down to a small boat, which would have carried his coffin across the loch to the island. Dugald's father, Peter, was a carpenter and made coffins. I wonder whether he made his son's? He could have had no idea, as he shaped the wood, that a century after Dugald's death the grave would be tended by an organisation dedicated to remembrance.

I joined Robert Ross by Grant's stone. He had scrubbed it with a stiff brush and was now repainting the letters. I was curious about all this effort. The dead of the world wars died a long time ago; in many cases it is likely that no family members visit the graves. Yet the CWGC team work their way around them dutifully, cleaning and repairing, making the names legible for whoever happens to pass. Why go to so much trouble?

'We do it for the guys in the ground,' he said. 'We do it for them. It's quite a deep-rooted thing. It feels a bit like a debt you owe. But not like a grudging debt. You want to pay your respects. That's a word that's used and abused. For me, respect isn't just a word, it's an action. Being able to say to somebody, "This is your relative's grave, and we've made sure you can read it and it's clean and cared for, and even if you can't come and visit, we'll still go back." That's special.'

*

RICHMOND CASTLE, Yorkshire. 19 May 1916. Three men are in the cell block. They are singing a hymn. One, on an upper floor, beats on the flagstones to help his comrade below keep time:

> *Though like the wanderer,*
> *The sun gone down . . .*

These men. One was a footballer and accounts clerk; the second, a miner and fine tenor; the third, a teacher and lay preacher. They are all now prisoners. Held within the castle's thick stone walls and the even stronger keep of their own faith.

> *Darkness be over me,*
> *My rest a stone . . .*

Norman Gaudie. Alfred Myers. John Hubert Brocklesby, known as Bert. They and thirteen of their fellows will come to be known as the Richmond Sixteen. They are conscientious objectors, conchies, cowards to many, respected by few. They will not fight, and they will not do any sort of work that helps the fight. For this they have lost their freedom, though not, it seems, their voices.

> *Yet in my dreams I'd be*
> *Nearer, my God, to thee.*

The castle, a great Norman fortress, was used during the First World War as a base for the northern companies of the Non-Combatants Corps. Following the introduction of conscription in early 1916, men who refused to fight were often posted to the NCC, the military unit in which those who refused to bear arms were put to work supporting the war by other means. This included moving supplies of weapons. Those so-called 'absolutists' who refused to do even this sort of work, on the grounds that one might as well fire a rifle as load one on to a truck, were kept prisoner in a grim cell block which had been built in the nineteenth century. It was unheated and unfurnished; prisoners ate bread and drank water, and were allowed outside for as little as an hour a day.

Of the approximately 16,300 men who expressed a conscientious objection to fighting in the First World War, 1,300 were absolutists. The uncompromising group imprisoned at

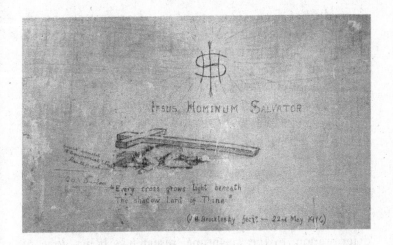

IESUS HOMINUM SALVATOR

"Every cross grows light beneath
The shadow Lord of Thine"

(J. H. Brocklesby fecit — 22nd May 1916)

Richmond Castle were a mix of socialists and committed Christians; their pacifism was informed by their most deeply held beliefs. They must have felt that their faith – whether religious or political – was being tested. How to keep their spirits up? By singing, yes, and through games; they found a way to play chess through a small hole between two cells. They also wrote on the walls. We know this because the writing is still there.

I stepped off the bus in Richmond's cobbled market square on a bright and bitter day just before Hallowe'en. A group of teenagers were gathered around the obelisk in the centre of the square, throwing a pumpkin as if it was a basketball. The Holy Trinity Church had a curtain of woollen poppies cascading down its tower, a display created ahead of Remembrance Sunday. Above all of this loomed the castle, its twelfth-century keep seeming to glower down at the town.

The prison block, a brutish slab of blond brick, is attached to the keep. There are eight solitary-confinement cells over two storeys, each about nine feet long by six wide. Inside, the air smelled of damp. The afternoon sun was strong enough to light the cells, through windows narrow as arrow-slits, and illuminate the remarkable walls. Graffiti was everywhere. Written in pencil, grey on grey. Bible verses, sketches of loved ones, lines from Tennyson, a little pornography, scenes from war, a mini-Hitler like a proto-emoji. There are more than 2,300 inscriptions dating from the nineteenth century through to around 1970. It is a wonder that they have survived. Fluctuating levels of humidity have meant that the limewash is coming away from the walls and bringing the writing and drawings with it. Historic England is monitoring the situation, and hopes to find a way to conserve what remains, but has had to close the cell block to the public to prevent further deterioration. In the meantime, research is being done to learn more about the men who made these markings.

The best of them are by the conscientious objectors: 'The only war worth fighting is the Class War'; 'You might just as well try to dry a floor by throwing water on it, as try to end this war by fighting'; 'Though shut in away from the world, I am shut in with my Lord.' These scrawled messages of steadfastness, mingling politics and religion, give something of the atmosphere of the cells. The word 'cenotaph' comes from the Greek for empty tomb, and these empty rooms derive their peculiar power from a sense of mingled absence and presence; the men imprisoned here are long gone but their own sacrifice – for an ideal which found little sympathy at the time – is expressed in every pencil stroke. One drawing which takes up the length of an entire wall imagines the official process of tribunals and appeal courts and prison as a *Pilgrim's Progress*-style journey through a landscape of hills and valleys. Another shows a man pressed to the ground and trying to crawl under the weight of a huge fallen cross.

'It's interesting to think what it meant to them when they

wrote on these walls,' said Megan Leyland, a senior proper-
ties historian with English Heritage, who was showing me the
cells. 'Here is where they made their stand. Here is where
they were going to face the consequences. Their future was
uncertain. There was always the looming threat that they
would be sent to France.'

Life at Richmond was uncomfortable. The conscientious
objectors were put under immense pressure to do war work,
and there seems to have been a degree of physical brutality. But
the prospect of being sent to France was deadly serious. There,
in the theatre of war, they would be judged to be on active
service and, if they again refused orders, court-martialled.
The penalty for disobedience? Being shot at dawn.

'That threat was very real,' Leyland said. 'This graffiti
may have been the last mark that they thought they would
leave to the world. If you got hold of a pencil and thought
you might soon die, what would you put on the wall?'

On 29 May, just a week after Bert Brocklesby had drawn
that man struggling beneath the cross, the conscientious
objectors left Richmond Castle for Le Havre and Boulogne,
singing hymns by rail and bus and boat. They knew that they
might be going to their deaths. Huge numbers of casualties
meant the army needed men. The execution of the Richmond
Sixteen would surely serve as a deterrent for those who
thought to avoid combat.

Among their number was Alfred Martlew. He worked as
a clerk at the Rowntree chocolate factory in York and was a
member of the Independent Labour Party. His pacifism was
rooted in socialism. He believed, he said, in the brotherhood
of man.

Before visiting Richmond, I had made contact with a
relation of this particular conscientious objector. 'He was
my second cousin,' explained the Reverend Andrew Martlew.

'My father's father's brother's son.' Andrew Martlew is a former British army chaplain. He first visited the castle in 2003, shortly before deploying to Iraq. 'I went there in uniform and blagged my way into the cells,' he recalled. 'I found it very moving indeed.'

Growing up, he hadn't known anything about the conchie in the family. But, as a soldier, albeit one who never carried a weapon, he came to admire his relation and the other men who refused to serve. 'They were all incredibly brave. Far braver than I would ever be or have ever been. He was a Martlew, so he was pig-headed, but there is still courage there. I can't imagine the social pressure they were all under. There was no street in this country where there was not somebody who had lost a son or a brother or a father. If you are committed to your fellow working man, then the slaughter of your fellow working man must also have been awful.'

In France, the Richmond prisoners were court-martialled and sentenced to death. But the sentences were commuted to ten years in prison with hard labour. There had been an intervention at the highest level. The Prime Minister, Herbert Asquith, never comfortable with conscription in the first place, was unwilling to have his government sanction these executions.

There was, however, a feeling that the men should not escape entirely. Suffering was in the air and why should they not breathe it? They were sent to civilian prisons in England and then offered work of 'national importance' under a new Home Office scheme. At the end of August 1916, Martlew, along with other conscientious objectors, was sent to work in a granite quarry at Dyce, near Aberdeen. Conditions were wet and miserable. They slept in tents and worked breaking rocks. One young man died of pneumonia. A group photograph taken in the quarry is a portrait of exhaustion.

Martlew is standing at the back looking thin, tired and cold. It is possible to feel sympathy for these outcasts while still acknowledging the greater hardships experienced by those who went to fight. Though the Flanders trenches were hell, the work camp sounds a sort of purgatory.

When it closed at the end of October, Martlew was given other employment, but became upset that the jobs he was being told to do, in Dyce and elsewhere, had a military purpose. Feeling that the government had betrayed him, he went on the run.

He was last seen alive on 4 July 1917. Back in York, where he had lived and worked, he told his fiancée, Annie, that he was going to give himself up to the authorities as a deserter. In a state of some distress, he gave her his money and watch. Seven days later, the body of an unknown man was recovered from the River Ouse, near Bishopthorpe Palace. 'He is dressed in a sporting suit of brown tweed, is wearing a white celluloid collar, black tie, a navy blue stripe cotton shirt,' reported the *Yorkshire Evening Post.* 'His boots are of the black ammunition pattern, and the socks are army grey. A pair of gold-rimmed pince-nez were found in his pocket.'

The body was identified the following day. He was twenty-two.

Alfred Martlew lies in the churchyard of St Andrew's, Bishopthorpe, North Yorkshire, near the foot of a young oak. He is buried right on the eastern boundary, separated from a busy road by a hedge. Cars zoom by within five feet. It had been suggested to me, ahead of my visit, that this was an example of the Church being judgemental, placing him, a likely suicide, within consecrated ground, but only just. Seeing the grave, though, his does not seem a dishonourable position. The decisions he made put him on the margins of society, the edge of acceptable thought, and finding his final rest on the hallowed fringe seems of a piece with that; integrity has its own honour.

Placed in the earth by his headstone was a small wooden cross which must, at one point, have had a poppy attached. The paper petal, vanished in the rain, had left behind a red stain, and this too felt appropriate. His blood was shed as a result of the war, and his courage, though not the sort recognised in silences and gun salutes, was real. The edge of a churchyard and the ghost of a flower? Those may not seem much to show for a life and a death, but age has not wearied Alfred and the years have not condemned him. Quite the opposite. Almost a century after his passing, he seems strong and admirable.

Was he, I asked Andrew Martlew, a hero?

'Yes,' he said. 'Undoubtedly, unequivocally, without any qualification, yes.'

Why? In reply, he drew on his own military experience. 'I've seen people who were awarded the Military Cross because, in the heat of battle, when they've been shot, instead of lying down they got back up again and carried on shooting. Actually, that's more about adrenalin than courage.'

He recalled being part of a supply convoy driving around Basra after nightfall, without lights, delivering water to British positions; on the previous evening, the convoy had been ambushed. This required bravery of a sort, he said, but was really a matter of following orders. What his second cousin did, he felt, was different. 'The sort of courage that Alfred showed had no adrenalin content. The sort of courage which requires, in the cold light of day and in the dark hours of the night, that you do what you think is right? That, for my money, is more heroic than rushing towards the enemy with fixed bayonets.'

It is not known which of the Richmond Castle cells Alfred

Martlew occupied. He left no mark on those walls; at least, no writing or drawing by him has so far been confirmed. I had, however, brought with me something he had written. It was a copy of his official notice of appeal, a pink document on which he had set down, on 20 March 1916, the reasons he would neither fight nor do any work that would assist the fighting. A cell of the upstairs corridor felt like a good place to read this out: 'I hold, and have held for some years, a conscientious objection to warfare, as it involves the killing of human beings, which I firmly believe is, from a moral, sociological and humanitarian point of view, absolutely wrong.'

His words were written in a neat and steady hand. There was a slight echo as I read them. 'I am prepared to be myself sacrificed rather than be the means of sacrificing others.'

*

IT WAS RAINING over New Irish Farm Cemetery on the morning they buried the Royal Fusiliers. Grey skies, green lawn, white stones, and, of course, red, white and blue flags draped over the two coffins borne shoulder-high to the graves. Later, when the guns fired in salute, crows rose from the stubble field and then settled once more among the broken stalks.

These men had died in 1915. Now, over one hundred years later, the funeral. Found during an archaeological dig, their regiment had been identified but not their names. That was why the headstones bore those three words which sanctify anonymity: 'Known Unto God'.

A burial with full military honours is a stirring experience. Whether you are militarist or pacifist, hawk or dove, this solemn pageant cannot fail to impress. One might think, 'What a waste of life', or 'What an honourable way to die', or a little of both, but there is no denying the force of the service itself: death and grief made bearable and even poetic

through the application of discipline and ritual. Is it possible to hear the Last Post played on a bugle here, amid Flanders Fields, and not feel a clutch at one's throat?

New Irish Farm is a Commonwealth War Graves Commission cemetery near Ieper, a Belgian city better known to students of the First World War as Ypres. That is an infamous name. Like Verdun and the Somme, it carries a freight of horror. Around 600,000 people died on the Ypres Salient between October 1914 and October 1918, among them those two soldiers of the Royal Fusiliers.

The service was conducted by Father Patrick O'Driscoll, chaplain of the Royal Regiment of Fusiliers. 'We come this morning on a day these soldiers probably would have known all too well over a hundred years ago,' he had begun. 'We come in the rain . . .' He spoke of love and dust and lest we forget. The coffins were carried and lowered by young soldiers wearing khaki uniforms and expressions of such solemnity that there was no question of this being some sort of historical re-enactment. The soldiers were to be buried as if they had been killed the day before. 'It could have been us,' the company sergeant major, Matthew Hale-Smith, told me afterwards. 'Once a Fusilier, always a Fusilier. The gap in time doesn't matter.' These were fallen comrades. It was a privilege and honour and a duty to bury them right.

Such burials, decades after death, are not uncommon. Between early 1919 and the spring of 1920, dedicated units searched for and recovered bodies from the First World War battlefields, burying them in the neat new cemeteries with their orderly rows of white stones. This was unpleasant and dangerous work, the ground murderous with rusting metal, treacherous with unexploded shells. One thinks of Edmund Blunden's words: 'The whole zone was a corpse, and the mud itself mortified.' The dead, still decomposing, had to be examined carefully for anything that might identify them. The exhumation teams learned to look for discoloured grass and mud and water, for rat holes which might contain tell-tale pieces of bone or other relics indicating a body was below. They carried long metal poles, hollow in the middle, which they'd plunge into the ground and then smell the earth brought up. Thus the fallen were found.

Or not found. It is estimated that in France alone there are still 100,000 British and Commonwealth soldiers missing. They turn up, a few here, a few there, during construction work and ploughing. A family in Belgium, renovating their home, discovered a soldier beneath their living room floor. By the time of the funeral I attended near Ieper, in early October 2019, a total of fifty-one bodies had already been recovered that year. Seeds sown long ago still yield their blighted harvest.

I had driven to Belgium from Arras in northern France with Steve Arnold. He is fifty-one and has been with the Commonwealth War Graves Commission for his entire adult life. In a sense, he grew up in it. His grandfather Sidney started working as a Commission gardener in 1946; during the Second World War he had been a gunner with the Royal Artillery, and, billeted in Belgium, met his wife, Marie-Louise. Steve Arnold was born and raised in Ieper, though he is a UK citizen. As a boy, during holidays, his grandfather would give him little gardening jobs in the cemeteries – pulling up weeds, clipping the borders around graves – and when he left school the Commission recruited him. It is like the army in that way; more a culture and extended family than a regular job. Arnold is now horticultural manager for France and heads the exhumation and reburial team. As we drove, he took business calls on speakerphone, holding conversations about the dead in French, English and Flemish.

'Hi, Jules, how's it going?'

'It's absolutely tipping it down. I've just uncovered another three skulls, so this is going to take a bit longer than anticipated.'

Julian Blake was calling from a construction site. A hospital was being built near the town of Lens, and workmen had, that morning, uncovered part of a skeleton while digging a trench. They had called it in to the CWGC and Arnold had sent his colleague to take a look. Blake, excavating, had found four bodies, but the weather was against him. Should they protect the area and wait a couple of days for the heavy rain to pass?

'Maybe we just sit on it until Friday,' said Arnold, 'but the problem is scavengers. I tell you what Jules, carry on for a bit and then we'll make a decision when I get there. Okay, bye.'

'Scavengers,' I said. 'Is that really a problem?'

Arnold sighed. 'Oh, more than you know. There's lots of collectors around. We try to finish our work by day's end because it's dangerous leaving things overnight. But sometimes, if there's multiple casualties, we can't finish in a day, and then we try to secure the site as best as we can by putting diggers over it, so that thieves can't get to where we're working.'

There is a black market in battlefield memorabilia. Rifles, belt buckles, bullets – anything that has survived, a scavenger will either take to sell or keep for himself. It is dismaying to think that anyone who has an interest in the world wars, who has some feeling for the scale of the loss, would disturb a grave for pleasure and gain. Yet they do. Worse, the removal of army-issue and personal artefacts makes it much less likely that the soldier will ever be reunited with the most valuable item of all: his name.

'It's the same as killing them again, isn't it?' Arnold said. 'It might be that the body could have been identified and his family notified. Now, he will have to be buried as an unknown soldier. Those people ought to be ashamed.'

Speed is therefore vital. CWGC staff aim to be on site within an hour of the initial phone call, and to work fast when they get there. Arnold believes that their reputation for quickness of response is one of the reasons the numbers of bodies being found is increasing. Road builders and con-tractors involved in large infrastructure projects do not like their work being held up. It costs them money. Easier perhaps to just rebury and build upon any bodies found, with no one any the wiser. 'If these people go to the trouble of calling us and we take three days to get there and then another two days to do work, they won't call us again,' Arnold said. 'I'm one hundred per cent sure that's happened a lot in the past.' Later, as we passed along a busy stretch of road, he returned to the subject. It was built, he said, quite recently, and no remains were reported. Yet this was in a part of France which had been the scene of heavy fighting over many years, and near to a site where the CWGC team had recovered more than fifty bodies in a short period. Arnold was sceptical that the road workers had found nothing. 'It's impossible. I just can't believe it.' Most likely, we were driving over the dead.

Names matter. Part of the horror of the First World War is that so many were never found, or were found but could not be identified. How to respond to this double loss was one of the most difficult questions for the War Graves Commission. Their answer was the huge memorials which dot the hills and fields of Belgium and France. Thiepval, which commemorates the missing of the Somme, is the largest Commonwealth war memorial in the world and has 72,318 names carved into its Portland stone. Menin Gate, at Ieper, bears 54,610 names; every evening, at 8 p.m., the Last Post is sounded by buglers beneath its great arch. It was at the inauguration of Menin Gate, in 1927, that Field Marshal Lord Plumer made his famous address to the relations of those whose loved one had no known grave: 'He is not missing; he is here!' For Siegfried Sassoon, however, the Menin Gate was a 'sepulchre of crime': complacent, swollen with misplaced pride and carved with 'intolerably nameless names'.

This, I think, is a tension at the heart of all CWGC cemeteries and memorials. They are too pretty, too peaceful. All those dainty headstones, all those Crosses of Sacrifice silhouetted against the twilight in a million poignant photographs – they are so distant from the chaos and violence that put these men in the ground that they function not as warnings against war but as seductive monuments to it.

I wonder what Wilfred Owen would make of these cemeteries, if he could rise up from the one where he lies – in the French village of Ors – and tell us. Would he consider them a lie, a 'Dulce Et Decorum Est' of stone? I would like there to be one cemetery, just one, carved with the poet's cynical dismissal of glory and sacrifice, but I wouldn't like my great-uncle, Captain Alexander Ramage, a doctor killed by German shelling in Normandy in 1944, to lie in it. That's the contradiction when considering war graves. Candour is for other people; consolation is what one wants for oneself.

None of this is to denigrate the CWGC. Their mission, begun in the heat of battle at a time when the outcome of the war was uncertain, was impressive and visionary. As Rudyard Kipling said of the creation of the cemeteries and memorials, this was 'the biggest single bit of work since the Pharaohs – and they only worked in their own country'. The scale of the task can be best illustrated, perhaps, by the fact that the Australian National Memorial at Villers-Bretonneux, the last great monument of the Western Front, was unveiled in the summer of 1938, just in time for the Second World War to begin.

The work continues now. The Commission's headquarters in France are at Beaurains, just south of Arras. This is where headstones are made for cemeteries all around the world, replacing those that have become illegible or to mark the graves of newly found soldiers. At the visitor centre, the public can see headstones carved, and observe the skills of other workers, including gardeners and carpenters. Also on display are a few artefacts found with recovered bodies – a helmet, cap badges, an officer's whistle – but the dead themselves reside in the mortuary, off-limits to everyone except CWGC employees. Behind the mortuary door, on the day I visited, were 182 men awaiting identification.

It was clear from talking to staff that this is more than just a wage. Christian Cousin has been a blacksmith here for thirty years. He was busy repairing one of the bronze swords which can be seen set into the front of the Cross of Sacrifice in most CWGC cemeteries. Someone had damaged it while trying to steal it and melt it down. It is not uncommon, sadly, for the cemeteries to be targeted by vandals and thieves, and so there is always plenty for the blacksmith to do.

'But I know what I'm doing and why I'm doing it,' he said. 'Whenever I touch this metal, the memory of the soldiers and their families is in my mind always. If you don't have this feeling and this sense of history you shouldn't work here. *Le travail c'est la mémoire.* Working is remembering.'

*

BACK IN THE CAR with Steve Arnold, we were approaching the place where, that morning, the bodies had been found. We drove down a rough track on the boundary of a field. Two massive slag heaps, Europe's highest, were black pyramids on the horizon. A kestrel flew out of the trees and hovered, graceful and deadly, above the mud.

A new hospital for the town of Lens will be constructed on this twenty-six-hectare site just south of the A21 motorway. Before anything can be built, the land must be thoroughly de-mined, and it was in the course of this work that a body had been disturbed. This is fertile ground for the exhumation team. Arnold pointed out where he had found the bodies of seven Scots soldiers in a shell-hole, and the site of the tunnel where, on his last visit, he had found Germans.

Bodies will be recovered by different organisations depending on the country in which they are found. In France, the CWGC has responsibility. The process for the recovery of a soldier is similar to that used by an archaeologist, Arnold explained. It is done with a trowel and with a care. Gentling up the bones is important, but so too is the detection of any artefacts. They dig around the general area in case something which might be useful in identification has been thrown or rolled away at the moment of death. Once the body has been lifted, the soil beneath is explored, making sure nothing has been missed. Lots of photographs are taken and the positions of any objects noted.

Back at the mortuary, the bones are washed and left to dry. The shape of the skeleton is reassembled as well as can be done. Sometimes there are parts missing. The artefacts are examined in every detail. 'These boys had a lot of time on their hands, and sometimes scratched their names on their things,' Arnold explained. A spoon can be the key to a life.

The remains are boxed up; details and photographs are sent to the CWGC's UK headquarters in Maidenhead, where the process begins of trying to work out who has been found. They look at the dates when there was fighting in that area and which regiments and battalions suffered casualties. They look at who among those men is missing. It is a narrowing down. Even for a single body, an extensive report will be produced. 'Once that is done,' Arnold said, 'there will be a list of potential candidates for that soldier. It can have hundreds of names on it, or sometimes it can just have one.'

This report is sent to the relevant military authority: for those serving with British forces, the Ministry of Defence's Joint Casualty and Compassionate Centre, where investigators, sometimes known as war detectives, attempt to formally identify the deceased. Close examination of bones can give estimates of height and approximate age, which are then checked against service records, if they still exist. If the list of potential names can be reduced down to a manageable length, typically a maximum of fifteen, old census records are explored for details of children or, as most young soldiers died childless, siblings from whose line of descent a living family member can be traced. If one is found, attempts are made to contact them; they are asked to give a DNA sample via a mouth swab.

It is surprising how moved family members can be by this process. A telephone rings in Australia and they are told that a man whom they have never met, who may not be a direct relation, who died long ago on the other side of the world, has been found in the field where he fell. Despite these several steps of remove, it is common for people to become personally invested and tearful. They have a great desire for a DNA match. It is as if war, in all its electric sadness, has reached a jolting hand out of the past.

'Every time we find a body, the first thing you do is think of his family,' Arnold said. 'You start thinking about his parents, his wife, girlfriend, who lived out their lives not knowing where he was. Suddenly, here we are, and we've found them.'

It must be extraordinary, is it not, to come face to face with the dead? That man in the ground exists as an old photograph somewhere. People longed to see him again, or at least to know where he was, and now you are the first person to touch him in more than a hundred years. 'Yes. You sometimes find his personal items. A pencil, scraps of paper. There might be a little ring still on his finger. It's really special. It's a privilege, really, to do this job.'

Arnold parked the car and we walked across the field. He spoke, in French, to the two workers who found the first body, and then carried on to the lip of the trench. 'Are they Brits, Jules?' he asked.

The trench was about a metre deep. Julian Blake had widened it on one side, and was still busy down there, but stood at our approach. He was wearing white protective clothing over a shirt and tie. He has worked for the CWGC for thirty years. A lifer.

'Um,' he replied, 'well, they're Commonwealth.' It was possible to tell that from the belt buckles, the little that was left of the boots, and a few unfired bullets scattered around. The uniforms had rotted away.

'So,' said Arnold, 'what this looks like is a battlefield burial. See the skulls? Because they are all close together, they were probably just thrown down here.' He turned to Blake. 'Have you got a trowel?'

We climbed down into the grave. Heavy clay clung to my shoes, giving an infinitesimally small idea of what it must have been like to try to live and fight in such conditions. Four bodies had been partly exposed: three skulls were visible, in a row, and to their right the legs and pelvis of a fourth man. One of the skulls had gold teeth. These had been set aside. For fear of scavengers, they would not be left overnight.

'It's going to be slow going, isn't it, a jumble like that?' Blake said. It was difficult to make out which bones belonged to which body. 'I don't really want to move anything until we can see whose is whose. The skulls are so fragile. It's a wonder they have survived this long.'

Arnold nodded and pointed. 'That is where the feet should be. That's the hip here. So the other half of his body is gone. It's probably in the spoil over there. There's his ribs. Really, the best thing to do, Jules, is leave them in situ.'

It was almost 2 p.m. and not much light left in the day. They would cover the pit and return early tomorrow with a bigger team. Still, Arnold was intrigued, and didn't want to leave quite yet. He crouched to trowel around the right shoulder blade of one of the bodies. 'I'll just gently scratch away here.' He was busy for a few moments, and then: 'Oh! We've got it!' He straightened up, holding a small piece of oxidised metal in the shape of an arch. 'You know what that is? It's a shoulder title. *Ça c'est Canada!*'

This regimental badge was worn by soldiers of the Canadian Corps. These men were a long way from home.

Arnold pulled out his phone and called up an old map of the First World War trench system. The 5th Infantry Battalion of the Canadian Corps was here in 1917, he said. The front line was a hundred metres to the north. It was likely that the four soldiers had been killed in August 1917 during the fighting for Hill 70, an important strategic victory, but one which came at a cost: around 5,700 Canadian lives lost, and more than 20,000 Germans. These men would, Arnold thought, have been buried in haste, by comrades, during the fighting.

'Okay, Jules, we've got a plan of attack,' he said. 'You carry on for a bit. We'll be back.'

We got in the car and headed back towards Beaurains. Arnold was upbeat. He thought it probable that the soldiers would be identified. Canada kept good records, and the gold teeth would help. 'Before they even start taking DNA, they'll already have a shortlist.' The soldiers would be buried with full military honours in the nearby cemetery at Loos, and their headstones would carry their names.

To our right, as we drove south, I could see a structure on a hillside – two huge limestone towers. The Vimy Memorial is carved with the names of 11,240 Canadian soldiers with no known grave. If the four from the Lens hospital site are identified, their names will, eventually, be removed from the great monument. They are not missing; they are here.

But so many are still out there. When the work of recovering the dead began in 1919, it was estimated that it would take ten years. 'A hundred years on, we're not done yet,' Arnold said. Two had been laid to rest that morning, four were found in the afternoon, and so it goes.

Can you foresee a time, I asked, when the last soldier is found in the last field and laid in the last grave?

He shook his head. 'That day will never come. There's just too many lost.'

ANKH

ETON, MID-NOVEMBER. The town was dark and cold, the Thames high, the swans – spectral against the black water – beginning to preen and settle for the night.

Inside the College, in the drawing room of the Provost's Lodge, the atmosphere was cosy, expectant; not quite of this century, and barely the last. A bell chimed eight. We were gathered to hear a ghost story. This was a novelty for the boys among our number – pupils in their white ties and tail-coats – who had likely never heard this particular tale before. But even those of us for whom it was a familiar troubling pleasure would not have missed the opportunity to hear it told like this.

A man sat in an armchair by the fire. He poured whisky from a decanter, sipped, spoke: 'Up to the present day there is much gossip among the Canons about a certain hidden treasure of this Abbot Thomas . . .' Candlelight was reflected in his small round spectacles. The flames flickered with his breath and cast his shadow on the walls – that great cliff of a forehead, that great claw of an outstretched hand.

He was an actor – Robert Lloyd Parry – but this did not feel like an acting job. It was more like a channelling, a kind of benign possession. A thought occurred: this could almost *be* Montague Rhodes James, who some regard as the greatest writer of supernatural fiction in the English language, giving one of his celebrated Christmas Eve readings to an audience of students and fellow academics. It could be 1918, the year in which James became Provost of Eton and took up residence in these very lodgings, where he would spend the rest of his life. His portrait hangs on a wall in the room next door, but his atmosphere was all around – that distinctive ambience found in his stories in which calm, rational men are deeply comfortable until, all of a sudden, they are none of those things. What better place for a literary manifestation?

Lloyd Parry, who is in his late forties, has been telling the ghost stories of M. R. James since 2005. He has a dozen (and counting) committed to memory, and travels the country performing them. It is a tremendous feat of recall. He spends his summers learning the texts, tramping the streets of Southport where he lives, wandering the beach, muttering to himself. He likes, when he can, to give his performances in places which have close associations with James, such as here at the Provost's Lodge in Eton. To sit at a fire where the author sat, and to tell a tale in the spot where he told it, is in itself a rather Jamesian act, a summoning of the past into the present. The objects with which Lloyd Parry surrounds himself – the decanter, spectacles, candles – are not simply props, but seem more like ritual objects necessary for invocation. James lived and worked in these rooms, he died in them; it does not seem unreasonable to call him forth through the medium of ghost stories.

I say 'ghost stories' because that is how they are generally known, but the creatures within them are not ghosts. Not exactly. Demons might be nearer the mark. Indeed, one of the stories, 'Casting the Runes', was adapted as the great 1957 film *Night of the Demon*, from which Kate Bush later sampled the line 'It's in the trees! It's coming!' for her song 'Hounds of Love'.

Demons, though, isn't quite right either. The truth is that it's often hard to say just what are the *things* which appear in a James tale. A child-murdering toad. A coarse-haired beast, yellow-eyed, scimitar-clawed. A tentacled horror down a well. It is almost as if some of the scuttling fiends of Hieronymus

Bosch have fetched up in English academe, squirming around the ivory towers.

I met Lloyd Parry the morning after his performance. We were going to visit a grave. It was a short walk from the college, up Keate's Lane and along Eton Wick Road. The small cemetery is accessed through a lychgate, the arch of which frames a fine old chapel. We walked past this, over a damp carpet of fallen leaves, almost right to the low brick wall at the rear. And there it was, the stone. 'I'm sorry to see that his name is becoming obliterated,' Lloyd Parry said. 'But I'm glad that it isn't a spooky gothic gravestone. He doesn't require pinnacles and weeping angels. That's not what M. R. James is about. This is somewhat suitable to what I think I know of the man.'

The headstone of M. R. James is small and, Lloyd Parry noted, as restrained as one of his stories. Beneath the rounded top is his name, now almost unreadably worn, and his dates: 1 August 1862 to 12 June 1936. It notes that he was Provost of King's College, Cambridge, between 1905 and 1918, and from then until his death was Provost at Eton. There is a biblical text – 'No longer a sojourner, but a fellow citizen with the saints and of the household of God' – but no mention of his gifts as a storyteller.

Why would there be? The stories were, for James, no more than a sideline; not even that, an amusement. He was a serious scholar, a pioneering specialist in the cataloguing of medieval manuscripts and the study of apocryphal books of the Bible. The tales which he wrote between the 1890s and the 1930s were composed, at least at first, for the pleasure of friends. He wrote them to read in company, usually at Christmas, at Cambridge and then Eton. He would go into his bedroom to fetch the manuscript; returning, he would blow out all the candles save one, and then read his latest party piece. 'The stories themselves,' he wrote in the preface to his debut collection, 1904's *Ghost Stories of an Antiquary*, 'do not make any very exalted claim. If any of them succeed in causing their readers to feel pleasantly uncomfortable when walking along a solitary road at nightfall, or sitting over a dying fire in the small hours, my purpose in writing them will have been attained.'

I had found it amusing, yet also rather moving, to watch the candlelit faces of the boys at Eton – in their early teens – as Lloyd Parry delivered the most horrible lines in 'The Treasure of Abbot Thomas'. They had steepled their hands over their noses and mouths, and their eyes were as wide as could be. They were, in other words, pleasantly uncomfortable, and it was easy to imagine James himself smiling in some shadowed corner at this demonstration of his power, more than a century after the story was written.

Despite his modest intentions, the stories were understood, by greats of the genre, to have elevated James at once into a position of supremacy. On reading 'Canon Alberic's Scrap-Book', the first to be published, Arthur Machen wrote to congratulate James on his debut and to say it had been a long time since he had read anything so good. H. P. Lovecraft, in his study *Supernatural Horror in Fiction*, observed that James was 'gifted with an almost diabolic power of calling horror by gentle steps from the midst of prosaic daily life ... Dr James, for all his light touch, evokes fright and hideousness in their most shocking forms; and will certainly stand as one of the few really creative masters in this darksome province.'

Those gentle steps. That light touch. I wonder whether they are one reason why James has remained so popular? Settling down to read one of his stories feels like slipping on a familiar tweed jacket; it smells of tobacco and country walks, and perhaps there will be a book of matches and a library ticket in one of the pockets. Despite the moment of terror which invariably arrives, his works are soothing in a way, and they have, mostly, an innocence about them. They are, or at least *feel*, pre-1914. Theirs is an Albion in which every village did not yet have its war memorial and empty pews where, once, young men had sat. 'For the ghost story, a slight haze of distance is desirable,' James wrote. '"Thirty years ago", "Not long before the war", are very proper openings.'

His heroes (not quite the word, that) are professors on golfing holidays; affable chaps on bicycles; Englishmen abroad and out of their depth. A discovery of an antiquarian nature – a bronze whistle, say, unearthed from the ruins of a Templar church – precipitates a moment of crisis. Something ancient and malevolent is disturbed.

In the preface to *More Ghost Stories of an Antiquary*, James explains something of his method: 'Let us, then, be introduced to the actors in a placid way; let us see them going about their ordinary business, undisturbed by forebodings, pleased with their surroundings; and into this calm environment, let the ominous thing put out its head, unobtrusively at first, and then more insistently, until it holds the stage.'

'A Warning to the Curious', first published in 1925, is, I think, his best work. Lacking that characteristic innocence, the very pages feel heavy with sorrow; even haunted. It's in the leaves, it's coming. 'It strikes me as the most profound of his stories,' Lloyd Parry said. 'It packs an emotional punch that the others don't. I'm certain that it's a response to the war.'

That story, in manuscript form, was set in April 1917. In its published version, the last two numbers have been struck out. The action takes place in Suffolk. A young antiquary called Paxton digs up a Saxon crown from its hiding place in a burial mound. It is, we learn, the last of three holy crowns buried near the coast to keep foreign invaders – 'the Danes or the French or the Germans' – from landing. In taking this sacred object, Paxton risks the security of England, and is harried and punished by a guardian set over it. This figure – the ominous thing – is difficult to see, if one looks directly; what Paxton and those who aid him experience is 'an acrid consciousness of a restrained hostility, very near us, like a dog on a leash that might be let go at any moment'. Cry havoc, indeed.

It was his last great tale. By the 1931 publication of his *Collected Ghost Stories*, James was in the final years of his life. His biographer, Michael Cox, wrote:

> The end came peacefully . . . at three o'clock in the afternoon on Friday 12 June, just as the Nunc Dimittis was being sung in Chapel.
>
> Monty left the beloved confines of the Cloisters and School Yard for the last time on the following Monday, 15 June. After a service in Chapel, during which the Dead March from Handel's Saul was played and the choir sang the prayer of Henri VI, '*Domini Jhesu Christe, qui me creasti*', the coffin was taken to the town cemetery . . . There, in bright sunshine, Cyril Alington said prayers over the grave and a hymn, 'Jesus lives! No longer now can thy terrors, death, appal us', was sung.

The impression James seems to have given during the course of his life, and subsequently, is of an amiable man whose progress from public schoolboy to head of a public school had a kind of frictionless inevitability. His interests as a child informed his work as an adult. The hobbies of his boyhood included exploring old churches and reading up on the martyrdoms of the saints, the more unpleasant the better. 'Nothing could be more inspiriting,' he recalled, 'than to discover that St Livinus had his tongue cut out . . .' He was deeply conservative, socially and artistically. He opposed allowing women to become full members of Cambridge University, and described James Joyce as 'a prostitutor of our language'. Eton he regarded as a joyful mother. As a pupil, he had lain in the sun by the river, breathed deep the scent of lime blossom, smiled at the sound of the clock and bells. One of his friends thought he had 'the mind of a nice child'. Lytton Strachey, reviewing James's memoirs, observed that he had lived 'a life without a jolt'.

The war, though; that had jolted him, all right. He was Provost of King's for most of those years, and seems to have felt the generational loss deeply. 'More than four hundred and seventy Cambridge men have fallen: a hundred and fifty of them, at least, should have been undergraduates still,' he said in a speech of 1915. Among those who had died was Rupert Brooke, whom James had first met in 1906 when the poet-soldier had been a freshman. The fallen, he continued, would not be forgotten, for 'the University bears them upon her heart, and will not, I know, neglect to perpetuate the memory of them in such sort that it may speak to the youth of England in time to come'.

In a speech the following year, intended to console Cambridge women who had lost husbands and brothers and sons, he said: 'Among much else that this war has taught us is its lesson about the dead. It has not lifted the veil and shown us what they do and what they know in the other life. But it has forced us to think of them . . . They are not at once made all-knowing and all-powerful. They have much to learn, and – it cannot be otherwise – much to unlearn, and to be sorry for. For the dead remember.'

The dead remember. It is a startling thought. At the rising of the sun and in the morning, they will remember us. What, I wonder, does Monty James remember, in his modest grave in Eton Town Cemetery? The things he loved, perhaps. The smell of pipe smoke and candlewax in long winter evenings; a ghost story told after dark.

*

AMELIA B. EDWARDS is buried in the churchyard of St Mary the Virgin, Henbury, once a village, now a suburb of Bristol. She shares a grave, as she shared a home for more than thirty years, with Ellen Braysher. They are buried hard by the northern wall of the church, beneath a stained glass window of Christ and his disciples. Braysher, who predeceased Edwards by three months, dying in January 1892, is described on the obelisk above the grave as a 'beloved friend' of the writer. Were they lovers? In 2016, Historic England designated the grave a Grade II monument in recognition of its importance to the LGBTQ heritage of the country. A large sculpted ankh – the Egyptian symbol of life – lies on the grave in tribute to Edwards's role as the so-called godmother of Egyptology. She also wrote some very fine ghost stories.

Her most anthologised work, 'The Phantom Coach', was first published in a Christmas 1864 edition of *All the Year Round*, a magazine founded and edited by Charles Dickens. This atmospheric tale takes place during a snowstorm on a moor in the north of England, where a foot passenger finds himself aboard the mouldering wreck of a mail coach which had crashed, with deadly consequences, nine years before.

'The Phantom Coach' is unusual in that most of Edwards's supernatural tales are set abroad – the galleries of Paris, a friary in Calabria, the Jewish cemetery on the Venice Lido – informed no doubt by her own extensive travels on the Continent. Her ghosts are often murder victims doomed to haunt their final fatal steps: a boy walks with a fishing rod to the tarn where his body has been concealed; a jilted lover

materialises by the pottery kiln where his remains have been burned. The dominant emotion in her stories is guilt. The eyes of her characters burn with it. A wanderer in the valley of the Upper Rhine calls in at a little church; thinking himself alone and pulling back the curtain of the confessional, he reveals a man in a black cassock who, despite having been hanged for a double murder more than thirty years ago, turns to regard the newcomer with a look of ferocious despair.

Who was the woman who imagined such things? For an 1891 edition of an American magazine called *The Arena*, Edwards contributed an article, 'My Home Life'. She had lived, she wrote, for more than twenty-five years 'with a very dear friend' – Ellen Braysher – 'in a small, irregularly built house' in the Gloucestershire village of Westbury-on-Trym. The house, which would be destroyed by bombs during the Second World War, was called The Larches. It stood in an acre of ground and was enclosed by a wall. She hoped to extend the property to include her collection of antiquities, but for that moment they were scattered throughout the rooms: in the entrance hall, a wood-and-ivory chair, two centuries old, once the seat of a Coptic bishop; in the library, in a tin box, shrivelled dates, nuts and lentils, food offerings found in the tombs of Thebes. 'There are three mummified hands behind Allibone's *Dictionary of English Authors*,' she wrote. 'There are two arms with hands complete – the one almost black, the other singularly fair – in a drawer in my dressing room; and grimmest of all, I have the heads of two ancient Egyptians in a wardrobe in my bedroom, who, perhaps, talk to each other in the watches of the night, when I am sound asleep.'

She would die the following year, leaving her antiquities and library as part of a bequest to University College, London, with the intention of founding a museum of Egyptian archaeology. She favoured UCL because it was, at that time, the only university in England which awarded degrees to women. The Petrie Museum – named for her colleague and friend, the pioneering archaeologist Flinders Petrie – now has a collection of more than 80,000 objects. It is the second largest assemblage of Egyptian antiquities outside of Egypt, after the British Museum. Petrie died in 1942, and his own head – not mummified, but preserved in fluid – is a specimen in the collection of the Royal College of Surgeons. Whether it murmurs in the watches of the night, who can say?

Cerys Bradley, a comedian and science communicator, worked at the Petrie Museum while a postgraduate student, talking to the public about the collection. We spoke amid cabinets packed full of artefacts, many of which had once belonged to Edwards herself. 'I don't think I met a single visitor who knew about her past or about the contribution she made to this museum,' Bradley said. 'We haven't done enough work to make people know who she was and what was her legacy. She gave all of this to UCL students and so I think it's unfair that she isn't remembered. I like talking about her because she's pretty bad-ass, but also people don't know anything about her.'

Amelia Ann Blanford Edwards was born in Islington on 7 June 1831, the only child of an Irish mother with a taste for the theatre and a retired lieutenant who had served under Wellington during the Peninsular War. She was a born writer; while other girls played with dolls, little Amy wrote poetry, her first efforts being published at the age of seven. She had a talent, too, for drawing; when she was twelve, George Cruikshank – who had illustrated *Oliver Twist* for Dickens – offered to take her on as a pupil. The success of her 1853 story 'Annette' began a literary career lucrative enough to allow her to travel to Europe.

She seems to have had a romantic feeling for grave-yards. On 20 February 1857, aged twenty-five, she visited the Protestant Cemetery in Rome, to see where Shelley was buried. 'I could have knelt down and kissed the stone,' she told her diary. 'I would have done it, had I been alone, were it only in memory of the strange worship I once paid to the memory of that man.' In Venice, two months later, she visited the Lido and examined the Jewish graves: 'I stayed by some to put aside the brambles and spell out the names and dates of those which were yet legible . . . Here, thought I, may lie what was once the dust of Shylock!' This experience seems to have inspired her 1867 tale 'The Story of Salome', in which a young man – the narrators of her ghost stories are invari-ably men – falls in love with a beautiful young Venetian, all 'grace and sorrow' in mourning sable, whom he sees lingering by what turns out to be her own grave. Salome is one of the many unattainable women who people Edwards's stories.

In 1860, her parents died; first her father, and then, within a week, her mother. Edwards went to live in Kensington with the Brayshers, a family with a wide circle of acquaintance among prominent people in the arts. John Braysher and his daughter, Sarah, died in 1863 and 1864, after which his widow, Ellen, set up home with Edwards in Westbury-on-Trym, where they were to live for the rest of their lives.

Among the locals with whom Edwards made friends was the poet and literary critic John Addington Symonds. In correspondence with Havelock Ellis, the pioneering writer on sexuality, in the year following Edwards's death, Symonds wrote: 'I have a few curious personal experiences in the region of female sexual inversion . . . I had another eminent female author among my friends, Miss Amelia B. Edwards, who made no secret to me of her Lesbian tendencies. The grande passion of her life was for an English lady, married to a clergyman & inspector of schools. I knew them both quite well. The three made a menage together; & Miss Edwards told me that one day the husband married her to his wife at the altar of his church – having full knowledge of the state of affairs.'

Though Symonds does not name the clergyman and his wife, it is very likely to have been Ellen Gertrude Byrne and her husband, the Reverend John Rice Byrne. In a letter of 1871, Edwards wrote that the Byrnes were moving from the area, and that she herself planned a trip abroad in order to recover from that loss, which she called 'that great blow – the greatest that could befall . . . It is like a death-blow to me.'

Edwards had a number of significant relationships with women, and travelled with them in Europe, Egypt and America, but whether these were close friendships, or something more, or a blurring of the two, is unclear. It is not known whether she was gay, or bi, or how she thought of herself, and does it even matter?

For Cerys Bradley, Edwards's sexuality *is* significant: 'She lived her life in a way that was very unconventional and bold. So bold that it withstood the way that history tries to erase the legacies of women like her.' If indeed she wasn't straight, that – in Bradley's view – would have been in keeping with the other ways in which she set herself against mainstream culture: her refusal to play the passive domestic role expected of a middle-class woman in Victorian society, for example, or her later campaign to save the ancient sites of Egypt from predation by unscrupulous excavators. 'If you are queer, or whatever word we want to use, you do see the world differently,' Bradley said. 'You have a kind of outsider's perspective.'

In 1870, Edwards met Marianne North, the botanical artist and sister-in-law of John Addington Symonds, whose beautiful paintings of exotic plants are on permanent display at Kew Gardens in a gallery named after her. The two grew close. Edwards's letters to North do not survive, but North's to Edwards suggest an imbalance in the relationship, with the writer desiring a greater intimacy than the artist was prepared to offer. In one, North scolds her gently for her offer of a keepsake of gold jewellery: 'Bless you! What love letters you do write, what a pity you waste them on a woman! Don't waste your money . . .' In another, she adds, 'in all truth, Amy, I have no love to give you or anyone . . . but that is no reason why you & I should not be true friends as long as we both live & bring much happiness to one another also'.

While travelling in Italy, in late 1871, Edwards confided in her notebook. 'As life goes on, one's heart deadens & wearies from many disappointments, & one ceases to look for heart in others. My heart no longer beats faster at the sight of a new or kindly & beautiful face. I hope nothing from it. I have come to the turn in the road of life when I expect no more love, when an act of genuine kindness, or an expression of genuine interest startles me & surprises me & fills me with gratitude, but ceases to give me hope.'

If Edwards had indeed given up on love, she put her energy into work. In 1872, she made the journey through the Dolomites – at that time, rough terrain and not on the tourist trail – which became the subject of her first great success as a travel writer, *Untrodden Peaks and Unfrequented Valleys*. This was followed, a few years later, by her masterpiece, *A Thousand Miles up the Nile*.

She and her travelling companion, Lucy Renshaw, with whom she had experienced the Dolomites, had sailed to Alexandria in late 1873, travelling first to Cairo and then up the great river on the *Philae*, a large passenger boat of the type known as a *dahabeeyah*. Her great joke was that they had made the trip simply because it was intolerably wet in France, and had 'taken refuge in Egypt as one might turn aside into the Burlington Arcade or the Passage des Panoramas – to get out of the rain'. If so, it was a fortuitous impulse, for the journey gave her not only a subject but a crusade: on her return to England, she was determined to do what she could to explore, document and preserve the heritage of ancient Egypt.

Edwards, who taught herself to read hieroglyphics, had been alarmed to see so many monuments damaged and despoiled for their riches. 'The work of destruction goes on apace,' she wrote. 'There is no one to prevent it; there is no one to discourage it. Every day, more inscriptions are mutilated – more tombs are rifled – more paintings and sculptures are defaced.' In 1882, she founded the Egypt Exploration Fund, later renamed the Egypt Exploration Society, with a mission to fund systematic archaeological excavation so that the ancient culture might be better understood and preserved for future generations. She raised the money to hire the most skilled archaeologists, most notably Flinders Petrie, whom, according to one of her biographers, she came to regard almost as a son.

Their portraits hang side by side in the Petrie Museum, he in oils, she in a large black-and-white photograph. She is regal, stately; silver hair swept back from a strong face. In a letter to her friend Kate Bradbury, she referred to herself as 'Owl' – a pet name between them – and indeed the portrait does speak of a certain fierce wisdom. The photograph, by William Kurtz, was taken towards the end of her life. She autographed copies of it while on a lecture tour of America in 1889 and 1890, commanding appearance fees surpassed only by her former editor, Charles Dickens. The *Boston Globe* called her 'the most learned woman in the world'.

This tour was the late triumph of her life. In the summer of 1890 she had surgery for breast cancer. 'It was successful –,' Kate Bradbury later wrote, '. . . the dreaded evil never returned; but the loss of blood, & the nervous exhaustion, & the shock, she never recovered from.'

Ellen Braysher died on 9 January 1892, at the age of eighty-seven. Edwards, though very unwell herself, was at the deathbed. 'When Mrs Braysher saw her,' Bradbury wrote, 'it was beautiful to see the strong faithful love of years rising to dominate all that weakness and unrest.'

They were not apart for long. Edwards succumbed to flu on 15 April, at the age of sixty, and Braysher's grave was opened to admit her. It was Petrie and Bradbury, on a visit to the churchyard soon afterwards, who decided that a stone ankh should be laid on the grave.

When I journeyed to the spot in early November, rainwater and a mush of fallen leaves had gathered in the symbol's loop, and the obelisk bore a delta of scars where ivy had been stripped away. I was alone in the churchyard, and had the feeling that I would have been alone no matter what hour of the day I visited. The peace was disturbed only by the crows flying in and out of the belltower, passing through a window above a clock face inscribed with the words of Horace: '*Pulvis et umbra sumus.*'

We are dust and shadows – it seemed an appropriate phrase for a writer so famous in her day, so nearly forgotten now.

*

In Mount Jerome Cemetery, a little south of Dublin city centre, a busy funeral was taking place. Staff in black tailcoats and top hats stood outside the Victorian chapel, directing traffic with a waft of their silver-topped canes. Piped music drifted out of the grand arched doorway: *Drove my Chevy to the levee but the levee was dry . . .*

I hadn't come for the funeral. I was after a man long dead.

I found him on the Nun's Walk, three graves in from the wall, very near the tall brick chimney of the neighbouring hospice. The carving on the grey limestone slab was too eroded to read, but a small stone plaque at its foot – a recent addition – made the identity of the occupant clear:

Here Lies
Dublin's Invisible Prince
JOSEPH SHERIDAN LE FANU
28th Aug. 1814 – 7th Feb. 1873
Novelist and Writer of Ghost Stories

'Dublin's Invisible Prince'. Was there ever a title so apt to intrigue? Le Fanu was a very popular author in his day, and had an enormous influence on the writers of the supernatural who came after. He has been described as the father of modern horror. M. R. James, in particular, took much from him. Le Fanu, James wrote, 'succeeds in inspiring a mysterious terror better than any other writer'. E. F. Benson, no slouch with a tale of dread, wrote with delicious appreciation of the dynamics of Le Fanu's stories: 'They begin quietly enough, the tentacles of terror are applied so softly that the reader hardly notices them till they are sucking the courage from his blood. A darkness gathers, like dusk gently falling, and then something obscurely stirs in it . . .'

Le Fanu was born in Dublin, the son of a clergyman. He studied for the bar, but did not practise, becoming instead a newspaper editor and proprietor. Although his first ghost story was published in 1838, his finest work – the collection *In a Glass Darkly* – was written as he neared the end of his life, and published in 1872, less than a year before his death at the age of fifty-eight. The stories include 'Carmilla', a homoerotic vampire novella believed to have been a strong influence on *Dracula*. And then there is 'Green Tea'.

If I tell you the premise of 'Green Tea' you might laugh. If you read it, you would not. The Reverend Mr Jennings is travelling by omnibus from central London to his home in Richmond when, in the gloaming of the interior, he encounters the spectre of a small black monkey with eyes of ember red – it follows him home and begins to haunt him day and night. Risibly absurd, right? Or it would be if the story were not so grim, serious and unflinching. The monkey is a presence of 'unfathomable malignity' which drives Jennings to cut his own throat.

'Green Tea' was first serialised, like Amelia Edwards's 'The Phantom Coach', in Dickens's *All the Year Round*. But is it even a ghost story? It reads more like a psychological breakdown. Visual and auditory hallucinations, suicidal ideation, intrusive thoughts: one might diagnose Jennings with all of those symptoms before calling upon the exorcist.

Much the same can be said of 'The Familiar', which M. R. James considered one of the best supernatural stories in the English language. If James's works feel like wintry tales lit by a cheery fire, the works of Le Fanu seem dim and cold, half glimpsed by guttering candle. 'The Familiar' is one such. Towards the end of the eighteenth century, Captain Barton, a navy veteran, arrives home to Dublin, where he becomes engaged to a young woman, Miss Montague. It is his last happiness. Returning late one night from the house of his fiancée, he is followed through the lonely streets by a small man in a fur cap and a state of fury who calls himself 'The Watcher'. This figure pursues him wherever he goes, and Barton comes to believe it is a demon bent on vengeance for a sin from his past. 'I stand in the gaze of death,' he tells a preacher to whom he turns in desperation, 'in the triumphant presence of infernal power and malignity.' Yet, once again, Le Fanu's writing suggests not a possession but a disordered mind – paranoid and delusional.

'He is masterful at dramatising psychology. His stories work on a subconscious level, they have multiple meanings, and he gets at what really frightens people,' the writer and film-maker Matthew Holness told me. I had been keen to hear his thoughts. Holness, whose psychological horror film *Possum* was based on his own short story, is a Le Fanu admirer of long standing. Growing up in Whitstable, Kent, he first read 'Carmilla' in his teens, but it is only as an adult that he has come to appreciate the Irish writer's beguiling bleakness.

'Le Fanu taps into our private innermost anxieties and fears, and for that reason his ghost stories are very disconcerting; they go right inside you,' he said. 'There's no sense in which you are being entertained. I have a theory that Le Fanu is not as popular as M. R. James because people like to be scared, but they don't want to be really disturbed.

They don't want to confront too much about themselves. Reading James, you feel that it is a performance of sorts. You are waiting for that pleasurable frisson of fear. Le Fanu never gives you that. He's very modern, and properly dark and horrifying.'

It is tempting to seek a correspondence between Le Fanu's life and his remarkable late work. The grand Georgian house where he wrote these stories still stands – at 70 Merrion Square, overlooking St Stephen's Green. It is now the headquarters of the Arts Council, but a circular plaque on the front tells of its illustrious former occupant.

Le Fanu married Susanna Bennett shortly before Christmas in 1843, and they moved to Merrion Square in the 1850s. They had four children. Susanna seems to have had problems with anxiety and morbid thoughts – 'the idea of death was constantly present in her mind,' her husband wrote – which were intensified by the passing of her father in 1856. She dreamed one night that he appeared by her bed, drawing back the curtain, and smiling down on her with the words, 'There is room in the vault for you, Little Sue.' She considered this not a dream but a vision from God. Le Fanu felt that she longed to be lying in the grave with her father. If so, she had her wish. She died in 1858.

Badly affected by this loss, struggling with debt, and with children to raise, Le Fanu withdrew from Dublin society for the last decade or so of his life. His reclusiveness earned him that nickname, 'The Invisible Prince'. He could be spotted in old bookshops after dark, examining aged texts on demonology and the walking dead. His taste for the supernatural appeared to intensify following the loss of Susanna. 'Any more ghost stories for me?' he would ask.

But he wasn't only reading, he was writing. He worked in bed by candlelight, fuelled by strong tea, 'in that eerie period of the night when human vitality is at its lowest ebb and the Powers of Darkness rampant and terrifying', according to an essay of 1916 by S. M. Ellis, based on the memories of Le Fanu's son Brinsley. In this way, 'Green Tea', 'The Familiar' and the other stories of *In a Glass Darkly* came to be written.

It is from the S. M. Ellis essay that we have the famous account of Le Fanu's end: 'Horrible dreams troubled him to the last, one of the most recurrent and persistent being a vision of a vast and direly foreboding old mansion (such as he had so often depicted in his romances), in a state of ruin and threatening imminently to fall upon and crush the dreamer rooted to the spot. So painful was this repeated horror that he would struggle and cry out in his sleep. He mentioned the trouble to his doctor. When the end came, and the doctor stood by the bedside of Le Fanu and looked in the terror-stricken eyes of the dead man, he said: "I feared this – that house fell at last."'

This has so much of the flavour of one of Le Fanu's own ghost stories that it is hard to resist. It is likely to have been based on the later recollections of Brinsley, but appears to be contradicted by a letter from Le Fanu's daughter Emmie. Writing two days after her father's death and possibly in the presence of his body, she gives an account of a more peaceful end: 'He had almost got over a bad attack of Bronchitis but his strength gave way & he sank very quickly & died in his sleep. His face looks so happy with a beautiful smile on it.'

However it happened, Le Fanu was buried on 11 February 1873, on a cold afternoon of light snow. His coffin was lowered into the family vault beside that of Susanna. There was room.

One hundred and twenty-seven years passed. His name, scoured by Dublin wind and rain, vanished from the grave.

Then, one day, a young American arrived in the city. Brian J. Showers had a taste for ghosts. He had first encountered

Le Fanu in horror anthologies in school in Madison, Wisconsin. Now he found himself living in the city where those stories were written, where their creator had lived and died. In October 2000, sitting in his flat and reading about Le Fanu, he realised that Mount Jerome cemetery was only a fifteen-minute walk away. He could try to find the grave. 'So,' he told me, 'I chucked the book in a bag, and went off and did that.'

Mount Jerome, though nowhere near as grand and celebrated as Dublin's other great cemetery, Glasnevin, is still a fascinating place to visit. It opened in 1836. Le Fanu is not the only important cultural figure buried there. It is also home to the playwright J. M. Synge and the artist Jack Butler Yeats. The writer Máirtín Ó Cadhain has, since 1970, lain at the foot of a rough stone cross which resembles some of those on St Finnan's Isle. He is a laureate of the shroud; his 1949 Irish-language novel *Cré na Cille* is told entirely through the voices of the dead – a coffiny cacophony – as they gab and gob, blether and curse, beneath the sod of a Connemara churchyard.

Managing, after some difficulty, to identify the correct vault, Showers scraped the moss off the top to try to read the inscription. It was clear that the grave was not in good repair. He began making regular visits, clearing weeds and so forth, but felt more ought to be done. Working with the Le Fanu family, he organised a restoration, including the installation of the new plaque. People now leave little tokens on the slab – stones and chestnuts and trinkets – as signs that they have been there, and thought about Le Fanu, that his stories have meant something in their lives. Showers himself has a proprietorial feeling towards the grave. And not only this one. He tends the Dublin graves of other writers of the fantastic, and is a pilgrim to such graves elsewhere. He has visited Amelia Edwards and M. R. James, yes, but also Arthur Machen in Amersham and H. P. Lovecraft in Providence, Rhode Island. Edgar Allan Poe, in Baltimore, is on his list. 'I make a personal connection with these writers,' he said, laughing. 'I enjoy reading Le Fanu, and I have for decades, and before you know it you're looking after the guy's grave.'

Showers is the founder of the Dublin Ghost Story Festival – 'For such a small country and small population, Ireland's contributions to supernatural and gothic literature are substantial' – and runs Swan River Press, the Republic's only publishing house dedicated to that genre. Lately, Swan River has produced a beautiful hardback of 'Green Tea', with an introduction by Matthew Holness and a postcard of Le Fanu's death-mask. Two months after we had met, and as the 150th anniversary of the story approached, Showers visited the grave with the unbound pages, laying these on the slab together with some flowers and a freshly brewed cup of green tea.

Was the Invisible Prince visible once more?

'I hope so,' Showers said.

DUBLINERS

AT AROUND HALF-PAST TWELVE on 20 March 2014, two women were walking through a cemetery in Dublin, returning to their car after visiting the grave of a family friend who had been buried that morning. It was a large cemetery, an easy place to become lost, and to get their bearings they were looking for the round tower which rises, as if in a fairy tale, not far from the main gates. As they turned on to the path leading to the tower, the younger of the pair glimpsed, some twenty or so feet away, a man in a tree, dead. She recalled, later, the shock of it. Maybe it was the shock that meant she took in every detail, like the way he moved with the wind. She remembered, too, that the tree was beautiful. 'I felt like I was meant to find him,' she said.

The cemetery was Glasnevin. The man was Shane Mac-Thomáis. This is the story of both.

What can I tell you about Shane MacThomáis? Shane was gas. Shane was a true Dub. Shane was a good auld Dublin skin. These are the things people say. I can tell you that he was forty-six at the time of his death, that he was the best-known guide at the most famous cemetery in Ireland, that his knowledge of Irish history was such that his suicide was likened to a library burning down. There are other things.

'I don't think Shane liked the airbrushing of faults,' his nephew, Niall, told me. 'You look at history books about certain people and they get rid of the humanity of them, y'know? Sometimes the humanity is what makes the story interesting in the first place.'

In that spirit, this.

Glasnevin, known in its early days as Prospect Cemetery, opened in 1832. Enclosed within its high walls and watch-towers – built to deter body snatchers – are 124 acres thickly sown with the bodies of around 1.5 million people, more than the present population of Dublin. It is a city within the city, a sinkhole nucleus at the centre of the cell. The cemetery attracts 200,000 visitors each year, but for a little while, at around half past eight on a fine morning in early July, I had it to myself. This was my first visit, and I couldn't get over the theatricality, the sheer swaggering drama of the place. It felt like walking on to the abandoned set of some early Hollywood epic.

The sky was blue, the sun slanted low and dazzling. Marble angels loomed in silhouette, spreading their wings as if to drape the day in mourning black. The O'Connell Tower gleamed white in the summer light. Rapunzel might have found it familiar, except the tower isn't a prison, it's a tomb. It stands 168 feet. The granite cross on top is seven feet tall and weighs three tonnes. God knows how they got it up there. There are 198 steps inside. The top offers views over Dublin to the water and hills. At the foot of the tower is the crypt of Daniel O'Connell, 'the Liberator', who did so much to advance the rights of Catholics in the nineteenth century, including establishing this cemetery in which they – and anyone else who wanted – could be buried. O'Connell died in Genoa in 1847. His coffin is visible through trefoils in the marble sarcophagus; I touched it for luck and went on my way.

Not far from the tower, I found the grave I was after. Someone had left offerings: a lily, a scallop shell, a fading plastic windmill of the sort a child would stick in a sandcas-tle. Shane MacThomáis is buried with his father, Éamonn, who predeceased him by twelve years. Their names and dates are written in gold letters on black, along with the words, 'Patriots, historians, writers & Dubliners' and the Irish phrase, '*Ní bheidh a leithéid ann arís*' – we may never see their like again. This sounds stupid, but standing there, in the sun, I promised Shane I would try to do a good job in writing about him. I would do my best not to balls it up.

'I love this place,' he had once said. 'I walk through the back gate in the morning, and I'm not always in a good mood, and I'm not always mad into Glasnevin, but I look at all the headstones and I imagine all the people here, all the stories that are yet to be discovered and told. And it lifts my spirit.'

That quote is from *One Million Dubliners*, a documentary about Glasnevin made by the film-maker Aoife Kelleher. It is a wonderful film with two stars, one of flesh and blood, the other of earth and stone: Shane and the cemetery itself. Shane is an impish figure, dashing around in a duffel coat, grave to grave, name to name, tale to tale. He seems to be driven by sheer storytelling energy. You can almost see the words streaming behind him, a vapour trail of breath and ink.

His love for Glasnevin and the force of his personality are such that you spend the first eighty minutes of the film falling for the guy. Then the kick in the guts: the slow coming into focus of his nameplate on the coffin. It is beautifully done. *One Million Dubliners* does not explain how Shane died. There would have been no need for that. The point was that he had joined the multitude whom he once hymned, gone beneath the earth over which he had walked with such purpose and passion. The final shot is of Shane, and, for one last time, his voice. Some day, he muses, he too will be buried in Glasnevin: 'Where better, y'know? Where else would I go?'

Where indeed? Glasnevin is extraordinary. It was described in 1907 as 'an open-air Pantheon or Westminster Abbey of Catholic and Nationalist Ireland', but, like a lot of big cemeteries, it later fell into an awful state of disrepair. 'The people of Dublin used to say you wouldn't bury a bleedin' dog in Glasnevin, and they were right,' the former CEO, George McCullough, told me. 'But it has been resurrected.' It is state-of-the-art, has all the facilities, including – that holy of holies for those of us who like to spend our days in graveyards – decent toilets. There is a café, a museum, a gift shop. You can buy Countess Markievicz fridge magnets, Easter Rising keyrings, Éamon de Valera mugs.

The grave of Michael Collins, very near the museum, is always covered in flowers. Perhaps because the revolutionary leader was played by Liam Neeson in the 1996 film, the site has a greater romantic – even erotic – allure than would otherwise be the case. The cemetery florists told the story, in *One Million Dubliners*, of the young woman who used to holiday in the city and leave fresh roses on every day of her trip. 'She was in love with Michael Collins,' one recalled. 'She said she would never marry because no man would come up to his standard.' The grave even receives Valentine cards and balloons. Shane used to love to talk about that as a way of publicising Glasnevin. 'Next year,' he once said, 'there'll be thongs – and if people don't leave them, I'll put them there myself.' A good yarn, he seemed to believe, deserved to be spun ever finer.

Despite being a great reader, and the author of two books – *Dead Interesting* and *Glasnevin: Ireland's Necropolis* – Shane didn't find writing easy. He was probably dyslexic, his family think. He was a decent writer, but a genius talker. All those clichés about Irish charm and verbosity were proved true in him. The Blarney Stone? Forget it. He had a million stones to inspire his quicksilver tongue.

'He would walk around in this cemetery of stories,' his daughter, Morgane, told me. 'I don't think he saw it as a place where dead people were laid to rest. I think he saw it as so much information stored around him, and he could just pick a name and go with that. It was like a library almost. I remember going for walks with him in the cemetery at twilight. He never saw it as spooky. It was a very calm and peaceful place for him.'

To explore Glasnevin, you can take a guided tour, or, as I did, wander around with the help of a map. Having been in so many cemeteries that felt neglected, I was struck by how much care was being taken of this one. The grass was clipped, leaves had been blown from paths, and there was very little litter. Workmen were digging a trench for the resetting of a headstone, and a number of memorials carried blue signs indicating that they had been restored. A squirrel scurried up a sequoia. I noticed, on the grave of Brendan Behan, a pint glass musky with the dregs of stout; someone must have drunk him a toast. They had brought it in, no doubt, from the lovely old pub next to the Prospect Gate entrance. The sign above its door says John Kavanagh, but everyone calls it The Gravediggers.

There is no shortage of famous names buried in Glasnevin. Luke Kelly of The Dubliners and Liam Whelan, one of the Manchester United players killed in the Munich air disaster of 1958, are in the newer section across Finglas Road. The poet and priest Gerard Manley Hopkins, dead from typhoid at forty-four, lies in the Jesuit Plot. The precise location of his grave is unmarked, but his name, in Latin, is one of many listed on the base of a granite crucifix: P. GERARDUS HOPKINS OBIIT JUN. 8 1889.

Visitors to Glasnevin sometimes expect to see the grave of James Joyce, and are disappointed to be told that he is buried in Zurich. The confusion stems from the fact that his father, John Stanislaus Joyce, is buried here, and from a feeling that such a significant cultural figure should lie in what is Ireland's de facto national cemetery. Dublin city councillors had proposed repatriating Joyce's remains to coincide with the centenary of *Ulysses* in 2022. The Hades chapter of that novel is set in Glasnevin.

'In the midst of death we are in life,' Leopold Bloom, attending Paddy Dignam's funeral, observes. '. . . All these here once walked round Dublin. Faithful departed. As you are now so once were we.'

*

AT AROUND HALF PAST TWO on 14 June 1998, a young man was wandering around Glasnevin, reading the stones. Shane MacThomáis had a job interview and was passing the time. All those famous names, he thought. All that Irish history. It was thrilling. If the cemetery wanted a tour guide, he was the very man. 'I just so wanted to work here,' he later recalled. 'I would have given anything for the job.'

He got it. George McCullough interviewed him. You couldn't call it recruitment. It was more like inviting a star to step out on to stage. 'Shane could pick up a crowd,' McCullough remembered. 'He said the secret of a good tour guide was make them laugh, make them cry, tell them something they know, tell them something they don't. He just had a way of dealing with people, didn't matter who they were. I've seen him here with British royalty, and with our own President. Regardless of who you were, he could talk to you, and make you feel engaged.'

Shane was born in the summer of 1967. He was the second eldest of the four children of Éamonn and Rosaleen MacThomáis. There was only fifteen months between him and his younger sister Melíosa – 'Irish twins,' as she put it, with a laugh, when we met. He grew up in a northern suburb of Dublin. The family home was a small terraced house built in the 1940s for those displaced by the clearance of the inner-city slums. The area back then was called Ballymun, but has come to be known as Glasnevin North, perhaps in part to distinguish it from the Ballymun high-rise flats a mile away, which came to be so associated with the heroin epidemic of the 1980s. The last of the fifteen-storey blocks, Joseph Plunkett Tower – named, like the rest, after the leaders of the 1916 Easter Rising – was built in the year Shane was born.

Glasnevin Cemetery was a half-hour walk south of where the family lived. When would Shane first have come to know it? 'Oh, probably as a baby in a buggy,' Melíosa thought. 'Our dad used to love the place and show us around quite regularly. It was a lot more overgrown at that stage. And it wouldn't be like going to visit a family grave. It would be like "The History of Ireland" as we were walking through.'

Éamonn would, of course, point the great figures from Ireland's past: the tomb of O'Connell, the grave of Michael Collins and so on. But he also passed down to his children his taste for Dublin characters such as Michael Moran, known as Zozimus, the blind balladeer who scratched a living by reciting poetry in the streets and died in 1846.

'My dad loved bringing history to ordinary people that didn't have a chance to study it in school. Like bringing stories alive,' Melíosa remembered. 'And Shane got that, Shane did the same. Shane was great at picking forgotten figures from history and making them visible again.'

Éamonn MacThomáis was born in 1927. His father, a fire brigade officer, died when Éamonn was very young, and so he left school at thirteen to earn a living. He delivered laundry from a horse-drawn cart, worked as a messenger for a Grafton Street store ('By eighteen, I knew every street, road and lane in the city') and then found an office job. The politics of his family were republican. The introduction to *Three Shouts on a Hill*, a posthumous book of his articles, states that he joined the Dublin brigade of the Irish Republican Army as a young man and participated in Operation Harvest, the 1956–62 guerrilla campaign along the border. The book also claims that he was among those who raided a British army barracks in Armagh in 1954, stealing weapons.

A political prisoner, he was held in the Curragh internment camp from 1957 to 1959, and in 1961 was sentenced to four months under the Offences Against the State Act. In August 1973, now editor of *An Phoblacht*, the republican newspaper, he was arrested at his home and charged with IRA membership. He was convicted and sentenced to fifteen months. Within two weeks of completing this stretch in Mountjoy Prison, he was given another sentence of the same duration on the same charge, plus that of being in possession of an incriminating document. He was released in August 1975. 'Martin McGuinness was in prison with Éamonn,' Gerry Adams later recalled. 'They were in Portlaoise for a while, and he has very fond memories of Éamonn, like a *seanachaí*, telling them yarns and stories and the social history of Ireland and of the ordinary people.'

A *seanachaí* is a storyteller, a tradition-bearer, a bard. It was while in Mountjoy Prison that Éamonn wrote the book which established that reputation. *Me Jewel and Darlin' Dublin*, published in 1974, is a love letter to the city and its people. You might call it popular history, but it's more like a conjuring up of the life and atmosphere of the place, from the bustling trams, to kids kicking the can, to Bang Bang – a famous character, obsessed with cowboy movies, who used to run around with a large door key, pretending it was a Colt 45, and shouting the noise that earned him his name. 'James Joyce locked himself in the tower at Sandycove for twelve months to write his book,' Éamonn later wrote. 'I don't see much difference between the tower and Mountjoy.'

The success of the book led to a career as a writer and broadcaster. His television films about Dublin made for RTÉ in the 1970s and early 1980s are remembered with great fondness; they look, now, like time capsules of a city largely gone. Éamonn, on screen, is an ambling, avuncular figure, all beard and specs and tartan ties – he has the autodidact's trait of wearing his learning lightly; the delight he took in acquiring all that knowledge matched by the delight he takes in laying it out.

There was a bookish atmosphere in the MacThomáis home, Melíosa recalled, though not at all pretentious. Spines lined the walls, and the children would read the newspapers delivered each day. The conversation around the table was of politics and social justice issues. There was no pressure put on the kids to follow the republican path, although Shane did become a Sinn Féin activist for a time.

'My dad loved Joyce and Yeats, and he brought that love of literature into the house. So he talked about big themes, but, if anything, there was almost an anti-intellectual vibe,' Melíosa said. 'Certainly, we weren't brought up thinking university education was a goal that we should aspire to. You were brought up and you went out to work. None of us went to college when we left school, although probably the potential was there. But we were also brought up to believe that literature didn't belong to the middle class; it belonged to the working class as well.' Éamonn's copy of *Ulysses*, now owned by his grandson Niall, has tally marks in the back, indicating how many times it had been read. 'Forty-seven,' he wrote at the bottom. 'That's enough!'

Shane had a difficult childhood. His father's absence while in prison, and the fallout from that, seems to have cut deep. Éamonn was away for most of the two years between August 1973 and August 1975, from the time Shane was six until he was eight. 'The particularly traumatic bit was that our dad served six months and then he was released, and three days later he was rearrested and served another sentence,' Melíosa said. 'I remember that was really tough as a kid – waiting for your dad to come home, and then he's back in prison.'

Although Shane was too young to understand the situation properly, he was a deeply empathetic child, quick to pick up on atmosphere and the hurt of others. He didn't blame Éamonn for what had happened. He loved him deeply and regarded him as a patriot. 'He idolised and iconised his father,' his close friend Jack Gleeson told me. 'He just had this perfect vision of him. It was very important to him that his father was buried up at Glasnevin, and it was important to him to be buried with his father. He'd spoken about that quite a lot, that he wanted to be buried in his father's grave.'

On the day of his death, Shane left a final post on Facebook: 'Broken 1974 . . .' It accompanies a photograph of himself as a little boy, smiling at the camera while receiving a gift from a department store Santa. What looks like a happy memory is, in fact, a snapshot of one of the worst periods of Shane's early life. His father was in prison, the family struggled to cope, and the four children were separated for a time – sent to stay with friends and family. The picture has that fuzzy melancholy of old Polaroids, as well it might; it is a portrait of innocence lost.

'Childhood scars run deep,' Melíosa said, 'and I don't think Shane's ever healed.'

*

THE GRAVE OF Éamonn and Shane MacThomáis is in Glasnevin's republican plot – the area, close to the O'Connell Tower, containing the resting places of notable men and women of that movement. Here, too, lies Jeremiah O'Donovan Rossa, at whose funeral, in 1915, Patrick Pearse gave his incendiary 'the fools, the fools, the fools . . .' speech. O'Donovan Rossa's stone is marked with a bronze phoenix. The bird is an oxidised green, the flames bright from reverent fingers.

Not far away is what was Shane's own favourite grave, that of Elizabeth O'Farrell, a nurse who played a key role in the Easter Rising – going back and forth between the British and rebel leadership, through the barricades, past the fallen, carrying the terms of the surrender. She later became a personal friend of Éamonn MacThomáis and died in 1957. Shane thought that she hadn't been given her due, and was always keen to talk about her courage on his tours. Irish women were too often forgotten in the history books, he felt. This was all of a piece with his general philosophy. As resident historian at Glasnevin, he was on the side of the underdog. He celebrated the extraordinary in the ordinary: the Dubliners whose names and faces will never appear on mugs in gift shops but whose lives and deaths are part of the story of the city. 'Working in Glasnevin was a great outlet for his love of Dublin,' Niall said. 'That recognising of the regular people buried here meant a huge amount to him. It felt like he was fulfilling a purpose.'

His knowledge of history was picked up along the way. He wasn't academic. 'His intelligence never really fit school,' Melíosa said. 'It was more of a challenging, questioning intelligence rather than the ability to learn things off. If Shane was in school now, he'd probably have some sort of diagnosis. ADHD or something like that, and maybe they'd be able to support him a little more. Back then, school was tough and unforgiving and Shane railed against that. He was failing to pass English, but at the same time would be the only person I would know who was reading Nietzsche in his teens.'

Jack Gleeson hung around in the same group of teenage boys. He was a few years older than Shane. 'I can still see that cheeky grin on his face,' he said. 'I don't think he ever lost that.'

This was the late 1970s. 'We would have had pretensions of being street gurriers, but if a gang from Ballymun came down we'd quickly flee,' Jack recalled. 'We weren't real troublemakers; we would get up to harmless devilment.'

Shane left Ballymun Comprehensive at fifteen to start a painting apprenticeship, but at some point towards the end of his teens left Ireland for London. 'When I met Shane over there, he was living that bohemian life: living in squats and picking up furniture from skips, that kind of thing,' Gleeson said. 'He was very much at home in that environment, much more so than he would have been in Dublin. He had a very romantic view of life.' He saw himself, at times, as a character in a novel, or a black-and-white movie. It was the 1980s, but in photographs he looks more like an existential hero from an earlier decade – waistcoat and tie, slick hair, long dark coat and fedora. His Facebook avatar, towards the end of his life, was Albert Camus – upturned collar, insouciant fag. 'People say I look like him,' he posted, 'and I certainly think like him.'

In London he met Isabelle, his future wife. She was in her early twenties, and had left France for England. Fate, if one believes in that, brought her to King's Cross, to the squat next door to Shane. 'My dad fell head over heels in love with her,' their daughter Morgane told me. 'She wasn't so interested at the beginning.' Isabelle was waitressing at a nightclub. 'He would wait up till, like, four in the morning until he heard her coming home, and then stand there with a cigarette, going, "Oh, fancy seeing you here . . ." He was besotted. And then, over time, they developed a relationship.'

Morgane is in her late twenties. We met for coffee in Busy Feet, a café that was one of Shane's favourite hang-outs. I had been nervous about meeting in a public place, worried about how upset she might become, but she seemed easy and free. I could see her father in her; not so much his looks, but his manner. He hadn't really been an authority figure in her life, she said. It was a friendship.

Shane returned to Dublin, now with Isabelle, in 1989. Two years later, Morgane was born. The relationship was off and on. 'I don't know if you know,' Morgane explained, 'but while they were in London they were heroin-users. They were smoking it. The eighties was full of heroin.' In Ireland, Isabelle stopped taking the drug. 'But with my father, his using progressed and his life began to spiral down.

'In those few years, we were a bit distant. My mum didn't want him around me because he was using, and she didn't want to be around him either because she was trying to get her life up and running. He used to see me on the weekends and he'd be high; he would maybe take my pocket money, or he would do dodgy stuff like bringing me to the Ballymun flats, which were kind of a rough place, to score. He wasn't a bad person, but he was sick, you know?'

The heroin, she thinks now, was 'a form of self-medication' – a way of suppressing the pain from his earlier life. In any case, the drug culture in England was very different from that in Ireland. 'There was easier access in London,' Jack Gleeson explained. 'In Dublin it was more of a working-class thing. To get drugs you had to go to very rough areas, like Ballyfermot. Shane was always a bit of a snob and he wouldn't have fitted in well there. He would have been seen as a mark, somebody you could take money off. In London, you could indulge in heroin and it all appeared to be very civilised. You could go into a pharmacy and buy needles. It felt cleaner over there, for want of a better term.'

Isabelle gave Shane an ultimatum: until you beat your addiction, you can't see your daughter. 'So, I didn't see him for a year,' Morgane remembered. 'But when he came back he was nine months clean, he had joined Narcotics Anonymous, and he had gotten really into it. He picked me up, brought me to a restaurant in Dublin City centre, and told me everything. I was nine.'

Jack Gleeson became his sponsor in NA, helping him progress through the twelve-step programme and stay clean. 'It was like anything else with Shane. When he embraced something and got a passion for it, he went for it full gung-ho. He helped an awful lot of people. He got involved in organising recovery-based conventions, and would have been seen as a leading light in recovery circles.'

Morgane believes that it was in NA, sharing his story with groups of addicts, that Shane first came to appreciate that he had a talent for communication. 'That was maybe the beginning of him realising that people were drawn to him and he could talk to them with ease. He realised he had a gift.' It was a particular sort of gift: he could take a painful tale and tell it with humour and compassion; the sorrow of the story never went away, but laughter eased it into the minds and memories of those who heard it. Darkness was his material, light was his medium. What worked in group therapy would later work in the graveyard. He had found his voice. 'I think his life only really began,' said Morgane, 'when he gave up heroin and was able to realise what he liked and what drove him, which was history and storytelling.'

He began to give tours. He had three in his repertoire in those early days: James Joyce's Dublin, the Easter Rising, and

Glasnevin Cemetery. His great innovation was to talk about Irish history, so burdened with tragedy, without false solemnity. He told jokes. People laughed. They applauded. They took him seriously, regarded him with respect. For someone with a history of depression, the daily approval of strangers was validating.

'When you're doing a tour, any problems you're having in your own life are put to the back of your head,' Lorcan Collins told me. He runs the 1916 Rebellion Walking Tour, on which Shane had worked; indeed, he led one of those tours a week before he died. 'If you're in a bad mood,' Collins went on, 'you just try to close that off and concentrate on what you're doing. You're conscious of the fact that people are paying to be entertained as well as educated. You have to learn to do that, and I think Shane was good at it.'

To the public, he looked like a man without a bother on him. This wasn't so. He was, in a way, performing a less complicated self. But it must have felt good in the moment. Best of all were those occasions when his father turned up. Éamonn himself had given tours of the cemetery in the 1950s, so this was a kind of inheritance. 'My dad was enormously proud of Shane,' Melíosa said. 'Particularly when he started working at Glasnevin. He'd go down to his tours and stand at the back and watch him.'

What would he have seen? His boy finding a role in life. It had taken a while. There had been false starts. There was a period when he and Isabelle had broken up, and she moved to France with their daughter. Shane's response to this was, naturally, to join the French Foreign Legion. This period of his life, when it comes up, is often played for laughs, with a disbelieving shake of the head, and sometimes characterised as a grand gesture, a self-sacrificing response to a broken heart by a man with a taste for the dramatic. Morgane thought it was romantic, but in a different way from how it is usually understood: it meant Shane could be based in France, close to his family, and learn the language. Whatever the motivation, it didn't last long. He spent part of his service in Africa – Somalia or Chad, no one seems quite sure – and, eventually, absconded back to Ireland. George McCullough tells a story that the only VIP Shane ever refused to show around the cemetery was the French ambassador to Ireland – worried that he might yet be prosecuted for desertion.

Shane's renaissance coincided with that of the cemetery. They shaped each other. As a huge amount of government money was spent on restoration, he became the voice of the stones – talking Glasnevin up on the tours and in the media, celebrating its value as both an educational resource and a great monument to the complexity of the Irish story. 'The place is so vast you could tell the whole history of Ireland ten times over,' he said. Shane changed the way people saw Glasnevin, and Glasnevin changed the way people saw Shane. Perhaps even the way he saw himself. 'A creative person,' Melíosa thought. 'A person with vision and the capacity to negotiate with people and get things done.'

It's important not to make him sound like a saint, like he was born again. He was complex; let's not reduce him by making him simple. 'The Shane that a lot of people would have loved wasn't the side of him that I often saw,' Jack Gleeson reflected. 'He was probably the funniest person that I ever knew, but he could rip people apart like nobody else I've ever come across. He could be cruel and vicious in his humour, but he could also be kind and would reach out and help people.'

I suppose he was like most of us; he would let you see who he wanted you to see at any given moment. He liked attention, and knew how to play to his strengths – that Klieglight charm – in public appearances. When Aoife Kelleher started to research *One Million Dubliners* in the spring of 2013, the first thing she did was join Shane for a walk around the cemetery. 'It was a tour unlike any other,' she recalled. 'He was such a big personality. So engaging and funny. He was very comfortable in the space. You'd see him bounding over graves and jumping between them. I think people's views of Glasnevin, and of cemeteries in general, were changed by his attitude and by the tours.'

I had heard from other people that he would walk over the graves, and that, in the days when he still smoked, he would flick his cigs away any old where. He seemed to get away with this because it was understood he wasn't being disrespectful; his easy intimacy with the cemetery meant that the dead would not be troubled by feet and fags.

'He was so steeped in Irish lore, and had so much respect for the graveyard, that even where his behaviour might have been boundary-pushing it was all about this familiarity that he brought to every aspect of his relationship with Glasnevin,' Kelleher said. 'He *was* Glasnevin. There was a real sense of belonging and strong personal connection. Of course, his father was buried there. But I think that was only part of it. His love for Irish history created that connection, too.'

Éamonn MacThomáis died in 2002. His death hit Shane hard. The funeral, though, he found inspiring. He gave an account of it in the introduction to *Dead Interesting*: 'Lollypop women stood beside Trinity professors, while balladeers and newsreaders looked at each other's shoes. It was at that point that I realised that a funeral was, in a way, a short biography of a person's life … From that point on I never lifted a biography without skipping to the last chapter to see what was written about the funeral.'

His father was buried in the morning. That afternoon, he gave his tour as usual – 'for Da' – showing tourists around the cemetery where his own parent was the newest resident. 'I can understand that,' said his nephew, Niall, who now himself works at Glasnevin. 'It was a way of honouring Éamonn. Not by leaving flowers, not sitting in the house drinking tea. Doing a historical tour is a way of saying that history keeps going. It was a fantastic gesture.'

Shane knew, of course, that he would lie alongside his father one day. Was that day the beginning of the countdown, I wonder? 'I think Shane hung on for as long as he could,' Melíosa told me. 'We were lucky to have him for as long as we did. I think he found it very difficult to be alive.' I heard much the same from his friend Jack: 'He did want to die. He wanted to die for a long time. When I look back, particularly over the last nine months of his life, I can see things unravelling and him letting go.'

His depression manifested itself in various ways: suicidal thoughts, low appetite, poor concentration, difficulty sleeping. He took antidepressants and saw doctors. He was becoming bored, people told me, even with Glasnevin, but didn't know what else to do with his life. He was tired, they said. The darkness and pain, which he had overcome for so long, had come creeping back, and he felt too weary and old to fight them any more.

It was against this medical background that he began to participate in the making of *One Million Dubliners* and quickly emerged as its star.

I asked Melíosa what she thought was, for her brother, the significance of the documentary. 'It was incredibly important,' she said. 'I think Shane waited until it was finished before he did what he did. I think the reason he did that was because that film was his legacy in some way. I think Shane planned what he was going to do for a very long time, and wanted to leave something behind that his family could be proud of.

'My dad wrote his books for much the same reason. He [Éamonn] grew up knowing very little about his father, who had died when he was only about three and a half. When we were born, my dad decided he was going to write books about his childhood and about himself so that we would know him in case he died young. This is conjecture, but I think Shane felt the same about that film: that people would be able to know him through it, so he wasn't just leaving this big void.'

Melíosa believes he would have had his daughter in mind, in particular. 'What Shane loved most in the world was Morgane. She was fearless as a kid, and that was him. That huge amount of spirit she has, he would have encouraged that every step of the way. I think she was the great love of his life. Dublin, history, Glasnevin – those things would all have been a distant second to Morgane. I think the film was his gift to her.'

I had wondered whether the film was Shane saying good-bye. The way Melíosa tells it, though, it's more him, saying, 'This is your dad at his best.'

She nodded. 'Exactly. I think that's what the documentary was about. He really gave everything to it, and that was why.'

I asked Aoife Kelleher a couple of questions I felt bad about asking: does she believe that, during filming, Shane had known that he was going to take his own life? And did he regard the documentary as an opportunity for a final flourish? 'It's not really a thought that I would want to entertain,' she replied. 'I don't go there, because you then find yourself asking a series of what-ifs, you know? What if we had never come to the cemetery?'

No one whom I interviewed, I assured her, had suggested that the film-makers were in any way responsible. It was going to happen anyway, seemed to be the thinking, and the film was simply a way for him to make some sort of final statement. 'I just don't know,' she said. 'Shane loved being in the documentary and the version of stardom it afforded to him.' She had had no sense at all of what was going on in the background of his life. 'The reality,' she added, 'is that his death could have brought the entire project to a close had the family not wanted his footage to be used.'

It was not, in fact, his final appearance on camera. The last time he was seen it was by no human eye. At around 7 p.m., on 19 March 2014, he was picked up by CCTV entering Glasnevin by a staff entrance, heading in the direction of the main part of the cemetery – and what came next.

'He then turns around,' a police officer told the inquest, 'salutes to the camera and walks away.'

*

BEFORE THE FUNERAL, the rainbow.

It was a wet day, brightening later, as Shane MacThomáis lay in repose in Glasnevin's chapel. People still talk about that lush arc of colour, how it seemed to pass through the apex of the O'Connell Tower. Those who believe in such things took it as a sign that he was at peace. Shane himself might have laughed that off as sentiment, or he might have taken the rainbow as his due: the Irish weather at its most dandyish paying tribute to a man who knew how to cut a dash. He used to tell the story of the shooting star seen in the sky as Charles Stewart Parnell – the so-called uncrowned King of Ireland – was lowered into his grave. It would suit Shane's vanity to think he might have upstaged him.

Likewise, just as he had appreciated the social mix at his father's funeral, he would likely have been impressed by the attendees at his own. The President of Ireland. European ambassadors. Gerry Adams. Old pals from NA. They would have heard the recitation of Joseph Plunkett's poem, 'I See His Blood Upon the Rose'. They would have seen his family and friends drop lilies – Shane's favourite flower – into the open grave.

Choosing to end his life in the cemetery was meaningful, Morgane thought: 'To him, in some weird backwards way, he was back in the place where he started: "And here I shall end."'

'Has it changed your own attitude to the cemetery?' I asked her.

'In what sense?'

'Well,' I said, 'is it a place that you hate now?'

'No, not at all. I don't think that would be healthy. I don't really feel anything at his grave, so I'll usually walk down to the place where he did it. I feel more in touch with him there.' It is a beautiful spot, she says; sunken stones, ivy everywhere, a sense of peace.

I asked Morgane about that CCTV footage of her father entering the cemetery. The turn to the camera, the final salute. Had she seen it? She shook her head, no. But she thought she could understand what he was about.

'That's the way he was,' she said. 'He had pride, he had ego, he was a performer. Doing that was part of the perform-ance: "I'm out." It's the end of a movie.'

Or not quite the end. Shane had written himself into the story of Glasnevin for ever – among all the living and the dead.

LILIAS

I WAS LOOKING FOR the grave of a witch. I'd been told it is visible at low tide, which, on this December day, meant starting from shore at around half eleven. Out there somewhere, in the seaweed and smirr and mud of Torry Bay, was all that remains, if anything remains, of Lilias Adie.

I have called her a witch, but, rather, she was a victim of the Scottish witchcraft panic in which at least 2,500 people were executed between the late fifteenth and eighteenth centuries. It is said that more were put to death here in Fife than in any other part of the country, and the vast majority were women. Lilias Adie died in prison on 29 August 1704, having confessed before the kirk session to renouncing her baptism and having sex with the devil. He was both 'black and pale', she said; his skin was cold; he came and went like a shadow; he had hooves yet she could not hear him walk. These things, she is reported to have insisted, were 'as true as the sun shines on that floor, and – dim as my eyes are – I see that'. Her eyes were dim with age; she is thought to have been in her sixties and not in good health.

How she died isn't known. There has been talk about torture, which might explain the confession. She was buried beneath a large sandstone slab, and below the tideline of the bay so that the high water would cover her grave – choices indicative not only of the disdain of the Church, but also the fear of a people who sought to prevent her vengeful return.

Fifers these days take a different view. 'If you can, touch her stone, and tell her we're thinking of her,' Kate Stewart had said before I set off. Stewart is a local councillor and a founder member of a group, Remembering the Accused

Witches of Scotland, which is campaigning for a national memorial to the victims of persecution. She lives near the grave and had explained how to find it.

In the end, it didn't take much finding. The coastline was pushed back by about eighty metres in the late nineteenth century in order to reclaim land for the railway, meaning that the grave was once a good bit further out.

Flurries of black snow – jackdaws – swept across the shingle as I approached. The sun, sieved by cloud, fell as glitter. Across the water, dragonish fire and steam marked the oil refinery at Grangemouth. The retreating tide had exposed a great expanse of muck and rock. A sign warns walkers not to go on to the mudflats ('the depth in certain areas is over a couple of metres deep and the tide can race in at incredible speed'), but the grave is so close to shore that it seemed worth the risk.

Lilias Adie's stone, a block of around four by two feet, was fringed in treacle-brown channel-wrack. The ground was busy with the tracks of moorhens, beautiful prints that look very like birds in flight. My own tracks were less dainty. If I stood still even for a moment, the lonely mud clung hard to my boots. I thought of 'Tam O'Shanter'; that last needful tug on the grey mare's tail.

This is the only known grave of a witch, so-called, in Scotland. It was rediscovered in 2014 by the archaeologist Douglas Speirs, and has since become the focus of efforts to begin to atone for what was done to Adie and others like her. A few months before my visit, on the anniversary of her death, a group – including representatives of Fife Council – had gathered at the stone and laid wreaths. 'Three hundred and fifty years ago, Lilias Adie was cast out of this community,' one of the speakers said. 'Today she is welcomed back.'

Torryburn, where Adie lived, was notorious for witch-burnings. This appears to have been thanks to the obsessive fervour of the local minister, the Reverend Allan Logan. The persecution of witches can be seen as an expression of the Church's desire for social control, but it seems likely that a sadistic misogyny was also often at work. As the historian Christine Larner suggested in her book *Enemies of God*, 'witch-hunting is to some degree a synonym for woman-hunting'. This link to gendered violence is one reason the women of Remembering the Accused Witches of Scotland are so interested in Adie: male abuse of power is an old story but, like the waves that wash over her, ever new. They call her 'Lilias', talk about her with familiarity and gentle fondness; she could be an old friend who came to a sorrowful end.

Yet her end was not her end. In 1852, her remains were dug up and her skull sold to Joseph Neil Paton, a textile designer specialising in damasks, who liked to spend his money on antiquities and had a keen interest in both witchcraft and phrenology – inferring character traits and personality from the measurement and shape of the head. He had created a museum in his home in Dunfermline, and no doubt the skull was exhibited there. A report in the *Fife Herald* of 13 May 1852, relates that the 'coffin' – really just a wooden box with a roof-like lid – was six and a half feet long, and that examination of the thigh bones suggested a woman of considerable height. The story was headlined 'RELIC OF BARBAROUS TIMES'. It seems not to have occurred to the editor that exhuming a body for commercial gain and personal amusement is hardly the action of civilised people.

The skull passed eventually into the possession of St Andrews University, where it was photographed, and was exhibited in 1938 as part of Glasgow's Empire Exhibition. Two walking sticks were made using wood from the coffin. One came to be owned by the philanthropist Andrew Carnegie, and is in the collection of his Birthplace Museum in Dunfermline. The other is held by the museum which forms part of the town's Carnegie Library complex. Neither is on display very often.

No one knows the current whereabouts of the skull, or those other remains – at the very least, a femur and two ribs – which were taken from the grave. It is thought, or hoped, that some of those bones are still down there, but it is not clear how much damage was done to the coffin when it was opened. That said, heavy, wet foreshore mud and silt is anaerobic, so it may be that the box and its contents are in a good state of preservation.

The archaeologist Douglas Speirs is making an active search for the missing remains, writing to museums, universities, medical schools and anatomical collections, asking them to check their records for crania with pronounced maxillary flaring (Adie, we know from photographs of the skull, had buck teeth). 'I could recognise that skull at a hundred yards,' he told me. The Witch of Torryburn, so feared that she had to be buried beneath a great slab in the Firth of Forth, is likely in a box somewhere, in a loft or storeroom, her identity and history forgotten.

Kate Stewart hopes that, if the bones are found, the coffin could be exhumed and both sets of remains reburied at a new site, perhaps next to the proposed memorial to victims of the persecution. One witch would stand for all. What an extraordinary elevation for Adie that would be, a turning of the tide, to be raised up to a place of honour – an outcast become national martyr.

Or is that too grand a way of putting it? Better, perhaps, to think of this as a story about a village; about neighbours, about exile and regret.

'All we want,' Stewart said, 'is to bring Lilias back home.'

CRESCENT

WHITECHAPEL ROAD, a week before Christmas. Two crows, perched on the crescent atop the minaret of the East London Mosque, surveyed the scene below.

A busker in a Santa hat played 'Jingle Bells' on a trumpet, and a woman in a black niqab walked past without shifting her eyes, the only part of her body visible, even a millimetre in his direction. Shops sold halal fried chicken, garish ziggurats of *barfi*, and *jalebi* in sticky coils. Market stalls offered fish and vegetables: basins of limes, bags of okra. A sign in the window of The Blind Beggar, where Ronnie Kray had shot and killed George Cornell, advertised a gangster bus tour led by one Mickey Goldtooth; he might have found something to his taste on the jewellery stall opposite the pub, where a young woman in a headscarf was trying on a gleaming bracelet.

In this street full of life, I turned in the direction of death: entering the mosque through a side door, and down to the basement. I had been permitted to attend a *ghusl* – the ritual washing of a body. Oladayo Malami* was to be buried that afternoon.

There was something arboreal about his body; an old root grubbed up after a lifetime of work. He was Nigerian, and had died at the age of eighty. He lay on a steel table, a sink and shower attachment at the end closest to his head. He had thin dark hair and a grizzle of white stubble. There was no question of shaving him so that he appeared groomed for the viewing. In Islam, the body is treated gently, reverentially, as if still alive; it is said that the deceased retains

* In this chapter, the names of some of the deceased have been changed.

awareness, that they can hear and feel. 'We believe that not one hair should be touched,' I had been told. For this reason, and because they are considered to disturb the sanctity of the body, post-mortems are often regarded as desecration, yet it is not always possible to escape them. Mr Malami had a stitched line of incision from the bottom of his throat to below his belly. Had any family been present at the washing, they would likely have found that scar troubling.

But they were not. The ghusl was being carried out by Khaleel and Nurul, two employees of Haji Taslim Funerals, the oldest firm of Muslim undertakers in the UK and, they say, in Europe. Khaleel, who is twenty, is a great-grandson of the founder, Taslim Ali, after whom the business is named. Nurul, a good bit older, with a long black beard and a woollen prayer cap, is from Bangladesh. He is an *alim*, a scholar of the Qur'an. His colleagues, respectful of his understanding, called him Mama, meaning 'Uncle'. I had seen him around during the days I had spent with the firm. He was very quiet, spoke little English, and had an air of religious absorption. He wore a green apron and blue gauntlets while he cleaned the body, reciting Arabic prayers – *duas* – as he did so.

A ghusl is an obligatory part of Islamic burial. Just as a Muslim will perform *wudhu* – washing before prayers – a body must be purified ahead of meeting Allah. Women wash women, men wash men. Nurul and Khaleel were using vegan liquid soap and lukewarm water. There was a ritual order to the cleansing, beginning with the private parts; this was done beneath a plastic sheet, so as not to compromise Mr Malami's modesty. The washing complete, Nurul anointed the body with attar, a perfume, and then it was time for the shrouding. Men are wrapped in three sheets, women five, including a headscarf. Plain white cotton is used, regardless of wealth

or status. Iranian princess, Syrian refugee, London rapper –
Haji Taslim will bury you in exactly the same way.

'In Islam, there's no way of pimping up your funeral,'
Moona Green, one of the owners of the business, had told
me. She is Khaleel's mother. 'If you're keeping it real, you're
buried without a coffin, wrapped in white cloth.'

Mr Malami could now go upstairs to the mosque. His
head was wrapped, his face still visible. His eyes, which had
been half-open when he was brought from the mortuary,
had been closed. His body was placed in a coffin. Most of
those buried in London's Muslim cemeteries are wrapped in
shrouds, but the body is usually transferred there in a coffin,
which is then cleaned and reused.

Later, after funeral prayers, Khaleel's task was to get
Mr Malami's coffin from the mosque into the hearse, and
then drive it to the cemetery. It was Friday lunchtime, the
halls and corridors crowded with worshippers. Khaleel had
to shout to make himself heard as he wheeled the trol-
ley towards the exit. '*Janazah!* Sisters, make some space,
please! Janazah! Brothers, watch your backs!' The aftermath
of a Muslim funeral – a janazah – has none of the solemn
melancholy those of us raised in the Christian or secular
tradition know so well: the slow trudge from the church or
crematorium, the muttered platitudes, the first soothing draw
on a well-earned smoke. It is noisy, busy, jostling. Speed is the
important thing. There is a desire to put the body under the
earth as quickly as possible. Only then can the spirit enter
the afterlife.

Khaleel opened the back of the hearse. He was working
alone, and under pressure. 'Can I get some brothers to help
me with the janazah? This brother' – he pointed to the coffin
– 'has no family.'

A few men came over and helped lift the coffin into the hearse, from where Mr Malami would be conveyed to eternity, via the Romford Road. He was ready to go to his grave. The angels, traffic allowing, would soon greet him there.

*

HAJI TASLIM FUNERALS operates from a small office next to the mosque. From here, they carry out more than a thousand burials each year. In quieter moments, of which there are few, it is possible to hear the call to prayer broadcast from the minaret. Louder and more frequent are police and ambulance sirens on Whitechapel Road, and the ringing of the three phones used by Abu Khalid as he mans the desk, arranging funerals in three languages: Bengali, English and a little Urdu. He also has some Arabic; the phrase 'Inshallah' – God willing – is never far from his lips, and, as we spent time together, I grew to admire its mix of optimism and fatalism, Tigger and Eeyore. He spends his days coordinating coroners, bereaved families and cemeteries, always under pressure of time, always under the cosh of paperwork, trying to ensure that less than twenty-four hours passes between death and burial. This is complicated when, as is still quite common, the deceased is not to be buried in London, but flown to the country of their birth, or family origin. I once saw him break off from arranging to get a body from Southend to Tangier, in order to begin a separate conversation about sending one from Basildon to Istanbul. Then he stood up to do a spot of vacuuming.

Abu is in his early forties. His standard look: black beard, black hoodie, black cap. Early one afternoon, as I sat at a desk near his, two men walked into the office.

'*Salaam aleikum,*' the younger said.

Abu returned the Islamic greeting. '*Waleikum a-salaam.* Please take a seat.'

They had come to arrange the funeral of Mr Ali, their father and brother, who had died that morning. Speaking in Bengali sprinkled with the odd English word, the details were settled quickly. The man would be buried on the following day. 'That's how fast and simple our funerals are,' Abu told me, once they had gone. Had the men come to see him first thing, their relation could have had his funeral prayers at lunchtime and been on his way to the cemetery by 1 p.m.

Islamic law requires burial as soon as possible after death, cremation being forbidden. The widespread idea that it should be done within twenty-four hours, though cultural rather than religious, is taken very seriously. This haste can make the Muslim way of death appear, to an outsider's eyes, functional to the point of indelicacy. It is not uncommon – I witnessed this myself – for a family to contact the undertaker while their loved one is still on life support. Moona Green, during one of our conversations, had recalled a phone call from a man whose mother had died a short time before. Could they collect the old lady from the hospital? There would be a delay of an hour or two, Moona had explained, because her staff were all out at funerals. 'Next thing,' she told me, 'an estate car comes screeching around the corner and pulls up.' It was the man who had phoned. 'He had his dead mum in the back on a mattress.' She laughed. 'If Muhammad can't get to the mountain, the mountain will come to Muhammad.'

Haji Taslim Funerals opened for business in 1960. Taslim Ali, the founder, was Moona's grandfather. He was born in Assam, in what was then India, now Bangladesh, and arrived in Britain during the Second World War. He had left India to escape poverty. 'His family were so poor that they couldn't afford to buy salt,' his son Gulam, Moona's father, had told me. He went to Calcutta and found work on British merchant navy ships. Torpedoed in the English Channel, he was rescued and taken to Kent. Deciding to stay in Britain, he found a job in the Daimler factory. 'He met my mother in Coventry when bombs were dropping everywhere,' Gulam explained. 'She married him and converted.' Her name was Josephine, a Welsh coalminer's daughter who came to be known as Mariam. They started a family, lived in Cardiff for a time, before settling in London.

To be born in one country and die in another is the migrant's story in ten words. The Haji Taslim family embody this in both their own lives and in the service they have provided for half a century. Taslim Ali was deeply religious. He started arranging Islamic funerals not out of a desire to make money, but in answer to a need. In the early days of mass immigration from Asia and North Africa, Muslims struggled for the basics: halal meat, a place to pray, a good death.

There have been Muslims in Britain since at least the twelfth century. Imperialist expansion and eventual control of India meant that numbers began to increase significantly during the eighteenth and nineteenth centuries. In Brighton, I had visited the grave of Sake Deen Mahomed, who, in 1810, opened London's first curry house, and later had great success with his steam bath and massage venture. He was appointed 'shampooing surgeon' to George IV and William IV, and died – according to his headstone – in 1851 at the age of 101. He is buried in the churchyard of St Nicholas, on the other side of the church from Phoebe Hessel.

By the end of the nineteenth century, Britain was home to an estimated 10,000 Muslims, mostly clustered in ports, including Liverpool and South Shields. The country's first burial ground for their exclusive use was established in 1884 as part of Brookwood, a cemetery in Surrey known as the

London Necropolis. The architect Zaha Hadid was buried at Brookwood in 2016, by which time the Muslim population of the UK had risen to around three million.

'Where were you born?' is a question weaponised by racists. 'Where will you die?' has greater significance. It is, if we are lucky, a choice. With the mass immigration of the 1960s and '70s, more and more Muslims were dying and being buried in Britain. This, as much as starting families and businesses, was a putting down of roots, a claiming of space – six feet of English soil that would be for ever Islam.

Few would regard it that way, though. Death, in Islam, is seen as a kind of homecoming. Gulam Taslim had made it clear: 'When someone dies, we say the words, "*Inna lillahi wa inna ilayhi raji'un*" – Surely we belong to Allah, and to him we return.'

*

I KNEW THAT PHRASE. I had heard it. I wish I had not.

'*Inna lillahi wa inna ilayhi raji'un*' is what Rania Ibrahim had said, live on Facebook, looking down over London from the twenty-third floor of Grenfell Tower, as the flames rose. She sounded a little breathless, from either the smoke or fear, or both, but her faith was strong. She died there, in Flat 203, on 14 June 2017, with her daughters, Hania and Fethia, known as Fou-Fou. She was thirty-one, the girls were three and four. 'She was a beautiful soul,' her sister Rasha told the inquiry.

Of the seventy-two people who died in the fire, forty-two were Muslim, and thirty-four were buried at Gardens of Peace, the Muslim cemetery in Hainault, Essex. Rania and her children were identified after three months, and their funeral held on 29 September, a day of driving rain.

Mohamed Omer, a founder and board member of Gardens of Peace, conducted the burials of thirty-two of

the Grenfell dead, speaking at the gravesides. He is in his early sixties, with a short grey beard and a mild air. When we met, he was wearing a skull cap and a pale green robe. He had the smoothness of a politician, the warmth of a good priest.

An under-appreciated aspect of the Grenfell story is that the grief felt by affected families was exacerbated due to the time it took to recover, identify, and release remains. Given the religious significance of burying quickly, the delay was especially difficult for Muslims. 'The families couldn't get closure until they had something to bury,' Omer said. 'A mother's bones, or whatever it may be. That was the biggest challenge.'

The larger tragedy of the fire contained dozens of personal stories, each with its own unique pain. What we all saw on the news was a huge burning tower; we knew there were people inside, but the mind recoiled from imagining them as individuals. By the time each body reached the graveside, sometimes months later, Mohamed Omer had to find a way to respond to that particular loss.

Some of the burials have remained especially vivid. There was the young man who spoke to the fresh graves: 'I am so sorry, Mum; I am so sorry, Dad; I am so sorry, sister, that I couldn't do anything for you.'

How, Omer wondered, do you deal with that raw emotion? 'What words can you say that will be able to resolve his guilt? I found it upsetting. But I couldn't break down.'

He had stayed strong, and found some words: 'We feel your pain. We make prayers to the almighty that justice is done. It says in our scriptures that whenever anybody dies in a tragedy they will be given status equal to that of a martyr. This is a blessing. We hope these people will be going straight to heaven.'

Although almost every person buried at Gardens of Peace is placed in the earth in nothing more than a shroud, the Grenfell dead were in coffins. This was because of the condition of the bodies, a factor which also created complications during the ghusl, Abu Khalid had told me. Instead of the ritual washing, *tayammum* – a dry ablution using dust from a special stone – was performed over the top of the shrouds.

Moona Green, when we met, remembered something similar in the aftermath of the 7/7 bombings. A young woman had been caught in one of the explosions, and almost all that remained of her body was a limb. Moona had explained to the woman's mother that it wouldn't be possible to carry out a washing with water. 'But she just wanted to come, and she sat there and stroked the hand.' Picture that. An image beyond Goya. Was there ever an act of greater horror and love?

If you were to visit Gardens of Peace, you would find nothing to distinguish the Grenfell graves from the thousands of others. The idea is that all plots are identical as all Muslims were created the same by God. Each is marked by a mound of earth, to prevent anyone from stepping on the grave, and on that mound there is a square of black stone with the name and age of the deceased, the date of death and a grave identification number. Muslims visit cemeteries because, like anyone else, they miss the people who are buried there; but it is also regarded as properly Islamic to go and face one's eventual fate. People often say to Abu Khalid that he is blessed to be constantly reminded of death, and he is inclined to agree; he hopes his heart never becomes immune to it. The big picture, he says, is that it may look like the funeral directors are taking the dead to their graves, but in fact the dead are taking them, and saying, 'You're going to end up here.'

When Gardens of Peace was founded in 2002, its management estimated that it would last seventy-five years, but after just fifteen it was full – with 10,000 adults and around 4,000 children. A new site opened nearby at the end of 2017, and is reckoned to have four years of capacity left. A third site has already been purchased, and they are looking for more. The problem of how to find enough space for Britain's dead is especially acute in the Muslim community as they cannot cremate. Mohamed Omer believes that the current norm, where each grave is used by one individual, is not sustainable.

'Will British Muslims accept the idea of graves being reused?' I asked.

'They will have to accept it,' he replied, 'because they will be faced with the stark reality. There is so much demand on land.'

We were talking in the new cemetery on Five Oaks Lane. The skyscrapers of London were visible on the horizon. Through a veil of rain, I could see the light on top of Canary Wharf. The cemetery was muddy. Mourners wore plastic bags around their shoes. I did not find Gardens of Peace beautiful, but it was not intended to be. It had no interest in comforting or impressing; it was a waiting room for judgement day.

A sign asked visitors not to leave flowers or other objects on the graves. They had no religious value or significance, it said, and were only for personal gratification. Nonetheless, a few of the mounds did have flowers on them, and, in one case, a snow globe containing a white plastic rose. These felt like small acts of rebellion, incursions of the personal into the cosmic. Another sign asked visitors to observe the dress code: no revealing or low-cut clothing; skirts and dresses should reach below the knee. No one, as far as I could see, was flouting this rule, but then there were almost no women anyway.

It was just after 3 p.m., and a burial was taking place. A 92-year-old woman, originally from Bangladesh, was being laid to rest. I had travelled here in the hearse with her grandsons, the coffin in the back. They called her Nani. One prayed during the journey, the other kept his eye on Google Maps. Gulam Taslim drove. 'If you go to Saudi Arabia,' he told me, 'the only time a woman goes to the cemetery is when she's dead.'

In Britain, things are not as hard-line, but there is still segregation. Nani's coffin was brought close to the grave-side by men. Her shrouded body was removed by men and carried to the grave. She was placed inside at a depth of six feet, resting on her right side, facing Mecca. Wooden planks were arranged at an angle above her body, sheltering it from being touched by the earth, which was pushed in by a mechanical digger as the mourners, all male, looked on. There were brief prayers from an imam and it was over very quickly. A few women watched from around a hundred feet away. They were expected to keep back during the lowering of the body, and the burial, and could go to the grave after that point. The idea, I was informed, is to avoid close physical proximity of the genders and loud expressions of grief.

'The emotion's taken out of death in Islam,' Moona Green had explained to me. 'You're told how to mourn. You're given three days and then you have to get over it.'

The men returned to their cars. The women went no closer, but stood silent in the rain.

*

THE EAST LONDON MOSQUE dominates Whitechapel Road: a huge building of light brick with a dome and hundred-foot-tall minaret. The word 'Allah' is written above the main entrance in green Arabic script. The great cathedrals of medieval England must have exerted similar magnetic force.

Established on Commercial Road in 1941, the original mosque was created by converting three houses into one gathering place. That mosque, serving around six hundred worshippers, is the one Taslim Ali would have first known, and out of which he began offering a funeral service. This latest building, which opened in 1985, is busy every day, but the *jumu'ah* prayers at lunchtime on Fridays are especially popular, attended by crowds of five thousand. Before this extraordinary congregation, the dead are laid.

Given the emphasis on prompt burial, not every Islamic funeral takes place on Friday, but some families do choose to wait a day or so, hoping that their loved one will benefit from the prayers of such a large number of people on this most blessed day. Still, even on the Thursday when I visited, the main prayer hall was full.

Two coffins had been wheeled into a small adjoining room. Curtains had been pulled back on a window between the prayer hall and the room, allowing the caskets to be seen by the imam and those worshippers closest to the front. One of the coffins held an elderly woman, Nahida, the other a man, Muhammad, of similar age. They were both from Bangladesh, but were not related. In Islam, the funeral rite tends to take place at the end of the regular prayer, at around noon, and is a communal event; all the dead are dealt with at once.

Haji Taslim had four funerals that day, but the other two were taking place at another mosque. Neither of those others – a Turkish man and a Moroccan woman – would be buried in the UK. Their coffins, zinc-lined and sealed, would instead be carried as cargo to their home countries. Flying overseas for burial used to be the norm, but Abu Khalid estimated that only five per cent of Haji Taslim funerals now involve repatriation. Muslims, especially those born in this country and who already have family buried here, tend to regard Britain as their home, Abu had explained. There is also a reluctance to have bodies embalmed, a requirement of most airlines, as the fluid contains alcohol.

It can, however, be much cheaper to bury the deceased abroad. Pakistan International Airlines carries the remains of Pakistani nationals free of charge (and does not require embalming) and it will likely cost nothing to bury in the communally owned cemetery of the village from which your family comes. London is the most expensive part of the UK in which to be buried, with the average funeral costing almost £6,000, so, for those with limited means, repatriation may be a pragmatic choice. 'It's £1,800 to send someone to Bangladesh, and that don't even cover half the cost of the grave here,' Gulam Taslim had told me. 'But it's not about money. It's about sentiment. A lot of people who die in Britain feel they have never been welcomed here, so they want to go back.'

In the hall, the *zuhr* prayer had finished, and the imam explained what would happen next. 'Inshallah,' he said, 'the janazah today is for one man and one woman.' He named Muhammad, but not Nahida. She was described as 'wife of' and 'mother of' – her existence defined in terms of her husband and son. When I asked about this, it was explained that not using her name was intended to respect, not exclude, her.

The imam turned to face the coffins. Saying '*Allahu Akbar*', he raised his hands to the sides of his head, palms outwards, and then crossed his arms before him. Speaking quietly to themselves, eyes closed, he and the congregation said the janazah prayers, praising God, and asking forgiveness for the living and the dead. It was all over in two minutes. Fast and impersonal, yes, but it did not feel perfunctory. It was deeply serious. The coffins were wheeled out to one of the public halls, and the lids removed, so that anyone who chose could stare upon those faces one more time in this world. The shrouds were then folded closed, and it was off to Essex, and whatever lies beyond.

I had become fascinated, over the days that I spent with the funeral directors, with the Muslim attitude to death. It seemed to me a kind of radical acceptance paired with a consoling helplessness. Abu had told me, within half an hour of our first meeting, that he and his wife had lost two babies: one at four days, one after two hours. It hurt them as parents, of course, and it has taken time for him to be able to talk about it comfortably, but he knows that one should not question death, for it is something that Allah has decreed.

Gulam Taslim had put this in even stronger terms: 'Someone can murder you, but not without the permission of God. If God doesn't want you to die, you don't die.'

He grew up with death. I had seen archive footage of him in the 1960s, aged seventeen, carrying out a burial on behalf of his father, who was on pilgrimage to Mecca. The young Gulam wore a white kameez shirt and a karakul cap.

CRESCENT

These days his dress is that of a Western funeral director: white shirt, black waistcoat, black tie. He is a ball of energy, has a slightly pugilistic air, and is extremely practised at negotiating a path between Islamic purity and the demands of kaleidoscope London. 'A lot of Muslims would go mad with the stuff he does,' Moona had said. She remembered one occasion when the Catholic wife of a Muslim man had read the Lord's Prayer at her husband's graveside.

At seventy-one, Gulam has buried more than a thousand people. His life has been measured out in deaths: the old who slip away, the young who perish in fires, or by bomb or barbiturates, or behind the wheels of cars, speeding towards futures that will never arrive. He sees the cracked flesh; the spilled soul he senses.

God giveth and God taketh away. Allah is the maker and Allah is the taker. This is what he believes, what he tells the people who need to hear those words. His own belief, though – that intrigued me. Is it never tested, I asked, by the seeming senselessness of the tragedies to which he bears witness?

'Nothing shakes my faith,' he replied. 'I see all the violence, all the bad things that happen, and nothing shakes my faith. Because it don't matter. Whether you believe in God, or you don't believe in God, you're going to die. But who wants to live for ever?'

He was driving, and kept his eyes on the road.

SKULLS

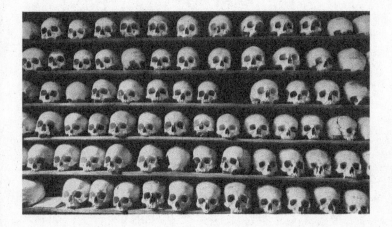

A WARNING TO THE CURIOUS:

> *Fragile bones*
> *Please do not touch*
> *These are our ancestors*
> *From 700 years ago*
> *So please respect them'*

The sign is hung upon a crate around six feet high, one of two down here beneath the Holy Trinity Church in Rothwell, Northamptonshire. This is the Bone Crypt, although it also goes by different names. The crates are full of bones – femurs, fibulas, scapulas, shanks – all stacked up. End on, they resemble a drystone wall. If anyone did decide to flaunt the sign and touch them, there would be witnesses. The crypt is lined with shelves and on the shelves are skulls. Hundreds and hundreds. A roomful of Yoricks. Jesters turned sentinel. One feels, in this sightless place, seen.

Before descending, I had spoken with the vicar, the Reverend Canon John Westwood. On first moving to the parish nine years ago, he had been rather shocked to find himself the custodian of the Bone Crypt. Of course he was. One of only two ossuaries in the UK which still contain skeletal remains (*os* is Latin for bone), it is not what anyone would expect to find beneath their church. His first instinct had been to wonder whether the skulls should really be on public display. 'Let's leave the dead in peace,' he thought. As time has passed, however, he has come to an understanding of the crypt as a place of worship in itself. He even prays down there sometimes. 'It is a place where you can reflect. Being brought face to face with the reality of mortality raises questions: "What does death mean? Is there life beyond death?" It has become much more meaningful for me.'

It helps, of course, that his parishioners value it. Some of the pew cushions are decorated with skulls in elegant needlepoint. The local football club, Rothwell Town, until it folded a few years back, was nicknamed 'The Bones'.

The church is pretty. I had walked up a tree-lined lane and there it was: a looming tower, sandstone against a blue sky, starlings making a stave of the weathervane. You enter the crypt by an arched door and narrow passage. 'Shall we go down?' asked Dr Jenny Crangle. She is an osteoarchaeologist in her thirties, a passionate authority on this place. We ducked our heads and went. Only a few steps and we had gone back centuries, and there they were – the bones, the crates, the shelves, that warning.

From the thirteenth century until the Reformation, human remains were taken down to the crypt and stored. Dug up from the churchyard after decomposition, the bones may have been washed ritually in holy water or blessed wine before being deposited. It is estimated that the remains of 2,500 people lie here. It is difficult to say for sure. There are only 1,000 or so skulls. Only. When you are in the crypt, 'only' doesn't come into it. The feeling is one of abundance, gluttony, a feast of death.

The crypt is nine metres long by four and a half wide. There are perhaps three and a half metres between the floor of compacted earth and the ribbed vault of the roof. Electric strip-lights, damp air, spiderwebs and dust. Two high windows, blocked.

At the bottom of the stacks, I noticed, the bones were crumbling in the damp and under their own weight. Not much can be done about this. Making the room more effective for preservation would cost a lot of money and involve a substantial period of closure, and the bones would have to be removed for the duration of the work. This last point is the most significant. The remains have been down here for so long, in this neutral zone between heaven and earth, that there is little appetite to disturb them.

'To put them in storage in a university for a couple of years would be doing something good for the bones, but it would mean taking them out of consecrated ground which would have been a big no-no for medieval people,' Crangle said. 'It would have been a comfort to them knowing that they would have ended up here. The whole point is that you didn't want to be forgotten. You wanted to be remembered, your name said in prayers.'

The first written reference to the place comes from John Morton, rector of nearby Oxendon, who wrote in 1712 about 'the great Multitude of Men and Women's Sculls that lye heap'd up in the famous Charnel-House at Rowel'. I like that word 'famous'. The Bone Crypt has long attracted stories and notoriety. It was rediscovered, it is said, around the year 1700, when a gravedigger fell through the roof, and, finding himself surrounded by skulls – 'this awful assemblage of past generations' – lost his mind. One thinks of Julian Litten falling into the vault of St Mary's. It would nice, though not for the poor gravedigger, to believe that the story is true.

So who were these people? Radiocarbon dating has revealed that the bones – men, women and children – range in age from the thirteenth to the nineteenth centuries, though most are medieval. There is something about the human imagination, when confronted with a room of empty skulls, that wishes to fill the vacuum with tales. They were, it has been said, plague victims, or Vikings, or soldiers killed in the Battle of Naseby, which was fought nearby in 1645. The truth appears to be less dramatic: these skulls are simply *us*, or, rather, they are ordinary locals – Rowellians, as they are known – dug up from the churchyard after decomposition and placed here until, it was thought, the coming of the Last Judgement, when the dead would rise from their graves and put on their flesh like discarded clothes.

Why, though, are they here at all? It would appear that this was not simply a storehouse of bones, the functional solution to the problem of a churchyard full to capacity. Jenny Crangle has identified it as a charnel chapel – a type of building constructed in England and elsewhere in Europe from the early thirteenth to mid-sixteenth century. She is a specialist in this field and was one of the founders of the Rothwell Charnel Chapel Project, based at the University of Sheffield, dedicated to the study of the building and remains. Crangle feels that charnel chapels are under-appreciated – 'English people don't really understand what these bones were here for' – and that her own Irish Catholic background (she is now an atheist) has helped her to grasp their meaning.

The development of charnel chapels, she says, emerged partly from Pope Innocent IV's establishment in 1254 of the doctrine of Purgatory: the realm of the afterlife in which those who had committed minor sins would have to spend time being cleansed by fire before ascending to heaven. The duration of the stay in Purgatory could be shortened by the prayers of the living. Where better, therefore, for exposure to the prayerful life of the church than an ossuary immediately below the floor on which worshippers knelt? This is why Crangle says the bones of Rothwell have been 'compassionately curated'. They are not there simply to free up space for new graves; they are halfway to paradise.

There was, moreover, a symbiotic relationship between the living and the dead. The souls of the latter were helped by the prayers of the living, and the living profited from the presence of the dead because, in reminding them of their fate, it strengthened them in their faith. That is why the bones were meant to be seen. The two windows high in the south wall of the Rothwell crypt would have meant the skulls were visible by those entering and leaving the church, a memento mori intended to concentrate the mind on the world beyond. There also appears to have been a vent at the top of the east wall, now sealed, which would have opened in front of the altar, allowing the bones to 'hear' mass as it was celebrated and to benefit from exposure to the sacred ritual. One can imagine the sound of the liturgy, the scent of wax and wine passing down into the dark. What rose upwards? The knowledge that, one day, you too would come to this pass and this place.

It seems likely that some form of worship took place inside the crypt itself, perhaps on apt dates in the Church calendar such as All Souls' Day and the Feast of the Holy Relics. Crangle led the way past the skulls to the wall at the far end. 'So much has been lost,' she said. 'On this east wall there was a painting of the Day of Judgement, the Doom, but most of the plaster is gone.'

The fresco would likely have shown Christ; on his right hand would have been people ascending to heaven, helped by angels, and on his left, demons dragging sinners to hell. The lower part of the picture would have shown the dead rising from their graves. 'Can you see tiny traces there? And over here, three black lines and three red lines? This whole wall would have been covered. It would have been the first thing you saw when you came in: the bones stacked around the edge, and this painting facing you.'

'Do you not wish with all your heart you could see that?' I asked.

'Yes! If I had a time machine, I would be back here, definitely. There's just so much to know.'

Crangle is not only an academic engaged in studying the charnel chapel, she is an advocate of the place, a defender of its reputation. She cannot abide the idea that it might be seen as macabre: 'These aren't scary places. They're not places of evilness or ghosts. They are places of rest and commemoration.'

Many of the skulls have numbers written on them, from previous research. It looks awful, appears disrespectful, and suggests that whoever did it had forgotten that these were people before they were specimens. I wondered aloud whether, seeing the remains heaped up en masse like they are, meant that Crangle ever has difficulty remembering that these were individuals? She shook her head. 'Not really. I see them as people who lived and died in the surrounds. I'm not a very social person and I prefer my people dead, so for me it's like these are just people you would walk out to Rothwell and see. They're all still individuals. I can see who was old, who was younger, who had some tooth decay . . .'

We were standing by the south wall. Beside us, on the top shelf, were five skulls. Labels had been placed in front of them, like place cards at a dinner party, giving their dates. One, from the late 1700s, had been sawn through above the brows, probably during an autopsy. Although the charnel chapel fell out of use in the sixteenth century, remains seem to have been deposited following its rediscovery, most likely medical specimens and the like.

Crangle ignored the sliced skull and instead reached for one to its left, dating from half a millennium before. Entirely missing its face, it was a deep brown in colour. It looked like an old burst football, a smashed Easter egg. 'This is the one, what's left of him, that had a sharp-force blow to the head,' she said. 'We can't tell if that actually caused the death.' She turned the skull to show the injuries. 'One blow here caused the radiating fracture – that's one hell of downward blow to make that crack – and also created another that went that way; don't know what it did to his face. And it looks like we have a second glancing blow – see that shiny bevelled edge? – caused by a sharp instrument. It's likely that this person was attacked in some way.'

She returned the skull to the shelf, next to one from the 1300s, and smiled. 'I think these two are my favourites because when these people were alive, they would have seen this place being built; they may have even helped to build it, and this is where they are now resting.

'If you do believe in the afterlife, that these people are dead and looking down, they would be very happy that their remains are still here, being touched and talked about.'

Some of the Rothwell crania show evidence of having been touched repeatedly. They have small shiny patches on their foreheads. Crangle thinks that this may be evidence of ritual practice. It is not hard to imagine a worshipper entering the crypt, making the sign of the cross on their own body, and then touching their fingers to a skull. There would have been nothing unseemly or morbid about this. Think of it as a tender and spiritual act – flesh and bone coming together under the gaze of God.

So why and when did all this stop? The Reformation, which saw England transformed from a Catholic to a Protestant country, was the death of ossuaries. Purgatory was no longer part of orthodox ideology so there was no need for places where the dead's passage to heaven could be accelerated by prayer. More than that, though, these buildings and their contents were visibly Catholic; they represented Popish ritual and had to go. In almost every case, the bones were removed or covered with earth, and the chapels either demolished or put to other use. Crangle has identified sixty or so former ossuaries in England, yet only Rothwell and St Leonard's at Hythe in Kent still have their bones. The others are eggless nests, treasure-less chests.

'The reason why, I think, this place survived is because Rothwell remained a staunchly Catholic town after the Reformation and they were reluctant to get rid of their old ways,' Crangle said. 'I think what happened is that when reformers came to shut down the nearby nunnery, locals would have known they were coming and arranged to hide this site, pretend it wasn't here, so that it wouldn't be destroyed. It's a very easy place to hide, if you don't want its existence to be known.'

Seen from outside, it is obvious how simple it would have been to make the ossuary disappear. All it would have taken would have been for the entrance to be blocked and concealed, and for the light wells on the south wall to have earth shovelled into and against them.

If the charnel chapel was hidden at the time of the suppression of the nunnery then this would date its closure to 1536. That would mean 160 or so years passed before the gravedigger fell through the roof, if that is indeed how it happened. Easily long enough for the place to pass from memory.

It is fanciful, but as I walked back down the avenue of trees away from the church, I thought about how much the skulls had missed during their period of darkness. A tyrannical king, a chopper of heads, succeeded, in time, by his virgin daughter; the birth and death of a playwright who made a jester's skull immortal; the beheading of a monarch, and the posthumous decapitation of the man – Cromwell – who had signed his death warrant. The England into which these skulls awoke would have been very different from the one they had known, and they themselves became objects of historical curiosity. And so they remain. You walk down a few steps and are brought face to face with the medieval world. It is, in a way, rather moving.

I obeyed the sign, of course. I did not touch the bones. But there was something in them that touched me.

*

'Now,' SAID BETTY, leaning over the glass counter of the church shop. 'You know the situation with the mummies, don't you?'

The Americans shook their heads. They were visiting Dublin from Pennsylvania and hadn't been following the local news. Luckily, Betty, one of the nice older ladies who volunteers at St Michan's, was able to bring them up to date.

'Someone broke in and stole two of the heads,' she explained, 'so we can't open that crypt just now.'

The Americans, being American, expressed their sympathy with earnest politeness.

'Yes,' said Betty, 'it's an awful thing. *But*,' she added, brightly, 'we did get the heads back.'

The heads had been recovered, the Gardaí were investigating, and the mummies would, everyone hoped, be back on display soon. In the meantime, a sign on the counter explained, tour prices had been reduced. It wouldn't be possible to pay one's respects to the famous St Michan's mummies, but visitors could still, if they wished, go down to the other crypt and admire a few coffins. 'Three tickets, please,' said the Americans.

Some explanation at this point, perhaps.

St Michan's, a church just north of the Liffey, was founded in 1095, although its oldest surviving part, the tower, is fifteenth century. Sandwiched between two astonishingly hideous modern buildings, the church appears under siege from ugliness and offers a moment of aesthetic respite to anyone passing along the street. Its fame, however, lies not in anything visible, but in a phenomenon below the level of that street. In the crypt of the church are the so-called mummies: four individuals whose coffins long ago fell apart, exposing their leathery, kipperish remains to public view.

They have been a tourist attraction for many years. M. R. James visited in July 1892 and described them as 'nightmare figures'. They inspired one of his most troubling ghost stories; a tale of child-murder, and vengeance from beyond the grave.

'His description of what he saw reminds me of what I once beheld myself in the famous vaults of St Michan's Church in Dublin, which possess the horrid property of preserving corpses from decay for centuries,' James wrote in 'Lost Hearts': 'A figure inexpressibly thin and pathetic, of a dusty leaden colour, enveloped in a shroud-like garment, the thin lips crooked into a faint and dreadful smile, the hands pressed tightly over the region of the heart.'

The names of the mummies are lost. We do not know who they were in life. But they have, in death, developed identities of a sort. On the right, as you peer into the vault, is a woman who has come to be called 'The Unknown'. On the left is 'The Nun'. In the centre is 'The Thief'; he is missing his right hand and both feet, the theory being that they were cut off as a punishment. Lying perpendicular to the others is 'The Crusader', the star of the show. Said to be the corpse of a soldier, he would have been around six and a half feet tall, although his legs appear to have been broken and tucked under him so that he would fit in the coffin. This giant is thought to be eight hundred years old. There was a long-standing tradition that visitors were invited to touch his hand for luck, it being slightly raised within the casket, but this hasn't been allowed for a few years. In any case, The Crusader has, lately, suffered a far greater indignity – his was one of the two heads which were stolen.

Shortly before lunchtime on Monday, 25 February 2019, Peter Condell, the tour guide at St Michan's, was preparing to open for visitors when he discovered that an atrocity had taken place. The metal doors, which give access to the crypt from the grounds of the church, had been broken open and the vault containing the mummies was in disarray. The Nun had been badly damaged, the head of The Crusader had been severed, and another skull – which usually sat on top of a coffin – was missing. Condell wasted no time in informing his boss, Archdeacon David Pierpoint, the vicar of St Michan's.

'My initial feeling was one of utter despair, revulsion and anger,' Pierpoint recalled when we spoke on the telephone. 'Within the first hour or so, I had all these emotions coming through. But then that horror turned to a sense of questioning. Why would someone do such a thing?'

It is a question Peter Condell has pondered, too. The guide, a former professional musician in his early sixties, is not very tall, which must be handy if your job involves spending much of each day stooping down among the dead. When dealing with visitors, he has a stone-faced lugubriousness bordering on the macabre, a manner pitched somewhere between Frankenstein's Igor and the comedian Dave Allen.

'Who wants to see the crypt?' he asked the Americans, who had been looking around the church, admiring the organ on which, according to popular local tradition, Handel first performed his *Messiah*. 'Come on, so. Enough culture.'

Leading me to one side, Condell explained that he couldn't take the tourists to the vault with the mummies, but he'd show it to me afterwards if he had a minute.

We went outside, round the side of the church. The guide undid the padlock, unwound the chains from the handles, and led the way through the heavy doors. The steps were steep. It was easier to turn and come down backwards. 'He's the bravest . . .' Condell observed, Igor-ishly, of the visitor who descended first. 'Or the most foolish,' he added in Dave Allen mode. We entered a low barrel-vaulted corridor with rough stone walls and an earth floor. The air felt neither cold nor hot. On either side of the path were arched doorways, most of them barred and dark. In these midnight nooks, the coffins lay.

While the church above had been rebuilt, Condell explained, the crypt was original, making it nine hundred years old or so. The families who had paid to be buried here were wealthy, but the vault, once bought, was theirs for ever. One is still used by a Dublin family; the most recent interment – of cremation ashes – took place just three years ago.

Stopping beside one vault, Condell pointed out the ornate stacked coffins of the Earls of Leitrim; green and red with golden fittings. The Third Earl, assassinated in 1878 while travelling in his carriage, was so unpopular with the public – regarded as a tyrannical landlord – that a hostile mob shouted abuse at his coffin as it passed on its way to St Michan's. They wanted to seize the body and throw it in the street.

'So much for the aristocrats,' Condell said. 'Now, for the finale, the rebels! You can't come to Ireland and not see rebels.' He led the way to the other end of the corridor. Behind a set of railings were the coffins of John and Henry Sheares, brothers executed in 1798 for their part in the uprising of that year against British rule. Condell gave a few of the gory details, but his heart didn't seem in it. 'Mmm,' he said, 'it's a bit early on a Monday morning for hanging, drawing and quartering.' It was the end of the tour and the

Americans had to be off sharpish. They had tickets for Kilmainham Gaol.

'C'mon, we'll see if we can get a quick peep next door,' Condell said to me. He meant the mummies. He unlocked a different steel hatch and we went down once more.

'Right,' he said, 'this is the scene of the crime.'

He switched on the light. The word 'mummies' conjures an image of a corpse wrapped in bandages, but that is not what these look like. They are more like bog bodies, stained and tanned and tough, except that they are so very dry. They bring to mind wood shavings, wasp nests, dead leaves, dust. They are skin stretched over bone stretched over time. More parchment than person. Autumn made flesh.

Condell explained how these bodies came to be mummified. It was all natural, he said; an accident, really. 'In the crypt, the temperature is constant, winter and summer. Secondly, it's very dry; the limestone walls absorb humidity. And the land underneath releases methane gas into the atmosphere. Those three things together − temperature, dryness and gas − cause the preservation.'

It was obvious what a mess had been made of The Nun. The Crusader, though, was right away at the back, and I couldn't get a proper look at him, which might have been a mercy. It had been four months since the break-in, and his head was due back that week. Since it had been recovered (found in a hedge on the church grounds with a note saying 'sorry RIP') it had been in the care of the Museum of Ireland. There had been great concern about decomposition and water damage, but conservators had managed to save most of it. His ears had been lost, and part of his nose. It wouldn't be possible to reattach the head; not without glue, which didn't seem right, so it would simply be placed back in position resting on the spine. The Nun, meanwhile, was to be moved into a new coffin and sealed up; it was felt that it would be undignified for the public to see her damaged body. The Archbishop of Dublin had visited the crypt and performed a ceremony of reconsecration.

The mummies of St Michan's occupy an odd niche in the life of Dublin. David Pierpoint told me that he feels protective towards them, regarding them both as parishioners and as the central objects in a long tradition drawing people to the church. He is both their priest and their custodian. He says a prayer whenever he enters the crypt. He is also frank about their financial importance. The crypt receives around 28,000 paying visitors each year, the church's only income. It is a delicate balance. There is certainly something of the Victorian freakshow about the mummies, but you never quite forget you are in a sacred space. Perhaps it is the uneasy tension between these two atmospheres that makes being in the presence of the mummies feel transgressive, even ill-starred.

I asked Peter Condell what the mummies mean to him. On the one hand, it's just a job; on the other . . . something else. 'I'm here twenty-five years,' he said. 'I started in 1994, my sister died in 1998 at the age of thirty-two, and my brother died in 2003 at the age of forty-eight. And I kind of said, "Is this some sort of karma going on with me messing around with dead people?" So I'm a bit ambivalent about it.'

The head and skull were stolen, it turned out, by a man in his thirties. He had been drinking and taking drugs. He said that he didn't remember damaging the coffins or bodies, and that, when he woke, he discovered, in a panic, the grisly objects in his bag. He was identified on CCTV and arrested. His lawyer told the court that he was deeply ashamed of having desecrated human remains, and that he had mental and behavioural disorders as a result of addiction. The judge said that intoxication could not be used as an excuse, adding, 'These skulls represent a lot to people of religious belief.' The man pled guilty and was sentenced to twenty-eight months. David Pierpoint intends to visit him in prison. 'I'm looking forward to meeting him,' he told me. 'Even if he doesn't give me an answer as to why he did this, it will put my mind at rest to have at least met him. And if he's remorseful, I'll certainly forgive him.'

Our phone connection was poor and I misheard that word 'remorseful'. I thought the Archdeacon had said 'a lost soul', which might have done as well. You'd have to be a bit lost to do what that man did.

Lost souls, lost names, lost hearts, lost heads – the story of St Michan's is, for me, unsettling. I can't regard it lightly. It isn't just a visitor experience to be given a star rating. These mummies, they were people. What are they now? Exhibits? Relics? Ambassadors of the dead? You look into those black pits which once were eyes and you wonder who – or what – is looking back.

*

EVENSONG AT St Leonard's, Hythe. Choirboys in white surplices and scarlet cassocks sang 'All Things Bright and Beautiful' as night fell and the stained glass faded to black. There were twenty-one of us in the congregation, twenty-two if you count Ziggy, a grey cockapoo seated at the back, named for the Bowie-esque flash of white over his right eye. 'We try to be dog-friendly,' the priest, Andrew Sweeney, would say later. This church welcomes all creatures great and small.

I had walked here from the seafront. An early-autumn day was fizzling out in drizzle; the English Channel a grey blur. In the High Street, Union flags flapped damply above vacant

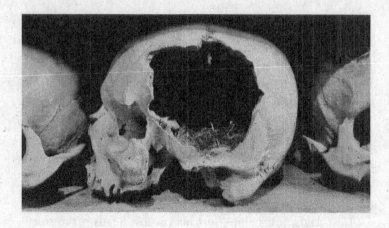

shops and charity shops. A homeless man called Alan, wearing a straggly blond beard and a heavy jacket, was lying in a doorway. He was trying to raise the bus fare to Canterbury and had slept in the church the night before – 'Not with the skulls, like' – in order to get in out of the cold. He had offered to show me the way, pointing up through a passageway to a short, steep hill. St Leonard's was at the top. Its bells were tolling six, calling the faithful to sing. Alan expresses himself in a different way. Beside him was a tin of watercolour pencils. He had been sketching the quaint houses and shops opposite. 'You don't really notice the character of England unless you go abroad and come back and look at it,' he had said. I wished him well and went up the hill.

St Leonard's is a Norman church dating from the eleventh century, although it incorporates elements of an earlier Saxon place of worship. The magnificence of the building is a clue that Hythe was once a more significant and prosperous place than it is now. It was one of the Cinque Ports, part of England's naval defence system, along with Hastings, Sandwich, Dover and New Romney. Medieval graffiti on the pillars shows ships, witch marks, a dragon, a demon, a cat. It is thought that some of these were made by pilgrims on their way to Thomas Becket's shrine at Canterbury Cathedral as a way of giving thanks for a safe crossing from France. From the high point of the churchyard, among graves carved with anchors, one can see the hazy Côte d'Opale.

That coast has perhaps more often represented a threat than a promise. Stained glass tells this story. The great east window shows anti-aircraft guns and a ship full of archers, bows and barrels and hackles up, England's defence against invasion across the centuries. A small window to the south of the nave is a tribute to 2nd Lieutenant Robert Hildyard, killed at the Somme five days before Christmas 1916, aged nineteen. A fragment of the wooden cross which was the first marker of his grave sits at the foot of the window. He is buried at Maricourt, France, in one of those immaculate war cemeteries with clipped grass and unchipped stones. It is very different from the method chosen by the French for laying to rest many of their own war dead: the Douaumont Ossuary, where the bones of 130,000 unidentified soldiers from Verdun are piled in vaults. Douaumont is remembrance as brute realism. The Hildyard window, by contrast, depicts death as a peaceful dream or religious vision; the young officer lies still and pale, his right hand touching the foot of the crucified Christ who appears, out of a blue haze, above the battlefield mud. Hildyard was killed by a shell while sheltering in a dugout, but the window shows him unscathed except for a small cut, as if from a thorn, just below the neat parting in his hair. This arch shines out towards the Channel with the consoling force of a beautiful lie.

St Leonard's is the only parish church in Kent that still retains a traditional choir of boys and men; they have been singing here since at least 1442. It is very likely that the skulls of choristers past are among the 1,001 gathered in a room beneath the chancel. Their days of hymns and music are behind them, but those bones still send out a siren song, drawing the curious to the church. It was 30 September, the final day of the visitor season, and I was keen to see the skulls before their months of isolation began.

My guide was Brin Hughes. He is seventy-eight and sings in the choir. He had swapped his surplice for civvies, the better to show me around. 'Welcome to our bone house, ossuary, crypt,' he said, unlocking the door. 'We loosely call it a crypt although, technically speaking, it's not.' The room was originally an ambulatory, a ceremonial passage-way allowing for ritual processions. It is directly beneath the high altar of the church, a deeply symbolic location: mortal remains below, the promise of immortality above.

It is fairly narrow and has a large wooden door at each end. As you walk in, there is a vaulted archway on either side; shelves full of skulls rise to the ceiling in a sort of human pyramid. This arrangement is repeated at the back of the room. In between is a long stack of thigh bones – around twenty-five feet long by six tall – with a few skulls peering out; this represents an estimated four thousand individuals. In a display case there is a pile of hair, reddish-gold, some of it done up in plaits, which was found among the stacks. On a side table, several lower jaws are laid out like lucky horse-shoes. One had fallen on the floor; I picked it up and brushed dust from the teeth, wiping clean the mouth which may have spoken Middle English or Norman French.

The earliest bones, it is thought, date from the thirteenth century. They first appear in the written record in 1678. Samuel Jeake, the town clerk of Rye, wrote that 'On the north side of the church is a charnel house, or Golgotha, full of dead men's bones, piled up together orderly, so great a quantity as

I never saw elsewhere in one place.' No one knows why the bones were not removed during the Reformation. Perhaps the crypt was concealed, as with Rothwell.

It all feels very different from that other ossuary. There are windows, so there is light, and, perhaps as a result of this, the skulls are mostly white. Skulls are like snowflakes: seen in their multitude they appear uniform, a dismal blizzard; close up, each is different. A few of the Hythe skulls stand out. Some show signs of sword blows; one has a hole just above the hairline on the right-hand side, either a stab wound or the result of medical trepanning. My favourite is a skull with a hole smashed in its left-hand side; a robin, seizing its chance, has flown in and built a nest. It wouldn't be a bad way to end up, I think, a nest-box for a robin's lovely blue eggs.

'Who were these people?' I asked Brin.

'Locals,' he replied. 'You've probably read there have been various theories as to who they might be.' Yes – Danish pirates, victims of the Black Death, Saxons killed at the Battle of Hastings. 'But,' he continued, 'all the more recent evidence suggests that they were simply people who lived and died in and around Hythe.'

The vast majority of the skulls are adult, with both men and women represented. Many of them had arthritis, one had a large tumour, and they were deficient in iron. Their teeth, however, were in better condition than many modern people – the result of a lack of sugar. A comment from a French tourist in the visitors book feels apt: '*On pense à la vie de toutes ces personnes.*' One thinks of the lives of all these people. Does Brin ever wonder who they were as individuals? 'Oh, yes, frequently. Whether they knew each other, and whether they commune with each other at night. Who knows? Maybe they have a skull choral society.'

They do this, the skulls – invite this sort of whimsical familiarity. They are us, so we feel we know them, but they are also deeply unknowable. They come from a time we struggle to imagine, and they have, all of them, gone through an experience which we cannot – may not wish to – comprehend. 'However young or old, however rich or poor, they have done the dreaded thing,' wrote Denise Inge in her study of ossuaries, *A Tour of Bones*. During the writing of the book she was diagnosed with cancer, and it was published posthumously. 'They have been where each of us fears and none of us has gone.'

Still, the ossuary was welcoming. There were informative leaflets aimed at children, and even souvenirs. You could buy a keyring or badge with a skull on it, or a postcard of St Leonard, the patron saint of prisoners, cattle and women in childbirth.

Earlier, I had spoken with the Reverend Andrew Sweeney. Since taking over at the church four years ago, he has felt a degree of ambivalence about the ossuary. 'There's a part of me that's deeply uncomfortable about the fact that we treat it as a visitor experience,' he said, 'and yet I remain committed to having the doors open. What I think it should be, and it only hints at this at the moment, is a memento mori. It should be a place where we help people spiritually or psychologically or emotionally look at death.'

He would like there to be a learning centre, and a chapel associated with the ossuary where people can pray. He would like, in other words, for the crypt to have a similar place in the life of the church to that of charnel chapels before the Reformation. To that end, he has started a new tradition on All Souls' Day – following Holy Communion, worshippers go down to the ossuary, light candles and say prayers for the dead. 'It's religiously quite unorthodox,' he said. 'In most parts of the Church of England, praying for the soul of the departed is frowned upon.'

Why then did he start the ritual? 'Because I was concerned that it was just a tourist novelty, and I wanted to make a public statement that this has a spiritual function as well.'

Just as Brin and I were finishing up in the crypt, we were joined by Margaret Pearce, one of the volunteers who keeps an eye on the place during visiting hours. It was the start of her shift: 'This will be my last stint until Easter.' As a steward here for fifteen years, she has witnessed some strong reactions from the public. A few people get to the door, see the skulls, and turn away, too afraid to enter.

'Sometimes we get people who are a little bit suspect, dressed like goths,' Brin said. 'Which is why we have a panic button.'

This seemed a little hard on goths, who have always seemed to me a gentle people, but I let it pass.

'One time,' Margaret recalled, 'there was a foreign student – a Russian girl – who rushed out, upset. I went after her and she said, "I no like. I'm vegetarian." I thought, "Well, I'm not trying to make you eat them, dear."'

What about Margaret herself? What is it like to sit in here, surrounded by skulls, during the long stretches when there are no visitors? 'Peaceful. I don't have creepy feelings, or anything like that.' Neither does she feel alone. 'I think of these people as parishioners. They were helping the parish when they were alive, and they are still helping the parish today.' Financially, she meant. The church earns around £10,000 a year from visitors.

Brin showed me a poem, written by a tourist, which the church has had laminated. 'Who knew the English did this kind of thing?' it asks. The poet has a point. Charnel houses are more commonly associated with Catholic countries.

Rothwell and Hythe are drab in comparison with the elaborate ossuaries of mainland Europe, among the most famous of which are the Capuchin Crypt in Rome, the Catacombs of Paris, and the Sedlec Ossuary in the Czech Republic. Death in such places is flamboyant, greedy, boastful: a glam reaper gloating over his spoils. Sedlec, in particular, with its skeletal chandelier, is a bohemian rhapsody in bone. Consider, too, the Beinhaus of St Michael's Chapel in Hallstatt, Austria, where the skulls are painted, very beautifully, with leaves, flowers, crosses, and other decoration; here a snake writhes out of an eye socket; there an ivy wreath snakes around bone.

Impressive though these are, I rather admire the plain English ossuaries. They seem in keeping with the best of the national character – quiet, demure, no airs and graces. They go with the potting shed and pints of mild, with even tempers and evensong. It may seem strange to describe dead people as survivors, but the bones at Hythe and Rothwell are exactly that. The ossuary at St Leonard's has survived the Reformation, when the statues of saints were torn down from the church, and the Blitz, when a German bomb landed in the churchyard and blew out the stained glass. If skulls could have stiff upper lips, these English skulls would have them.

I said goodbye to Margaret and Brin, and walked back down the hill towards the town and sea. Soon, the crypt would be closing for autumn and winter. A few months of resting in peace and then, come Easter, the resurrection: the key would turn in the lock, the salt air would waft back in, and visitors would be invited to consider their own mortality; two quid for adults, fifty pence for children.

PETER

NOBODY KNOWS who leaves the flowers.

There doesn't seem to be a pattern to it. It isn't only on the anniversary of his death, and it can't be the day of his birth because that is unknown. Suspicion rested for a time on a particular spinster believed to have sentimental inclinations, but she died and the flowers continued. Indeed, there were some lying on the grave when I got there, a wreath of artificial daffodils and irises laid at the foot of the small stone on which, roughly carved, are these words: 'PETER the Wild Boy 1785'.

It was an afternoon in late November, the sun low and strong, brightening the stone of St Mary's. The church has served the Hertfordshire village of Northchurch for more than a thousand years, and sections of the original Saxon building form part of its south and west walls. The grave, marked by that small and simple headstone, is on top of a steep bank directly opposite the porch. Inside the church, to the left of the door and beneath a stained-glass window, an engraved plaque gives the bones of the story.

> *To the memory of PETER known by the*
> *name of the Wild Boy, having been found*
> *Wild in the Foreſt of Hertswold near Hanover in*
> *the year 1725: he then appeared to be about 12*
> *years old. in the following year he was brought to*
> *England by the order of the late Queen Caroline,*
> *and the ableſt Maſters were provided for him.*
> *But, proving incapable of ſpeaking, or of receiving*
> *any inſtruction, a comfortable proviſion was made*

for him by her Majeſty at a farm houſe in this Pariſh,
where he continued to the end of his inoffenſive life.
He died on the 22d day of February 1785,
ſuppoſed to be Aged 72.

Peter was a feral child, found in the forest either naked or with the tatters of some clothes around his neck. His origins are mysterious, and accounts of his discovery vary in their details and the extent to which they sound fanciful. He was caught while suckling milk from a cow; he was enticed towards his captors by the offer of two apples; he walked on all fours; he hid in the high branches of a tree which had to be cut down before he could be caught. He had been raised, it was said, by a bear, or a wolf. There is a fairy-tale quality to the story of Peter, and it is in this spirit that some accounts claim he was spotted by King George I while out hunting. In fact, he seems to have been found by a man called Jurgen Meyer, a smallholder, who took him first to prison in the town of Celle from where news of the discovery reached Herrenhausen, the king's summer residence. George had Peter brought to London the following year, and he made his grand entrance to court and English public life in the drawing room of St James's Palace on the evening of 7 April 1726.

He was a sensation. He could not speak. His movements were animalistic. Having no concept of social status or etiquette, he did not defer to royalty or to the grand gentlemen and ladies. He ran straight over to the king. He tried on one of Princess Caroline's gloves. He had no taste for meat, having survived in the forest on tree bark and what could be foraged. He was not keen on wearing clothes, but a contemporary painting – part of a large-scale depiction of courtiers which can still be seen on the walls of the King's

Staircase at Kensington Palace – shows a puckish child in a green suit with a halo of curly hair, holding oak leaves and acorns; he looks like he might have stepped out of *A Midsummer Night's Dream.*

The striking facial features in this portrait – in particular the pronounced Cupid's bow of his upper lip – led in 2011 to a speculative diagnosis of the neuro-developmental disorder Pitt–Hopkins syndrome, the historian Lucy Worsley having brought Peter to the attention of Professor Phil Beales, an expert in medical genetics. This condition would explain why he had such severe communication difficulties, as well as his happy and excitable demeanour, and might be why he was abandoned by whoever were his parents, if that is indeed what happened.

Among the wits and thinkers and powdered gossips of Georgian England, Peter was regarded as a sort of 'noble savage' uncorrupted by society. Was he truly human? Did he have a soul? He was the subject of pamphlets, newspaper reports, satires. Daniel Defoe met and wrote about him, as did Jonathan Swift. He is thought to have inspired the Yahoos in *Gulliver's Travels.* His effigy appeared among the famous waxworks of Mrs Salmon in Fleet Street. He was commodified, intellectualised, became a creature of ink and paint and wax, and was almost certainly unaware of all the fuss. He was baptised, and attempts were made to educate him – by the Scottish physician John Arbuthnot, the subject of Alexander Pope's celebrated 'Epistle' – but these were not successful.

At some point, too, the court seems to have tired of Peter. The lack of civilisation which had seemed so delightful and charming was now vexatious. He would pick pockets and disrupt meals. He could never learn to say more than a few basic words. The pet had become a pest. With the deaths of Dr Arbuthnot in 1735 and Queen Caroline two years later, he lost his most influential supporters. As Lucy Worsley has written, 'Everybody was fascinated by the idea of the Wild Boy, but it seemed that no one really cared for the human child.'

He was sent to live in the countryside. He was, by now, in his early twenties and strong. He could be a useful man on a farm. One of the Queen's ladies-in-waiting had contact with a farmer in Hertfordshire, James Fenn, and Peter went to live with first him and then his brother Thomas. The crown paid for his keep, and the farmer charged visitors to meet him. Several accounts give a sense of what Peter was like in adult life. He liked gin, fire, walks, music, moonshine, sunshine, starlight, onions (which he ate like apples), bones and dung-carts. He followed the clouds where the wind blew. He could feel bad weather coming and would howl and growl at the thought.

He grew old on the farm. Late in life, he appeared very different from the forest sprite who first came to the royal court. He had long white hair and a great white beard. The novelist Maria Edgeworth, who met him often, thought he looked like Socrates. He may have felt more at home in the country than he did in London, or perhaps local people simply perceived him differently to city folk, but accounts of his life in Hertfordshire feel very different. 'All these idle tales which have been published to the world about his climbing up trees like a squirrel, running upon all fours like a wild beast etc are entirely without foundation,' runs an entry in the St Mary's parish register, 'for he was so exceedingly timid and gentle in his nature that he would suffer himself to be governed by a child.'

In his innocence, Peter sometimes went missing. He'd wander off. In 1745 – the year in which Phoebe Hessel was bayoneted on the Fontenoy battlefield – he was mistaken

for a Jacobite spy and was, for a time, in some danger. The worst, though, was in the summer of 1751 when, for months, he could not be found. He turned up in Norwich that October. He had been arrested for vagrancy and, unable to explain himself, was locked up in the Bridewell prison; when it went on fire, he had to be dragged out, not understanding that his life was at risk. In the aftermath of the blaze, his true identity was discovered and he was returned to Broadway Farm, where steps were taken to prevent his becoming lost ever again.

*

'HERE IS THE collar,' said the archivist. 'You're very welcome to hold it.'

Oh, it looked wicked. Just touching it brought on a phantom choke. It is leather, 25 cm across, with a small metal chain and clasp. Though light in the hands, it has a weight that cannot be reckoned in ounces. A brass plate bent around the curve is etched with its purpose: 'PETER the Wild Man from HANOVER. Whoever shall bring him to Mr Fenn at

Berkhamsted, HERTFORDSHIRE, shall be paid for their trouble.'

Peter was locked into this collar upon his return from Norwich. It is kept in a small wooden box with a red velvet interior within the archive of Berkhamsted School, which itself dates back to the sixteenth century. It has been in the school's collection since 1923. Around half a dozen visitors ask to see it each year. Lesley Koulouris, the school archivist, is always glad of the interest.

'This is a very powerful object, isn't it?' I said to her.

'Yes,' she replied. 'It makes you think of slavery. When people look at it, their automatic reaction is gosh, that's cruel. But it's not. Peter loved the farmers, according to the tales. This collar was a kind thing. It was made because they wanted to keep him safe.'

She loves having the care of the collar. She regards it as an expression of tenderness, made with a good heart and careful hand. What the collar does do, certainly, is wrench the story of Peter from out of the storybooks and into reality. A man wore this. It was taken from him only upon his death. It is intimately bound up with the physical reality of a living person. When he hummed tunes, or laughed, or howled down the rain, he did so with this band of leather around his throat.

Perhaps it slackened towards the end. He had, in his last years, what sounds like a stroke, and this seems to have lessened his great strength. It is said that he died of grief. Finding the farmer dead in bed, but having no understanding of death, Peter tried to rouse him. Unable to do so, he sat by the chimney, refused all food, and died after only a few days. This pining was, surely, an act of love, and perhaps, somewhere, a memory had stirred. The little German boy abandoned in the forest was now an elderly Englishman whose surrogate parent had gone he knew not where.

That is why those mysterious flowers are so moving. They speak of a community which, though many years have passed, has not forgotten the young man in need who came among them and grew old in their embrace.

'We were lucky,' the archivist said, 'to have him here.'

CROWS

IT WAS ALL SOULS' DAY, and Bridgitt Sanders was visiting the grave of her husband. 'This is Wayne,' she said, stooping to pick wet leaves from his flat slate stone, uncovering his name and the dates that showed he had died, the year before, at the age of forty-five. He took his own life.

We were on a hillside in Devon. Set into the ground around us were 242 other slates, just like Wayne's. At the foot of each, the earth had been heaped in a mound, suggestive of the body below. The grass, allowed to grow long over these, brought to mind Walt Whitman's line: 'the beautiful uncut hair of graves'. Anyone chancing upon this place would see a series of hillocks, evenly spaced, and only gradually realise that it is a cemetery of sorts.

Sharpham Meadow is one of three hundred or so natural burial grounds in the UK. There are around the same number of crematoria, but, while a little over three-quarters of deaths in the UK are followed by cremation, natural burial – sometimes called green or woodland burial – represents a very small but growing part of the sector. A natural burial ground will, often, be a field or lightly forested area; most bodies will not have been embalmed, will be in a biodegradable coffin or shroud, and may be buried at a depth of three to four feet – shallow and aerobic enough to allow for efficient decomposition, but deep enough so as not to attract digging animals. If there is any headstone at all, it will usually be modest and flat, like the Sharpham slates. The emphasis, always, is on treading gently on the land; to be humbly embraced by the earth, not to raise a monument upon it. In such places, stone angels fear to tread.

The first graveyard of this sort opened in 1993, as part of Carlisle Cemetery. It was the innovation of the then-manager Ken West. 'The essence is age-old elemental simplicity,' he wrote in *A Guide to Natural Burial.* 'It rejects the so-called traditional funeral with its stuffy, Victorian, urban look, in favour of an outdoorsy, homespun, back-to-nature look. It prefers an unspoilt landscape to that of a regimented conventional cemetery.'

Just outside Totnes, Sharpham Meadow – founded in 2013 – has a long view over the River Dart as it winds its way towards Dartmouth and the sea. It is said to be pretty in summer, a Monet blur of poppies and daisies and distant hay bales, but in November it was wild and bleak. Though a long way from Brontë country, one thought of moors and storms and ghosts.

All Souls' is a day to pray for the departed, to pray them towards heaven, to think on those we have lost. In Catholic and Anglican churches, the names of those parishioners who have died in the past year are written down and read out. At Sharpham Meadow, the day is marked, after sundown, with a secular ceremony. A candle is lit on every grave, a bonfire burns, the necrology is read. Think of it: the lights flickering on the wuthering hill, the names spoken into the wind, carried out to the lighthouse at Berry Head. Are the dead unquiet at such an hour? Do they swoon slowly, call faintly, on the other side of the gossamer night?

Bridgitt had attended the ceremony the year before, one of dozens who had gathered there, not quite seven months after her husband died. 'Stood out in the dark, listening to the wind howling, I felt like dead people were moving all around me,' she recalled. 'It was haunting and sad and crippling, but there was something very redemptive in it, too.'

CROWS

Sometimes, though, the wind blows too hard, even for All Souls'. Roads were flooded, rain was general across England, and this evening's ceremony was cancelled. Bridgitt and I had agreed to meet anyway, in the last of the daylight, to talk about Wayne, his life and death and burial. On this day of remembrance, it felt right.

Bridgitt is in her early forties. She has twin daughters in their mid-teens. Amie and Livvy tend not to visit this place. Bridgitt most often comes on her own, yet never feels alone. She speaks to Pam, who is on one side of Wayne, Alan on the other. She speaks to Holly, whose parents she knows. She plants seeds on her husband's grave, lies on a blanket, chats to him, walks around the whole meadow. Sometimes, after a day sunk in this eloquent silence, it is strange, and something of a struggle, to rise and return to the living world with all its noise and rush.

She and Wayne met in Bournemouth when she was nineteen and he was in his early twenties. She was waitressing in a restaurant where he worked in the kitchen. Before long, they moved to London, part of a group of friends, and became a couple. They worked jobs to pay the rent, but the focus was on music, partying, all-nighters. Wayne was a DJ. He was at his happiest behind the decks, dancing, lost in music. He loved hip hop, house, garage. He had bought his first record at nine and never stopped. Bridgitt still has thousands at home.

They married in Wandsworth Register Office. They both came from divorced families, had no illusions or fantasies of white weddings, but wanted to share a life, a name. The whole day was beautiful. Nothing fancy, but everything perfect. The pub to celebrate, Wayne doing the catering, music music music. When Bridgitt became pregnant, and they learned it was twins, they moved to Exeter to start their life as parents.

How was that life? Happy, largely, until it wasn't. Wayne had always had problems. He had a dependency on alcohol, which seemed to be a way of coping with depression and anxiety. That came and went. He was a committed father. Livvy was born with a rare condition called Goldenhar syndrome. 'Wayne was beautiful with her,' Bridgitt remembered. 'From the minute she was born, he was just like, "We're not victims. This isn't a bad thing. This is just the way it is, and we'll deal with it."' Still, there were a tough few years. Lots of time in hospital. The family closed ranks, existed within a bubble of their own love for one another.

There came a time, though, when Wayne began to struggle. Bridgitt dates this from the last five months of his life. He hated his job, felt he was useless, not bringing in enough money. He had a delusion that the bailiffs were coming, that the police were going to arrest him. None of this was true. It was paranoia, panic attacks, his head playing tricks. He was falling into darkness, ate little, began to find it difficult to leave first the house and then his room. He should have been sectioned, Bridgitt thinks, but was always sent home from hospital with medication. She never gave up on him. She had the hope he could never find. She remembers their last hug, both of them shaking with emotion, but a calmness in it, too. That hug meant different things to both of them, she realises now. For her: we move forward from here. For him: goodbye.

'We were both down in the hole, but I was climbing out,' she said. 'He was dancing with the abyss.'

*

WAYNE'S BURIAL was arranged by Rupert and Claire Callender of the Green Funeral Company. They are a husband and wife who describe themselves as alternative undertakers. Although separated, they still run the business together. He is Scottish – 'posh Scottish' – she is Welsh. They look a little like a bohemian version of Grant Wood's painting *American Gothic*, and in conversation act as one another's Greek chorus: interrupting, elaborating, amplifying, correcting.

We met in Totnes for coffee and cake. They have radical ideas about funerals, and are contemptuous of the way things are done by the death industry's big players.

They are against embalming ('Horrible, violent, invasive and unnecessary,' said Claire) and wary of cremation ('spiritually bankrupt') – which they regard as environmentally polluting, and too often a corporate conveyor belt that allows insufficient time and sense of occasion. Ru is into open-air funeral pyres – 'I want to be burned on the top of a hill at midsummer' – and looks forward to the day when UK law offers clarity on whether it is possible for him to offer this service professionally.

Claire would be happy to fulfil his wish should he die first ('I want to have the right to hold my husband's skull in my hand') but thinks the future is more likely to be alkaline hydrolysis, a green alternative to cremation. In this process, the body is submerged for four hours in a metal chamber containing a solution of water and potassium hydroxide heated to 150°C, dissolving the flesh and softening the bones, which are then ground down. The resulting fluid – 1,500 litres of it – is full of nutrients. 'You could have a meditative Zen water feature,' she mused. 'A death garden.'

The Callenders, who are in their fifties, came late to the undertaker business. Claire used to work in the music industry. Ru spent his twenties 'keeping a nervous breakdown at arm's length' – without, it seems, much sense of purpose. So why do they do this work?

'Because it's the best job in the world,' she said. 'We make really deep connections with people, and you learn that people are *good*. People are *strong*. And they are creative – when you give them the chance to be, when you tell them that there is no formula to this, let's just figure out what's going to be best for you and your friends and family.'

Ru nodded. 'I feel compelled to do it,' he said. 'I'm an undertaker, and I'm not okay with death. It frightens me just as much as it does you. My childhood experiences mean that it's that old-fashioned thing: a vocation.'

His father died when Ru was seven. He didn't go to the funeral. The first he attended was that of his mother when he was twenty-five, at which point he found himself fully experiencing the grief of that earlier loss. This is not to say that he spent his boyhood in denial of death. Indeed, he was steeped in it. His mother had a job at a hospice in Edinburgh; during school holidays he would have the run of the grounds, and would often find himself called inside to say goodbye at the deathbeds of old ladies whom he had never previously met.

'That's *weird*,' said Claire.

'It was quite weird,' he laughed.

The Callenders are keen on the idea that people take practical and creative ownership of the process of mourning; that they consider spending time with the person they have lost, perhaps washing the body; that they carry the coffin to the grave, so as to feel the weight and understand the truth of what that means; most of all, that they have the funeral they want to have – not one shaped by conventional notions of what is appropriate or what ought to be done for the sake of appearance. No need for the black suits, expensive coffin, shiny hearse. No need for formaldehyde and banal formalities. No need for anything but the one true need: a proper farewell worthy of the name.

In this, they are part of the so-called natural death movement. This began in 1991 when Nicholas Albery and his wife, the psychotherapist Josefine Speyer, founded the Natural Death Centre. The organisation promotes family-organised and environmentally friendly funerals, and publishes a handbook with practical advice on such matters as keeping a body at home between death and burial. Albery himself died in a car accident in the summer of 2001; he was buried in private woodland, by family and friends, in a coffin of woven bamboo, a pen in his hand. It was seeing Albery speaking on television that made Ru realise he wanted to become an undertaker. Reading *The Natural Death Handbook* 'radicalised' the Callenders.

Ru and Claire talk about the importance of inventing one's own rituals; ceremonies that are meaningful and beautiful, but not necessarily faith-based – 'Opening the door to wonder' is how Ru put it. The All Souls' ritual at Sharpham Meadow was their creation. Their thinking in all of this has been informed by esoteric influences: punk ('It's that DIY culture'); rave ('It's about connectedness, almost religious, but there's no Godhead'); and the wonder of crop circles ('numinous is the word that springs to mind'). If this all makes them sound rather out there, that is not how one feels in their company. Gentleness, humour and compassion are the keynotes of their presence.

That said, they are advocates for allowing space in mourning for negative emotions: anger and so on. When someone dies, those left behind often feel anger, either at the loss or at the deceased themselves, and this almost always goes unspoken and repressed during a conventional funeral.

The euphemism 'loved one' can mask complex feelings, Claire explained. 'Sometimes, if there has been a very complicated relationship, possibly abusive, I've said to the person, "Okay, come into the chapel of rest and just fucking let them have it. Just go and tell them everything you need to say while their body's there." That can be helpful, but obviously it's not for everyone.'

It is not common for such outbursts to occur during the ceremonies themselves, but it does happen. The Callenders recall the funeral of a man who had been a heroin addict for a long time. One of his brothers went up to the coffin and started roaring: 'You fucking dickhead. Everyone tried to help you.' It was done, they felt, with love.

'For us, a body is just that; a body,' Ru has written in a short essay on the subject of the straps they use to lower coffins into the grave. 'Something awkward and heavy to be treated practically between us, to be lifted and moved, dressed or washed. But when they are in the presence of those who loved them, they become people again, suffused with personality and history, mute vessels for love and longing, themselves but changed. It is to witness this change that we gently lead the living toward, no more certain as to what it means than they, only sure that it is as important as it is painful.'

This philosophy lies beneath their work. It shapes the services and rituals they conduct. 'Our funerals have got more and more stripped back,' Claire said. 'There's less viola-playing grandchildren, less poems, less readings. Just strip it back to the people who loved this person, standing around their body one last time on this earth, and talking honestly, and from the heart, about what they meant, how they've influenced them for good and bad.

'There's nothing more powerful than that.'

*

At Sharpham Meadow, I walked down the slope to the fire pit. A large iron ring had been engraved with the words, 'In my end is my beginning' – a line from T. S. Eliot's 'Four Quartets'. In the middle of the circle were the remains of a fire. This would have provided a blazing centrepiece for the All Souls' ritual had that gone ahead. It is lit, often, during funerals, for families to gather round. The ashes of at least six people have been scattered in the flames, according to Ru. Whenever it is lit, they are remembered.

One of the six was Frances Galleymore, a writer who died, aged seventy-one, in 2017. I had met her daughter Sophie earlier that day. Her mother, she told me, was 'a seeker' – always looking for ways to be happy and at peace. She had a deep interest in the elements, which Sophie wanted to reflect in the distribution of her ashes. Some, therefore, were interred in the Sharpham earth; some were scattered over the waves at Meadfoot beach; and the rest placed in the bonfire during an All Souls' ritual, a few blowing up into the night sky. 'It felt very good,' Sophie had said, 'to give her back to nature.'

A little further down the hill, I found the grave of Kate Woolner. I had promised her husband, Tom, when we met that morning, that I would look for her on the meadow. Kate had died of cancer at the age of fifty-eight. She had stood on this spot, I knew, on the day they both came to choose her resting place. Three months later, Tom and their daughters were among those who carried her coffin to the grave.

'Kate was part of us,' he had told me. 'So it was only natural and right that we should do as much for her as we could. Lowering her into the ground – who else would do that? It was our last act. She had chosen that place, and we were honouring her choice right through to the end.'

At the top of the meadow there is a building: a simple oval with a base of Cornish stone, walls of cob – mixed earth and straw – and a turf roof. It is not glazed; the front opens to the long view. It was in here, sheltered from the wind and rain, that Bridgitt Sanders continued her story.

The thing to understand is that it's a love story. Bridgitt and Wayne? That's a romance, not a tragedy. Yes, there is a deep sadness in it, but the love they had was – is – real.

'That day was the most beautiful,' she said. The day of the burial. Beautiful in the same way as their wedding day, in that it wasn't polished and manicured and stiff.

There weren't many people. Closest friends and family. Ru and Claire. A month had passed since her husband's death. Bridgitt pointed out to me the spot in the shelter where he was laid out. He was wrapped in a felt cocoon with a felt shroud over the top. They could see his outline. The outer shroud had been embroidered with four crows, one – Wayne – flying above the rest; the others represented Bridgitt and the girls.

They stood around the body as music played. Bridgitt and her friend Tom had been going through things in the house when they found a receipt tucked into Wayne's vinyl collection. Tom said, 'I think this is the last record he bought.' Bridgitt remembered him singing it: a remix of Josefin Öhrn & The Liberation's 'Rushing Through My Mind'. So this was what they played on the meadow – standing in silence for eight minutes, in the analgesic trance of the beats.

The words of the song inspired Bridgitt. She felt able to speak. She addressed Wayne: 'You're not only in my mind. You're in my blood, you're in my bones, you're everywhere. You're in your children, you're with us, you're here.'

Others joined in. Stories, memories. Two hours passed. It was time to go to the grave.

Their dog Heidi, a yellow Lab, was running around as they placed Wayne in the ground. Two strong lads were on hand for the burying, but Bridgitt asked if she could do it. 'I was really protective of him.' The soil there is very rocky, and she didn't want him to be crushed, so she started by placing the biggest stones around his body. 'Before we put the earth in, I said to everybody, "Do you mind if I have a fag?"' She sat smoking with her feet in the grave, touching his. She had put his camping socks on him, nice and cosy. It was like putting him to bed. All the while, she was talking to him. She finished the cigarette and placed the stub in the grave.

Then the earth. 'People were offering me shovels and gloves, but I needed to do it with my hands. I couldn't imagine somebody else doing that job. It was too sacred. It was too private. I wanted the dirt in me.' On her hands, under her nails.

'Once he was in the ground, I felt a complete peace. He'd been ill for so long, I'd been desperately trying to save him for so long.' He'd become the property of strangers: the doctors, the support workers, the system. No more. Where he was now felt completely pure and right. It wasn't a sweet little cemetery; that wouldn't have suited Wayne. It was, she felt, wild and chaotic and crazy, up there on the hill, in all the weather, under a bower of cloud. He would be part of that landscape for ever, while also existing in the intimate contours of his family's hearts.

'This is where we put him to rest,' she told me, 'and the rest of him lives in us.'

I said goodbye to Bridgitt, and wished her a safe journey. She was going to spend a little more time at the grave, this All Souls' Day, and then head back to Exeter and her children. I imagined her driving in the dark, radio on, thinking over the story she had told. I imagined her walking into the living room, into warmth and company, and what she might see there: Wayne's shroud, which had been taken off him, just before he was laid in the grave, and which she had hung over the fireplace of their home.

The mother. The daughters.
The husband and father.
The four crows.
'It has brought us a lot of comfort, me and the kids,' she had said of the shroud, 'to see him in flight, to see him free.'

BELOVED

Follow the pumpkins. It was as simple as that. A trail of jack-o'-lanterns, laid between the path and the graves, acted as smiling Sherpas: showing the way up the hill to where the vows would be said. It was Hallowe'en, and I was in Arnos Vale for Liz and Shaun's wedding.

This burial ground opened in Bristol in 1839, and is perhaps the finest Victorian garden cemetery outside of London. It is also the best example of a nineteenth-century graveyard being repurposed for the twenty-first, reborn as a place of leisure and pleasure. At one side of the gates when I visited was a billboard advertising a forthcoming theatre production of *Jekyll & Hyde* ('Following three sell-out gothic horrors here at Arnos Vale . . .'). On the other were hoardings noting the availability of burial space, coffee and cake. A blackboard outside the visitor centre listed that day's wildlife sightings: a cat, two bats, a peregrine falcon above the tomb of Rajah Rammohun Roy, and – in noticeably smaller writing – 'one rat'.

Is this place the future of graveyards? It certainly has an illustrious past.

Between the A4 and A37, covering a site of forty-five acres, home to around 290,000 dead, the cemetery is synonymous in this city with the life beyond life. 'I'll see thee down Arnos Vale,' is a typical line from Bristolians of a certain vintage; said with a smile, but serious, too, meaning that the speaker, and the friend being addressed, would end their days in the same ground.

There are worse places. Although bigger than Highgate, Arnos Vale feels much more compact, and there are many among its 200,000 annual visitors who would make a case that it is more beautiful. I think myself that 'pretty' might be a better word. On either side of the entrance on Bath Road are two small neoclassical gatehouses, one of which is now the cemetery reception and shop. Wander only a little further in, however, and you arrive at the real treasure: the two chapels, one Anglican, the other Nonconformist, both Grade II listed. The Nonconformist chapel resembles an Athenian temple. The Anglican is Italianate, and somehow more feminine; one admires the bell tower's long, slender neck.

Shaun and Liz had booked the Noncomformist chapel for their reception, though the ceremony itself was to be elsewhere in the grounds. The cemetery has been a marriage venue since 2014, and now hosts around forty each year. The coordinator is a young woman called Buffy. She gets a lot of goths. Wedding photographs taken at Arnos Vale tend to feature tattoos, black cakes, motorbikes. One couple walked down the aisle to Iron Maiden. Brides have been known to arrive by hearse.

'Last Hallowe'en,' Buffy told me, 'a couple had a Viking-themed handfasting. He wore a suit of armour. She had a massive red dress and a crown. They had wolfhounds running the aisle, and an owl ring-bearer. There was mead, and guests dressed as elves. I think they came from Southampton.'

I was a little early, so I visited the chapel. The room where the reception was to be held looked gorgeous: elegant and full of light, the tables dressed with gourds and ivy. Immediately below, and accessible to the public, was the site of the former crematorium. Between 1928 and the discontinuation of the service in 1998, 123,000 people were cremated down there. The area is now used to tell the story of Arnos Vale, but one of the great ovens remains. It is a rusty brown, the colour of dried blood, and looks like a hungry robot: tiny

black eyes, alimentary pipes and valves, a great gaping mouth full of blunt brick teeth. Across the way is the atomiser – a glass-fronted machine full of wheels and belts, which was used to grind the cremated remains into ash. Shaun, when we spoke on the phone a few weeks before, had suggested that any guests who found themselves bored could pass a little time inspecting this gizmo. It might also be used to chasten misbehaving kids. 'Watch out,' Liz had joked, 'or you'll get taken down to the bone-crusher!'

Liz Webb and Shaun McHale live in Bristol. He's thirty-two, a painter-decorator; she's twenty-nine and works for a serviced-apartment company. Liz grew up nearby and so has known the cemetery since childhood. They're not goths, or steampunks, or pagans, although Liz admits to 'witchy vibes'; they're just regular folks who are into Hallowe'en and fancied an outdoor ceremony, which Arnos Vale offers. The presence of the dead doesn't bother them. Quite the opposite. 'When we booked it,' Liz had laughed, 'Buffy was like, "So you've got about 300,000 guests coming to your wedding."'

Arnos Vale is owned by Bristol City Council, managed and leased by the Cemetery Trust. It has annual running costs of around half a million pounds. To meet these without local authority funding, the cemetery is used for a variety of purposes, including, of course, burial.

Some of the activities might have surprised the Victorians – weddings, for one, but also film screenings (*The Lost Boys*, *Corpse Bride*, etc.) held in the Anglican chapel. There is an annual festival called Life, Death (And The Rest) intended to bust taboos around dying. On the day of my visit, the crypt had been taken over by the city's Mexican community and turned into an *ofrenda* – an altar covered in food offerings, bright skull decorations and photos of the deceased – for *Día de los Muertos*.

More than any other cemetery in Britain, there always seems to be a lot going on. This is, perhaps, easier to sustain in artsy, liberal, hipster-ish Bristol than it would be in some other cities. Striking a balance in which the integrity and atmosphere of the cemetery are not compromised is a matter of instinct and ongoing debate.

'It's a constant conversation between the Trust and the staff and the Friends and the public: is this appropriate? Should we do this, should we do that?' said Janine Marriott, the public engagement manager. We were sitting in Arnos Vale's café, and she was all in black, having just come from walking around the cemetery with a bunch of little ones, reading *Room on the Broom*. 'For instance,' she continued, 'there have been situations where certain films have been proposed. *Psycho*, we decided, was a step too far. Someone else wanted to do a talk on necrophilia – we said no to that as well.'

She sees the cemetery as 'a sacred space' but also a 'heritage space', and insists that the two aren't at odds. She cited the great nineteenth-century cemetery visionary John Claudius

Loudon, who had written that a cemetery's secondary purpose, after burial, ought to be 'the improvement of the moral sentiments and general taste of all classes, and more especially the great masses of society'. That cemeteries might become places of education and entertainment is not, in other words, straying too far from their original social function. To see how Arnos Vale makes this work, representatives of other cemeteries make regular fact-finding visits to Bristol.

'Councils haven't the funds,' Marriott said. 'They're never going to care for a historic cemetery over a nursing home, or a museum, or a sports centre. And then you're just relying on Friends groups, which are really important, but they can't battle the tide of collapsing stones, falling trees and so on. So, some kind of income-generating activity is vital. For some of the smaller cemeteries, the future might be local communities taking over and them becoming more like nature reserves. But for large historic cemeteries, our model is probably a good one.'

That model relies heavily upon volunteers. Among the regulars is Howard Utting, although the word volunteer does not seem sufficient to describe his status. He is more like a patron saint, or a household deity; the guru of the graveyard. He is seventy-six, with long grey hair, a long grey beard, and a long association with Arnos Vale. The House of Utting is a famous dynastic line. Howard's grandfather William Utting was superintendent, responsible for running the cemetery, from 1908; William's son, Alfred, born in the cemetery in 1910, eventually took over the superintendent role. In 1941, Alfred married Betty Edgell, the daughter of the cemetery caretaker; she also lived in Arnos Vale, in the top lodge, and Howard can point to the exact place on the exact path where his father proposed to his mother one evening as he was walking her home.

Given his parentage, Howard was a true child of the graveyard. He lived here from his birth in 1943 until he married at thirty-one. Arnos Vale was his playground. His sister, Elaine, wasn't born until he was ten, so for much of his boyhood he was an only child. He'd ride his bike along the paths, climb across graves to reach the best conkers, share the sandwiches of the gravediggers.

As the family grew, the Uttings lived in different residences in the cemetery, settling eventually in the East Lodge, to the left of the main gates as you come in. Of an evening, he and Elaine would, at their father's behest, check the deaths column of the local paper. If Arnos Vale was down to perform more cremations than the council crem then all was well in the world. Forget Rovers vs City, this was the derby that mattered.

These days, on Fridays, Howard mans the reception desk of what used to be his living room; from the window he can see his parents' grave. As a young man, he loved living in the lodge. The walls were so thick you could play your records as loud as you liked, and in any case the neighbours, being dead, were unlikely to complain. He was cranking out 'Blowin' in the Wind' when his mother told him JFK had been shot. Even now, he feels a strong association between music and the cemetery landscape. 'Look out there,' he urged, standing at a window of the West Lodge, and sweeping an arm across the panorama of tombs and trees. 'That's Thomas Tallis!'

Howard didn't go into the family business. He became a postman. Still, he has ash in his blood, bones in his bones. Growing up in a graveyard shaped him in several important ways. It influenced his politics, made him realise that you can't take your money with you, so what's the point of grasping for it, and exploiting others to get it? Related to this was an appreciation of the importance of kindness; people suffer, they grieve, so treat them gently. 'Go out and be kind,' his father told him.

Even more significantly, Howard understood and accepted the inevitability of death at an age when most kids were having trouble understanding and accepting the inevitability of school. He remembers being sent out to tell his dad it was time to come in for dinner, and finding him in one of the chapels, closing up for the night. 'We were standing at the altar. My father said to me, "Life's like that candle. If you're lucky, you'll burn all the way down." And he licked his thumb and forefinger and pinched the wick. "Life can be snuffed out," he said. "But tomorrow, I'll light the flame again."'

Those words came back to Howard, recently, and gave him comfort, when he learned that a friend had had an accident and was unlikely to survive: 'She's halfway down the candle.'

Life in the cemetery gave him a taste for poetry; one of his daily jobs, as a boy, was turning the page of the Book of Remembrance – in which he would read the little verses, written over many decades, by families in commemoration of those they had lost. These were nothing fancy, nothing to trouble Dickinson or Larkin, but they were sincere, and they impressed him then, and still do.

'There is love in the world,' he told me. 'You might not think it, but there is.'

Arnos Vale is alive. The weddings, the funerals, the tours and talks – they keep its pulse steady. Things could easily have been very different. Had it not been for the determination of locals, I might have found the gates padlocked, the buildings collapsing, the graveyard dead.

The cemetery had been in decline since the late 1950s. It changed hands several times, and in 1987 came into the ownership of a businessman who announced that he wanted to build four hundred houses on a seven-acre section of the grounds. Families were asked to consider exhuming and removing the remains of their relations. This caused widespread outrage, and inspired a long campaign which would – in its quietly determined British way – revolutionise the way Arnos Vale was owned and run.

Joyce Smith, together with her husband, Richard, was one of the leaders of that campaign. Now in her mid-seventies, she met me in the café, and explained why she had first got involved. It was personal. Her father had died only a couple of years before, and been buried at Arnos Vale. 'My mother rang me up and said, "They're going to dig everybody up and clear the cemetery. What shall we do about Daddy?"' Joyce, indignant, replied: 'Well, we're not going to do anything about him, because he's not going to be dug up.'

The cemetery owner had a fight on his hands. 'He seriously underestimated the people of Bristol.'

A campaigning group, the Association for the Preservation of Arnos Vale Cemetery, was formed to resist the development plans. In the meantime, the grounds and buildings were allowed by management to become run down. Paths became overgrown. Visiting graves became difficult and unpleasant. Vandals got into the Anglican chapel and started a fire. 'They went down into the crypt, opened a couple of coffins, and took the bones up into the chapel,' Joyce recalled. 'We don't know what they were doing with them. Some sort of ritual, I guess.'

Things came to a head in 1998 when the crematorium failed to meet new environmental guidelines, and its licence expired. This meant the business had no income. The owner announced that he could no longer keep the cemetery open, and attempted to lock the gates. He was prevented from doing so by a crowd of around two hundred locals, who came to be known as the Arnos Vale Army. They established a caravan just outside the main entrance, and for several years made sure the cemetery was open in the morning for those visiting graves, locked up in the evening to protect it from intruders as best they could.

There followed a series of legal battles, first to establish the right of the Arnos Vale Army to be there, and then in defence of Bristol City Council's compulsory purchase order. This went to the High Court in London, and in 2003 the council, now the owners of Arnos Vale, licensed the new Cemetery Trust to manage it. Joyce and Richard Smith found themselves in charge of a graveyard that had one foot in the grave.

'We were so close to a real disaster,' she told me. 'The West Lodge was the worst. The staircase was gone, it was damp, rot everywhere, and the roof was leaking. It was only the spiderwebs holding it up.'

Richard Smith had been running an office out of the back of his car, but eventually they managed to clear out a corner of the Nonconformist chapel and install that invaluable item, a kettle. This was followed, in short order, by a second kettle, and then by a sign warning that boiling both at once would blow the fuses. Still, with a little care, tea could be made; and with a little tea, progress could be made. The resurrection of Arnos Vale was steaming ahead.

Money helped. The Trust was granted almost five million pounds by the Heritage Lottery Fund. This was to pay for the restoration of the buildings, but funds were still required for the day-to-day running of the cemetery. Joyce started giving tours. 'It was a real wartime effort,' she laughed. 'But people came. That was the amazing part. People wanted to see the cemetery. I found it so uplifting. I was inspired by everybody's support.'

Richard Smith died in 2009. His ashes are buried in one of the gardens of rest, as his wife's will be: 'Though not quite yet, I hope.' A plaque in the cemetery pays tribute to his passion, commitment and leadership. The main route through Arnos Vale is known as Richard's Road.

Had they known how the campaign to save and restore the cemetery would come to dominate their lives, Joyce is not sure whether she and her husband would have become as involved. 'But I hope,' she said, 'we made a difference.' They did. That Bristolians can still say to one another, with confidence, 'I'll see thee down Arnos Vale,' is thanks to the Smiths, as well as the many others who saw the meaning in this place and not just the money.

At last, it was time to follow those pumpkins. Shaun and Liz were getting married in the Underwood Centre, up a steep, winding path through the trees. It was in a part of the cemetery where, during Howard Utting's childhood, the horse and cart were kept. Now it is an outdoor wedding venue. The ceremony would take place inside what looked like a deconstructed barn: a steep roof, but open on all sides. This had been decorated with bunting, lights, candles, autumn leaves, and, of course, more pumpkins. Shaun looked sharp in blue tweed. Liz arrived in a burgundy 1934 Cadillac – 'The actual car from *Downton Abbey*,' Buffy whispered – and stepped out to the sound of Jimmy Cliff singing 'Many Rivers to Cross'. She wore white, with glossy green wellies.

The ceremony was short, but lovely. Champagne popped. Sinatra sang. Guests gathered around the fire for speeches and toasted marshmallows. A glass was raised to Shaun's late father, Rob: the dead remembered and named, brought a little closer to the warmth.

Afterwards, we all walked back down the hill, a line of suits and dresses passing along an avenue of graves. 'Till death do us part' never felt so real. As guests gathered by the steps of the chapel to smoke and chat and sip beer, Liz and her mother and uncle stopped at the white archway of the garden of rest. Her grandmother had died before Liz was born, and her ashes been scattered there. It was a quiet, still moment. They hugged, and Liz said: 'Let's go and get smiles back on our faces, have some champagne, and know that she's part of our day as well.'

First, though, a final ritual. Friends and family formed two lines, an honour guard, and Shaun and Liz ran between them in a shower of rose petals. Confetti in a graveyard; if one were looking for a symbol to sum up the way in which these great gardens of death can also be places of life, just follow the drift of those petals. Some fell, I noticed, on the shared grave of a couple. William Ring had died in 1886; his wife, Harriet, in 1908. Their life together had ended, that of Liz and Shaun was only just beginning, and so it goes.

The bride and groom went off for photographs. The day was fading fast, and it was important to make the most of the light.

Selected Sources

Author's Note

Pullman, Philip, *The Amber Spyglass* (David Fickling Books, 2000)

Ivy

Ford, John, *Memorials of John Ford* (Silvanus Thompson, ed; Samuel Harris, 1877)

Gammond, Peter, *Your Own, Your Very Own! A Music Hall Scrapbook* (Ian Allan, 1971)

Mellor, G. J., *The Northern Music Hall: A Century of Popular Entertainment* (Frank Graham, 1970)

Rose, Clarkson *Beside the Seaside* (Museum Press, 1960)

Highgate Cemetery Conservation Plan (Alan Baxter, 2019)

Angels

Arnold, Catharine, *Necropolis: London and Its Dead* (Simon & Schuster, 2006)

Bard, Robert and Adrian Miles, *London's Hidden Burial Grounds* (Amberley, 2017)

Chadwick, Edwin, *Report on the Sanitary Conditions of the Labouring Population of Great Britain: A Supplementary Report on the Results of a Special Inquiry into the Practice of Interment in Towns* (W. Clowes & Sons, 1843)

Clark, Ossie, *The Ossie Clark Diaries* (Bloomsbury, 1998)

Dickens, Charles, *Bleak House* (Bradbury and Evans, 1853)

Dickens, Charles 'The City of the Absent', in *The Uncommercial Traveller* (Chapman & Hall, 1861)

Selected Sources

Holmes, Isabella, *The London Burial Grounds: Notes on Their History from the Earliest Times to the Present Day* (T. F. Unwin, 1896)

Litten, Julian, *The English Way of Death: The Common Funeral since 1450* (Robert Hale, 1992)

Meller, Hugh and Brian Parsons, *London's Cemeteries: An Illustrated Guide and Gazetteer* (The History Press, 2011)

Stanford, Peter, *How to Read a Graveyard: Journeys in the Company of the Dead* (Bloomsbury, 2013)

Turpin, John and Derrick Knight, *The Magnificent Seven: London's First Landscaped Cemeteries* (Amberley, 2016)

Walker, George Alfred, *Burial-Ground Incendiarism: The Last Fire at the Bone-House in the Spa-Fields Golgotha, or The Minute Anatomy of Grave-Digging in London* (Longman, 1846)

Walker, George Alfred, *Gatherings from Grave Yards* (Longman, 1839)

Walkowitz, Judith R., *Nights Out: Life in Cosmopolitan London* (Yale University Press, 2012)

Reports from the Select Committees on Improvement of the Health of Towns – Interment of Bodies (1842)

Pasek, Benj and Justin Paul, 'This is Me', from the soundtrack to *The Greatest Showman* (2017)

LILIES

Beckett, Samuel, *Waiting For Godot: A Tragicomedy in Two Acts* (Faber & Faber, 1956)

Burns, Anna, *Milkman* (Faber & Faber, 2018)

Hartley, Tom *Milltown Cemetery: The History of Belfast, Written in Stone* (Blackstaff Press, 2014)

Hartley, Tom, *Written in Stone: The History of Belfast City Cemetery* (The Brehon Press, 2006)

Selected Sources

Henry, Paul, *Further Reminiscences* (Blackstaff Press, 1973)
Jack, Ian, 'Gibraltar', in *Granta 25* (Penguin Books, 1988)
McKee, Lyra, *Lost, Found, Remembered* (Faber & Faber, 2020)
Morrison, Danny, *All the Dead Voices* (Mercier Press, 2002)
Phoenix, Eamon, *Two Acres of Irish History: A Study through Time of Friar's Bush and Belfast 1570–1918* (Ulster Historical Foundation, 1988)
Stone, Michael, *None Shall Divide Us* (John Blake, 2004)

The Funeral Murders (BBC2, 2018; Vanessa Engle, director)

CHERUBS

Golledge, Charlotte, *Greyfriars Graveyard* (Amberley, 2018)
    Rankin, Ian, *The Hanging Garden* (Orion, 1998)
Verne, Jules, *Voyage à reculons en Angleterre et en Ecosse* (Le Cherche Midi Éditeur, 1989), trans. Janice Valls-Russell as *Backwards to Britain* (Chambers, 1993)

PHOEBE

De Pauw, Linda Grant, *Battle Cries and Lullabies: Women in War from Prehistory to the Present* (University of Oklahoma Press, 1998)
Erredge, John Ackerson, *History of Brighthelmston or Brighton as I View It and Others Knew It* (E. Lewis, 1862)
Hone, William, *The Year Book of Daily Recreation and Information: Concerning Remarkable Men and Manners, Times and Seasons, Solemnities and Merry-Makings, Antiquities and Novelties, on the Plan of the Everyday Book and Table Book* (William Tegg & Co., 1832)
Tennyson, Alfred, 'Rizpah', in *The Poetical Works* (Macmillan & Co., 1899)

CEDAR

Arnold, Catharine, *Necropolis: London and Its Dead* (Simon & Schuster, 2006)

Bard, Robert and Adrian Miles, *London's Hidden Burial Grounds* (Amberley, 2017)

Bulmer, Jane, *Highgate Cemetery: Saved by Its Friends* (Highgate Cemetery/Jigsaw Design & Publishing, 2016)

Dungavell, Ian, *Highgate Cemetery: Windows on the Past* (Friends of Highgate Cemetery Trust, 2017)

Gould, Philip, *When I Die: Lessons from the Death Zone* (Little, Brown, 2012)

Lydon, John, *Rotten: No Irish, No Blacks, No Dogs* (Hodder & Stoughton, 1993)

Meller, Hugh and Brian Parsons, *London's Cemeteries: An Illustrated Guide and Gazetteer* (The History Press, 2011)

Nairn, Ian, *Nairn's London* (Penguin Books, 1966; reissued 2014)

Turpin, John and Derrick Knight, *The Magnificent Seven: London's First Landscaped Cemeteries* (Amberley, 2016)

Victorian Society and contributors, *Great Gardens of Death* (The Victorian Society, 2019)

Wells, H. G., 'The Mode in Monuments', in *Certain Personal Matters* (T. Fisher Unwin, 1897)

Wheen, Francis, *Karl Marx* (Fourth Estate, 1999)

Highgate Cemetery Conservation Plan (Alan Baxter, 2019)

UNMARKED

Constable, John, *The Southwark Mysteries* (Oberon Books, 1999)

Dennehy, Emer A., 'Dorchadas gan Phian: The History of Ceallúnaigh in Co. Kerry', *Journal of the Kerry Archaeological and Historical Society*, series 2, vol. 2 (2002)

Dennehy, Emer 'Placeless Dead? Finding Evidence for Children in the Irish Landscape', *The Journal of the History of Childhood and Youth*, vol. 9, no. 2 (Spring 2016), pp. 213–31

Dennehy, Emer, '"What Damned You?" Changelings, Mylingar and Other Dead Child Traditions', *Archaeology Ireland*, vol. 30, no. 3 (Autumn 2016), pp. 21–5

Duckworth, George H., Notebook Police District 31 (digitised as part of Charles Booth's London, LSE website)

Flower, Robin, *The Western Island, or, The Great Blasket* (Oxford University Press, 1944)

Higgs, John, *Watling Street: Travels through Britain and Its Ever-Present Past* (Weidenfeld & Nicolson, 2017)

Holmes, Isabella, *The London Burial Grounds: Notes on Their History from the Earliest Times to the Present Day* (T. F. Unwin, 1896)

International Theological Commission, 'The Hope of Salvation for Infants Who Die Without Being Baptised' (Catholic Truth Society, 2007)

Maguire, Toni, *The Shoe-Box Babies of Ireland: Information on Cillíní and Unmarked Burials in Private and Institutional Cemeteries in Ireland* (2014)

Stow, John *Survey of London* (1598; The History Press, 2005)

Walker, George Alfred, *Gatherings from Grave Yards* (Longman & Co., 1839)

History Cold Case: The Crossbones Girl (BBC2, 2010; Neil Ferguson, director)

Limbo Babies (BBC2, 2010; Alison Millar, director)

ANCHOR

Blunden, Edmund, *Undertones of War* (R. Cobden-Sanderson, 1928; Penguin Books, 2000)

Selected Sources

Brassey, Bernard, *153rd Leicestershire Yeomanry Field Regiment R.A.,
  T.A. 1939–1945* (W. Pickering & Sons, 1947; The Naval &
  Military Press, 2015)

Brooke, Rupert, 'The Soldier', in *Collected Poems* (Oleander
  Press, 2013)

Crane, David, *Empires of the Dead: How One Man's Vision Led to
  the Creation of WWI's War Graves* (William Collins, 2013)

Ellsworth-Jones, Will, *We Will Not Fight: The Untold Story of
  World War One's Conscientious Objectors* (Aurum, 2007)

Francis, Peter, ed., *A Guide to the Commonwealth War Graves
  Commission* (Third Millennium Publishing, 2018)

Francis, Peter and Michael St Maur Sheil, *For the Fallen:
  A Century of Remembrance since the Great War* (CWGC/
  AA Publishing, 2014)

MacDonald, Charles, *Moidart, or, Among the Clanranalds*
  (Duncan Cameron, 1889; Birlinn, 2011)

Muir, Augustus, *Scotland's Road of Romance* (Methuen & Co.,
  1934)

Owen, Wilfred, 'Dulce et decorum est', in *Selected Poetry and
  Prose* (Routledge, 1988)

Sassoon, Siegfried, 'On Passing the New Menin Gate', in
  Collected Poems 1908–1956 (Faber & Faber, 1987)

ANKH

Brady, Sean, *John Addington Symonds (1840–1893) and
  Homosexuality: A Critical Edition of Sources* (Palgrave
  Macmillan, 2012)

Cox, Michael, *M. R. James: An Informal Portrait* (Oxford
  University Press, 1983)

Crawford, Gary William, Jim Rockhill and Brian J. Showers,
  eds., *Reflections in a Glass Darkly: Essays on J. Sheridan Le
  Fanu* (Hippocampus Press, 2011)

Selected Sources

Edwards, Amelia B., *The Collected Supernatural and Weird Fiction* (Leonaur, 2015)

Holness, Matthew 'Introduction', in J. Sheridan Le Fanu, *Green Tea* (Swan River Press, 2019)

Holness, Matthew, 'Introduction', in J. Sheridan Le Fanu, *Reminiscences of a Batchelor* (Swan River Press, 2014)

Holroyd, Michael, *Lytton Strachey: The New Biography* (Chatto & Windus, 1994)

James, M. R., *Ghost Stories* (Edward Arnold, 1931; Penguin Popular Classics, 1994)

Le Fanu, J. Sheridan, *In a Glass Darkly* (Richard Bentley & Son, 1872; Wordsworth Editions, 1995)

Lovecraft, H. P., *Supernatural Horror in Literature* (Ben Abramson, 1945; Dover, 1973)

McCormack, W. J., *Sheridan Le Fanu and Victorian Ireland* (Clarendon Press, 1980)

Moon, Brenda, *More Usefully Employed: Amelia B Edwards, Writer, Traveller and Campaigner for Ancient Egypt* (Egypt Exploration Society, 2006)

Ó Cadhain, Máirtín, *The Dirty Dust* (Yale Margellos, 2015; trans. Alan Titley). Originally published as *Cré na Cille* (Sáirséal agus Dill, 1945)

Rees, Joan, *Amelia Edwards: Traveller, Novelist & Egyptologist* (The Rubicon Press, 1998)

Lloyd Parry, Robert, 'Dim Presences' (documentary appears as a bonus feature on Lloyd Parry's *A Warning to the Curious* DVD (Nunkie & Thomthom Productions)

McLean, Don, 'American Pie', from the album *American Pie* (1971)

DUBLINERS

Chart, D.A., *The Story of Dublin* (J.M. Dent & Sons, 1907)

Joyce, James, 'The Dead', in *Dubliners* (Grant Richards, 1914) and in *The Essential James Joyce* (ed. Harry Levin; Jonathan Cape, 1948; Penguin Books, 1963, 2009)

Joyce, James, 'Hades', in *Ulysses* (Shakespeare and Company, 1922) and in *The Essential James Joyce* (ed. Harry Levin; Jonathan Cape, 1948; Penguin Books, 1963, 2009)

MacThomáis, Éamonn, *Me Jewel and Darlin' Dublin* (The O'Brien Press, 1994)

MacThomáis, Éamonn *Three Shouts on a Hill* (An Phoblacht, 2015)

MacThomáis, Shane *Dead Interesting: Stories From the Graveyards of Dublin* (Mercier Press, 2012)

MacThomáis, Shane *Glasnevin: Ireland's Necropolis* (Glasnevin Trust, 2010)

Kelleher, Aoife, *One Million Dubliners* (Underground Films, 2014)

LILIAS

Henderson, Ebenezer, *The Annals of Dunfermline . . .* (John Tweed, 1879)

King, Lillian, *Famous Women of Fife* (Windfall Books, 1997)

Larner, Christine, *Enemies of God: Witch Hunt in Scotland* (Basil Blackwell, 1983; John Donald, 2000)

Macdonald, Stuart, *The Witches of Fife: Witch-Hunting in a Scottish Shire, 1560–1710* (Tuckwell Press, 2002)

Neale, Chris, *The 17th Century Witch Craze in West Fife: A Guide to the Printed Sources* (Dunfermline District Libraries, 1980)

Pugh, Roy J. M., *The Deil's Ain: The Story of Witch Persecution in Scotland* (Harlaw Heritage, 2001)

CRESCENT

Ansari, Humayan, '"Burying the Dead": Making Muslim Space in Britain', *Historical Research*, vol. 80, issue 210 (November 2007), pp. 545–66

Dead Good Job (BBC2, 2012; Rob Cowling, director)
East End Undertakers (Al-Jazeera, 2018; Horia El Hadad, director)
God's Waiting Room (Channel 4, 2007; Heenan Bhatti, director)
Middle EastEnders (BBC1, 2010; Geoff Small, director)

SKULLS

Barker, Jack F., *St Leonard's Church: A Historical and Architectural Guide* (St Leonard's Church, 1994, 2014)

Barker, Jack F., 'A Study of the Crypt of St Leonard's, Hythe' (St Leonard's Church, 1985, 1998)

Craig-Atkins, Elizabeth, Jennifer Crangle et al., 'Charnel Practices in Medieval England: New Perspectives', *Mortality*, vol. 24, issue 2 (2019), pp. 145–66

Crangle, Jennifer, *A Study of Post-Depositional Funerary Practices in Medieval England*, Ph.D. thesis (Department of Archaeology, University of Sheffield, 2015)

Hawkins, Stephen, *Holy Trinity Rothwell: A Guide* (1986; 2009)

Inge, Denise, *A Tour of Bones: Facing Fear and Looking for Life* (Bloomsbury, 2014)

Koudounaris, Paul, *The Empire of Death: A Cultural History of Ossuaries and Charnel Houses* (Thames & Hudson, 2011)

Parsons, F. G., 'Report on the Hythe Crania', *The Journal of the Royal Anthropological Institute of Great Britain and Ireland*, vol. 38 (July–Dec. 1908), pp. 419–50

Ramshaw, Marcus, *St Leonard's Hythe: 'The Church with the Bones'* (Pitkin, 2000, 2017)

The Rothwell Charnel Chapel Project, University of Sheffield
   (www.rothwellcharnelchapel.group.shef.ac.uk)

PETER

Birtchnell, Percy C., *A Short History of Berkhamsted* (Clunbury
   Press, 1961; self-published, 1972)
Bland, Rev. W., 'Extract from the parish-register of
   Northchurch in the county of Hertford', *The Scots
   Magazine* (Murray & Cochrane, 1785)
Burnett, James, Lord Monboddo, *Antient Metaphysics*, vol. 3
   (J. Balfour and Co., 1784)
'Peter the Wild Boy', *The Berkhamstedian* school magazine
   (Feb. 1882)
Worsley, Lucy, *Courtiers: The Secret History of the Georgian Court*
   (Faber & Faber, 2010)
Yeoman, John, *The Diary of the Visits of John Yeoman to London
   in the Years 1774 and 1777* (Watts & Co., 1935)

CROWS

Brontë, Emily, *Wuthering Heights* (Thomas Cautley Newby,
   1847; Penguin Books, 1985)
Callender, Rupert, essay on lowering straps from the
   website of The Green Funeral Company, www.
   thegreenfuneralcompany.co.uk
Eliot, T. S., 'Four Quartets', in *Collected Poems 1909–1962* (Faber
   & Faber, 1985)
Joyce, James, 'The Dead', *Dubliners* (Grant Richards Ltd, 1914)
   and in *The Essential James Joyce* (ed. Harry Levin; Jonathan
   Cape, 1948; Penguin Books, 1963, 2009)
McCormack, Mike, *Solar Bones* (Tramp Press, 2016)
Natural Death Handbook, The, 5th edn (The Natural Death
   Centre, 2012)

West, Ken, *A Guide to Natural Burial* (Sweet & Maxwell, 2010)

Whitman, Walt, 'Song of Myself', in *The Penguin Book of American Verse* (Penguin Books, 1954; reissued 2011)

Woolner, Tom, *Let's Talk About Grief & Loss: A Discussion of the Aspects Commonly Experienced Yet Rarely Discussed* (self-published, 2018)

Callender, Claire and Rupert, 'Death, Grief, Ritual and Radical Funerals' (TEDx Talk, 2015)

BELOVED

Friends of Arnos Vale, *Arnos Vale Bristol: A Victorian Cemetery* (Redcliffe Press, 2007)

Loudon, John Claudius, *On the Laying Out, Planting and Managing of Cemeteries; and on the Improvement of Churchyards* (Longmans, Green, 1843)

Acknowledgements

Many people helped me tell the stories within *A Tomb with a View*. My agent, Kevin Pocklington at The North Literary Agency, and editor, Richard Roper at Headline, believed in the book when it existed nowhere else but inside my skull, and I am grateful to them for performing a literary craniotomy, allowing it to emerge. Richard has been such an enthusiastic and empathetic editor; it's been a pleasure to work with him. Thanks, too, to Edward Bettison, for the beautiful cover, and to Caitlin Raynor, publicity director, for spreading the word. My appreciation to Cathie Arrington, picture editor, for her efforts in sourcing photographs. I am grateful to Felicity Price at Reviewed & Cleared for her careful attention and legal advice, to Mark Handsley for his painstaking copy-editing, to Tara O'Sullivan for proof-reading, Jo Liddiard for marketing support, and to Georgie Polhill for her assistance.

A few chapters of *A Tomb with a View* had early readers who offered useful comments and much-needed encouragement. I'd like to thank, in particular, Dani Garavelli for responding to the work with great kindness, generosity and insight.

Lindsey Ward and Joe Hodrien put me up (and up with me) in London, and their only reward was listening to me talk about dead people all through dinner. My immense gratitude seems scant recompense for their hospitality, but I hope it will do.

I am grateful to Jackie Kay for allowing me to use as an epigraph a quotation from her memoir *Red Dust Road*, and for the cheering news that her dad – the late, great John Kay – loved my title. Many thanks to Yale University Press for permission to use a line from Alan Titley's translation of *Cré na Cille*. I am also thankful to Wayne Coyne of The Flaming Lips, and the band's manager, Scott Booker, for giving their blessing to my quoting the classic song 'Do You Realize??' as the third and final epigraph.

The chapter 'Dubliners' and its twin, 'Crows', contain appropriations from, and allusions to, 'The Dead' by James Joyce. 'Crows' also alludes to the final lines of Emily Brontë's *Wuthering Heights*.

I attended four funerals and a wedding in the course of researching this book. My thanks to the people, families and organisations involved in allowing me to be there.

It means a lot to me that the friends and family of Shane MacThomáis trusted me with their memories and stories. My thanks to them; I wish I had known him.

One of the most extraordinary experiences I had while working on this book was meeting Bridgitt Sanders on a wild All Souls' Day at Sharpham Meadow Natural Burial Ground. It was a privilege to be there to listen to her talk about Wayne. I had always known that my book about death was a book about life, but she made me realise that it is really a book about love.

I would also like to thank the following: Gonca Aksoy; Emma Bakel at Museum of London Archaeology; Shahera Begum and Khizar Mohammad of the East London Mosque & London Muslim Centre; Mary-Anne Bowring; Gerry Braiden; Emily Brazee at the Museum of London; the British Library; Peter Cheney in the Church of Ireland press office; at the Commonwealth War Graves Commission, Iain Anderson, Audrey Chaix, Peter Francis and Patricia Keppie; Dr Lizzy Craig-Atkins; Dunfermline Carnegie Library & Galleries; Alex Dean, *Prospect* magazine; Margot Eliadis of the Sharpham Trust; Sophie Galleymore Bird; Dr George Geddes, Historic Environment Scotland; Lynn Glanville, Diocese of Dublin & Glendalough; Professor Julian Goodare; the Rev. Canon Jonathan Gordon of St Mary's, Northchurch; Karen Green-shields; Jacky Hawkes at Blackstaff Press; Highgate Cemetery – in particular all of those whom I interviewed but did not quote; Layla Hillsden of the Special Collections department at Leeds University Library; Derrick Hussey, Hippocampus Press; Laura Hutchinson of Historic Royal Palaces; Rose Inman-Cook of the Natural Death Centre; Nikola Ivanovski; Helen John at Bankside Open Spaces Trust; Buffy Jones, wedding manager at Arnos Vale; Sara Ann Kelly; Robert Macfarlane; Greg McCarron, STV; Fiontann McCarry; Gerry McClory; Father Eddie McGee of the Diocese of Down and Connor press office; Alex McNeill at Belfast City Council; Denise Mina; the Mitchell Library, Glasgow; Catherine Munro; Dave Napier; Charlotte Newton, Royal College of Surgeons; Richard North; Andrew O'Hagan; Patricia Parfrey of St Michan's, Dublin; Tanya-Jane Park of WRAC Association; Derrick Pounder; Postal Museum, London; Baroness Gail Rebuck; Jacquie Shaw and colleagues at the National Museum of the Royal Navy; Alan Taylor; Transport for London press office; Margaret Utting; the Provost and Lady Waldegrave, Eton College; Tracy Watson; Daniel Weir; Tom Woolner.

There are a number of people whose interest, support and friendship have been important to me during the writing of this book. They include: Kelly Apter, Fiona Clark, Brian Donaldson, Jane Graham, Jamie Lafferty, Barry and Fiona Leathem, Damien Love, Paul McNamee, Alex Neilson, Stephen Phelan, Helen Ross, Alison Stroak, Graeme Virtue, and – for introducing me to the wonders and weirdness of Whitby – Paul and Christine Ward.

Finally, with all my love, to Jo, James and Jack – for walks in the graveyard, and everything else.

Index

Adams, Gerry, 88, 89, 226, 239
Adamson, Robert, 53
Adeney, Martin, 106
Adie, Lilias, 243–6
Aksoy, Mehmet, 127
Alan (homeless man), 282
Albery, Nicholas, 306–7
alkaline hydrolysis, 305
All Souls' Day, 302, 311
Allen, Jules, 159
Amiens, 60
Anatomy Act, 1832, 59
Anderson, Gavin, 128–9
Anderson, Sonny, 128–9
Anderson, Zoe, 128–9
Annett, Paul, 118–9
Arbuthnot, John, 293
Arnold, Steve, 183–5, 188–92
Arnos Vale Army, 323
Arnos Vale Cemetery, Bristol, 315–25
Asquith, Herbert, 178
Association for the Preservation of
      Arnos Vale Cemetery, 322–3
Austin, Joe, 73, 74–5, 76, 89
Austria, St Michael's Chapel, 288

Babbage, Charles, 35
Bainbridge, Beryl, 119
Ballycastle Golf Club, 142
Banff, St Mary's, 14
Bankside Open Spaces Trust, 140,
      159–60
baptism of desire, 154
Barnes, John, 4
Beadle, Jeremy, 123
Beales, Professor Phil, 293

Beaurains, 187
Behan, Brendan, 85, 223
Belfast
   anti-Catholic bigotry, 77
   City Cemetery, 78–83
   deaths of British soldiers, 86–7,
         89
   Friar's Bush, 76–8
   internecine tension, 69
   Lyra McKee funeral, 90–3
   memorials, 84–7
   Milltown Cemetery, 69, 70, 71–6,
         76–7, 78, 79, 86, 87–8, 89–90,
         150–4
   parades, 69–71, 71, 83–4, 89–90
   patriot dead, 69
   population, 77
   sectarian division, 81
   the Troubles, 84–9
Belfast City Cemetery, 78–83
Belfast News Letter, 78
Bell, Joseph, 105
Ben More Assynt, 165–6
Benson, E. F., 211
Berkhamsted, 295–7
Betjeman, Sir John, 112
Betty (St Michan's volunteer), 275
birth control, 153
Bishopthorpe, St Andrew's, 179
Blake, Julian, 184, 190–2
Blunden, Edward, 183
body snatchers, 40, 59–60
Bonamargy Friary, 143
Bonomi, Joseph, 26
Booth, Charles, 139
Bowie, David, 156

boy and the snake, the, 6–7
Boynton, Thomas, 17
Bradbury, Kate, 209
Bradley, Cerys, 204, 206–7
Brady, Kevin, 88–9
Braysher, Ellen, 202, 203, 206, 209–10
Brian (piper), xv–xvi
Bride of Frankenstein (film), 26–7
Brighton, 254
    St Nicholas, 97–101
Bristol, Arnos Vale Cemetery, 315–25
Bristol City Council, 318, 323
Brocklesby, John Hubert, 173–7
brokenness, beauty in, 160
Brompton Cemetery, 5, 12, 23–9
Brunel, Isambard Kingdom., 35
Buffy (wedding coordinator), 316,
    317, 324
Buggy, Kevin T., 76
Burial Acts, 36
Burke, Billie, 58
Burke, John, 72
Burn, William, 41
Burne-Jones, Edward, 25–6
Burns, Anna, 70
Burns, Robert, 53
Burt, Joseph, 117–9
Byrne, Ellen Gertrude, 206
Byrne, the Reverend John Rice, 206

Caledonian Railway, 13
Callender, Claire, 304–8, 310
Callender, Rupert, 304–8, 310
Calloway, Adeana, 56–7
Calloway, Jayne, 56–7
Cameron, Duggie, 172
Canadian Corps, 5th Infantry
    Battalion, 191–2
Cano, Frank, 107–8, 110, 130–2
Canongate, Edinburgh, 53
Capuchin crypt, Rome, 288

Carlisle Cemetery, 302
Carnegie, Andrew, 245–6
Carnmoney Cemetery, 92–3
Casati, Marchesa Luisa, 27–8
Casement, Major General Sir
    William, 45
Cathcart Cemetery, Glasgow, 7–11
Catholic iconography, 72–3
Caulfield, Paul, 123
Ceann Ear, 165
Ceann Iar, 165
cemeteries
    the future, 315–25
    numbers, 12–3
    secondary purpose, 318–9
Cemetery Club, 5
Chadwick, Sir Edwin, 37
charnel chapels, 267–74, 281–8
Chesterton, G. K., 32–3
cholera, 12
Christie, Agatha, 53
churchyard odours, toxicity of, 38
churchyards, numbers, 12–3
Chutnneagam, Siubhainin Ni, 152–5
cillíní, Ireland, 142–55
Clark, Ossie, 36
Clementson, Georgina, 33
Coates, Stephen, 26
Colette (Cola), 28–9
Collins, Lorcan, 233
Collins, Michael, 222
Collins, Wilkie, 35
Commonwealth War Graves
    Commission, 163–73, 181–92
Condell, Peter, 277–80
conscientious objectors, 173–81
Constable, John (aka John Crow),
    142, 155–60
    The Southwark Mysteries, 155–6
Cooper, Jennifer, 136–7, 158
Corner, Nichola, 92

coronavirus lockdown, xiii–xvi
cosmic unfairness, 49
Couchman, Father Anthony, 32
courage, 179–80
Courtoy, Hannah (Mysterious
    society woman with fabulous
    wealth), 26
Cousin, Christian, 187
Cousin, David, 58–9
Coward, Sacha, 26–8
Cox, Michael, 199
Crangle, Dr Jenny, 268, 269, 270–4
cremations, 14, 30, 108–9, 301, 305, 309,
    316–7
Crosby, Douglas, 6–7
Crossbones Girl, the, 139–40
Crossbones Graveyard, London,
    135–42, 155–60
Cruikshank, George, 205
cultural forgetting, 150
Curragh internment camp, 226
Czech Republic, Sedlec Ossuary, 288

Dawson, Margaret Damer, 97
De Quincey, Thomas, 53
dead, the
    company of, xiv–xv, 3–4
    needs, 29
Dean Cemetery, Edinburgh, 105
death
    democracy of, 36
    inevitability of, 321
death-masks, 124–6
Defoe, Daniel, 293
Dennehy, Emer, 149–50
Devon, Sharpham Meadow, 301–4
Dia de los Muertos, 318
Dickens, Charles, 38–9
    Bleak House, 38, 39
discovery, thrill of, 11–2
documenting, 61

dogs, devotion, 55–7
Dorrian, Bishop Patrick, 81
Douaumont Ossuary, 283
Dublin, 71
    Glasnevin Cemetery, 215, 219–40
    Mount Jerome Cemetery, 210–6
    Prospect Cemetery, 220
    St Michan's, 275–81
Dublin Ghost Story Festival, 216
Duckworth, George H., 139
Ducrow, Andrew, 45
Dundrennan Abbey, 5–7
Dunfermline, 245, 246
Dungavell, Ian, 113–6

easeful death, 47
East London Mosque, 249–54, 260–3
Edgeworth, Maria, 294
Edinburgh
    Canongate, 53
    Dean Cemetery, 105
    Greyfriars kirkyard, 53–7, 59
    Harry Potter tourism, 54–5
    the one o'clock gun, 64
    St Cuthbert's, 53
    St Giles's burial ground, 54
    Warriston Cemetery, 58–65
Edwards, Amelia B., 202–10, 216
Egypt, 208–9
Egypt Exploration Society, 208–9
Eliot, George, 5, 105, 115
Ellis, Havelock, 206
Ellis, S. M., 214
Enon Chapel, London, 40–3
eternal, the, 64
Eton College, 195–7
Eton Town Cemetery, 197–202
executions, First World War, 176–7,
    178
exploitation, 117
Eyles, John, 40

faded grandeur, 45
false intimacy, 101
Faraday, Michael, 105–6
Farrell, Mairéad, 70, 73, 73–5, 87–8
Fergusson, Robert, 53
film screenings, 318
Find A Grave website, 3
First World War, 108, 165, 166, 171–3,
    201, 283
    conscientious objectors, 173–81
    executions, 176–7, 178
    memorials, 185–6, 192
    recovered bodies, 181–92
    scavengers, 184–5
    the Ypres Salient, 181
Flower, Robin, 145–6
fossils, 83
Fowler, Sir Montague, 24
France, 37, 283
Franks, Bob, 17
French Foreign Legion, 233–4
Friar's Bush, Belfast, 76–8
Friends of Crossbones, 160
Friends of Highgate Trust, 113
Friends of Kensal Green, 29–32
Friends of Warriston Cemetery, 62
funeral customs, 29–32, 79–80, 306,
    307–8, 310–1
    Muslim, 249–52
funeral pyres, 305
future, the, 315–25
Gallagher, Angela, 86
Galleymore, Frances, 309
Galleymore, Sophie, 309
garden cemetery movement, 36, 78–9
Gardens of Peace, Hainault, 255–60
Gaudie, Norman, 173–81
gay, lesbian, bisexual graves, 23, 26–8,
    202–10
Gay, William, 78–9
Geary, Stephen, 106

Gentleman, Ebenezer, 4
George I, King, 292
ghost stories, 195–202, 202–3, 205,
    210–6
Gibraltar Three, the, 73–5, 87–8
Glasgow, xiii–xiv, 73–5
    Cathcart Cemetery, 7–11
    Necropolis, 7–8
    Southern Necropolis, 8
Glasgow Herald, 10, 11
Glasnevin Cemetery, Dublin, 215,
    219–40
Gleeson, Jack, 228, 230, 231–2, 232,
    234–5
Glover, Brian, 25
Gluebag, Tommy, 4
Golding, Samuel, 99
Goodman, Sheldon K., 5, 16, 23–5, 27
Gormley, Father Joseph, 91
Goths, 18, 287, 316
Gould, Philip, 119, 120
Grade II listings, 25–6
Grant, Dugald, 167, 171–3
Grant, Peter, 173
grave renewal, 115–6
grave space, 13
gravediggers, 119–21
graveyards
    function, xiv
    and imagination, 3–4
    as libraries, 16
    smallest, 15–6
    stories, 4–5, 9–10
Gray, John, 55–6
Green, Moona, 251, 253, 257, 260, 263
Green Funeral Company, 304–8
Green Isle, the, 163–4, 167–73
Grenfell Tower fire, 255–8
Greyfriars Bobby, 55–7
Greyfriars Kirkyard, Edinburgh,
    53–7, 59

grief, 306
Griffin, Susan, 152
Gunn, Martha, 100

Hadid, Zaha, 254–5
Haguenot, Dr, 38
Hainault, Gardens of Peace, 255–60
Haji Taslim Funerals, 250–1, 252–4, 261
Hale-Smith, Matthew, 182
Hallowe'en, 315, 317
Hampstead Cemetery, 5
Hartley, Tom, 79–83
hauntings, 56–7
headstones, 3, 14–5, 32, 82, 93, 98, 123, 128–9, 187, 197
Hemson, John, 18
Henbury, St Mary the Virgin, 202
Henry, Paul, 78
Heritage Lottery Fund, 323
Herman, Bill, 120, 121
Herman, Victor, 119–21
Hessel, Phoebe, 97–101
Hessel, William, 99
Highgate Cemetery, 5, 13, 24, 105–32
  Cedar tree, 106–8, 130–2
  decline and neglect, 109–11
  development risk, 115
  East Cemetery, 115, 117–32
  gift shop, 117
  income, 114
  island, 106–7
  lack of burial space, 115–7
  the Mound, 126–9
  West Cemetery, 111, 112, 115
Highgate Vampire, the, 111
Highland funerals, 171
Hildyard, 2nd Lieutenant Robert, 283
Hill, David Octavius, 53
Historic England, 175–6, 202

Historic Environment Scotland, 61
Hockney, David, 36
Holmes, Isabella, 45, 138
Holness, Matthew, 212–3, 216
Holy Trinity Church, Rothwell, 267–74, 285, 288
Hopkins, Gerard Manley, 223
Howell, Edward, 100
Howes, Corporal Derek, 89
Hughes, Bernard, 76
Hughes, Brin, 284–5, 287–8
Hulme, Andy, 140
Huntrodds, Francis and Mary, 19
Hythe, St Leonard's, 274, 281–8

Ibrahim, Fethia, 255
Ibrahim, Hania, 255
Ibrahim, Rania, 255
imagination, 3–4
Inge, Denise, 286
inscriptions, 3, 98
IRA, 73–6, 226
Ireland, cillíni, 143
Irish Famine, 77
Irish republicanism, 71
Islamic cemeteries and funerals, 249–63
Islamic law, 253
ivy, 9

Jackson, Elizabeth, 114
James, M. R., 195–202, 210–1, 212, 212–3, 216, 276
Jansch, Bert, 119
Janton, Jean-Baptiste Louis, 10
Jeake, Samuel, 284–5
Jizo, 157
Joint Casualty & Compassionate Centre, 189
Jordan, Pearse, 84

Joyce, James, 201, 223–4, 226
Joyce, John Stanislaus, 223–4

Kane, the Reverend Richard
    Rutledge, 82
Kaos, Katy, 160
Keats, John, 47
Kelleher, Aoife, 221, 235, 238
Kelly, Luke, 223
Kensal Green Cemetery, 24, 29–36,
    37, 43–9
Kensington Palace, 293
Khalid, Abu, 252–3, 257, 258, 261, 262
Kipling, Rudyard, 186–7
Knox, John, 7, 54
Koulouris, Lesley, 295–7
Küçük, Barış, 128
Kurtz, William, 209

Larner, Christine, 245
Laurel, Stan, 7
Laurentic, HMS, 165
Le Fanu, Joseph Sheridan, 210–6
Leadhills, South Lanarkshire, 15–6
Lego, 128–9
Leitrim, Earls of, 278
Leyland, Frederick, 25–6
Leyland, Megan, 176, 177
Life, Death (And The Rest) festival,
    318
limbo, 148, 153, 154
Limbus Infantum, 148
liminal spaces, 148–9
Litten, Dr Julian, 29–32, 33, 34–5,
    44–5
Litvinenko, Alexander, 106
Liverpool, 254
living, encounters with the, 57
Lloyd, Marie, 5
Lloyd Parry, Robert, 195–8, 199
Logan, the Reverend Allan, 245

London, 230–2
    7/7 bombings, 257
    Brompton Cemetery, 5, 12, 23–9
    Crossbones Graveyard, 135–42,
        155–60
    East London Mosque, 249–54,
        260–3
    Enon Chapel, 40–3
    Highgate Cemetery, 5, 13, 24,
        105–32
    Kensal Green Cemetery, 29–36,
        37, 43–9
    The Magnificent Seven, 24, 33,
        106
    Norwood Cemetery, 43
    population, 37
    Russell Court, 39
    St Olave's, 38–9
    Victorian, 36–45
London Necropolis, the, 254–5
London School of Economics, 43
Loudon, John Claudius, 318–9
Lovecraft, H. P., 198, 216
Lowe, Robert, 165–6
Luxton, Neil, 122–4
Lydon, John, 111
Lyness Royal Naval Cemetery,
    Orkney, 163

Macaulay, John, 167–8
McCabe, Nora, 85, 86
McCann, Dan, 73–5, 88
McCulloch, Horatio, 64–5
McCullough, George, 222, 224, 234
Macdonald, the Reverend
    Alexander, 167–8
MacDonald, Charles, 169
MacDonald, Kenneth, 170–1
MacDonald, Private Mary, 167,
    170–1
McDonald, Mary Lou, 83, 89–90

McGuinness, Martin, 226
McHale, Shaun, 315–7, 324–5
Machen, Arthur, 198, 216
Machon, Glyn, 6
McKee, Lyra, 69–70, 90, 90–3
Mackenzie, Sir George, 56–7
Mackesy, Charlie, 119
McLachlan, Margaret, 4
McLaren, Malcolm, 105, 124–5
MacLean, Angus Peter, 171
Macleod, the Reverend George, 168
McMullin, George, 82
McNeill, Lieutenant William, 165
MacThomáis, Éamonn, 220–1, 224,
    225–7, 227–8, 229, 233, 235–6
MacThomáis, Isabelle, 230–2, 233
MacThomáis, Melíosa, 224, 225, 227,
    228, 233, 234, 236–8
MacThomáis, Morgane, 222–3, 230–1,
    232, 233–4, 238, 239–40
MacThomáis, Shane, 219–23, 224–5,
    227–40
Magill, Father Martin, 92
Maguire, Toni, 143, 144–5, 146–8, 151,
    153
Mahomed, Sake Deen, 254
Maidenhead, 189
Malami, Oladayo, 249–52
Malmesbury Abbey, Wiltshire, 14–5
Manchester United, Munich air
    disaster, 223
Marriott, Janine, 318–9
Martlew, Alfred, 177–81
Martlew, the Reverend Alfred, 177–8,
    180
martyrdom, 4
Marx, Karl, 105, 113, 115, 120
Mehra, Mary-Anne, 46, 47–8
Mehra, Medi, 46
Mehra, Mehdi, 45–9
memorials, 122–4, 166

Menin Gate, 186
Michael, George, 5, 113, 118
Mills, Peter, 105, 111
Milltown Cemetery, Belfast, 69,
    70, 71–6, 76–7, 78, 79, 86, 87–8,
    89–90, 150–4
Mitchell, the Reverend David, 82
Mitchell, Elizabeth, 139–40
Monachs, the, 165
Monckton, Lionel, 24
monuments, 45–9
Morrison, Danny, 84–9
Morrison, Jim, 5
Morton, John, 269
mortsafes, 59–60
Mount Jerome Cemetery, Dublin,
    210–6
Mountjoy Prison, 226
Muir, Augustus, 168
Mulready, William, 45
mummies, 275–81
Murray, Father Raymond, 74
Muslims, 249–63
Myers, Alfred, 173–81

National Graves Association,
    Belfast, 73
natural burials, 301–12
Natural Death Centre, the, 307
natural death movement, 306–8
Navvies' Graveyard, South
    Lanarkshire, 13
New IRA, 70, 83
New Irish Farm Cemetery, 181–2
North, Marianne, 207
Northchurch, St Mary's, 291–7
Northern Ireland
    sectarian division, 81
    the Troubles, 69–71, 73–5, 84–9
Norwood Cemetery, 43
notice everything, 82

Index

Notorious Women of Brighton tour, 97–101
Nunn, the Very Reverend Andrew, 135, 136, 141–2

Ó Cadhain, Máirtín, 215
O'Connell, Daniel, 220
O'Driscoll, Father Patrick, 182
O'Farrell, Elizabeth, 229
Oileán na Marbh, 148–9
Old Town Cemetery, Stirling, 3–4
Omer, Mohamed, 255–7, 258
One Million Dubliners (film), 221, 222, 235, 237
Original Sin, 144
Orkney, Lyness Royal Naval Cemetery, 163
ossuaries, 267–88
overcrowding, 36–45, 78, 114, 115–7, 138, 258
Owen, Wilfred, 186

Paris, 27
   Catacombs, 288
   Père Lachaise, 5, 33
Parnell, Charles Stewart, 239
Paton, Joseph Neil, 245
peace, sense of, 311
Pearce, Margaret, 287–8
Pearse, Patrick, 71, 73, 229
Père Lachaise, Paris, 5, 33
Peskett, Louise, 97–101
Peter the Wild Boy, 291–7
Petrie, Flinders, 209
Petrie Museum, 204, 209
photography, 18
Pierpoint, David, 280, 281
Pigott-Smith, Tim, 127
Platts, Carole, 18
plot prices, 116
Poe, Edgar Allan, 216

pop occultism, 110–1
Potter, Beatrix, 29
Powell, Nick, 117
Prospect Cemetery, Dublin, 220
Provisional IRA, 69, 72
Pullman, Philip, *The Amber Spyglass*, xiv

Queerly Departed tour, 23, 26–8
Quigley, Jimmy, 85

Ramage, Captain Alexander, 186
Rankin, Ian, 60–1
rats, 39, 42, 79
Recchioni, Emidio, 35–6
Redcross Mary, 137, 157–8
Redgrave, Corin, 122
Reinhardt, Bob, 58–65
religious doubt, 109
Remembering the Accused Witches of Scotland, 243–4, 245
Renshaw, Lucy, 208
resurrection, 109
resurrectionists, 59–60
Reynolds, Bruce, 125
Reynolds, Nick, 124–6
Richmond Castle, 173–81
Richmond Sixteen, the, 173–81
Riddell, Thomas, 55
rituals, 307
Robey, George, 11
Rome, Capuchin crypt, 288
Rook, James, 100
Ross, Robert, 163–4, 166, 169–73
Rossa, Jeremiah O'Donovan, 71, 229
Rossetti, Dante Gabriel, 106
Rothwell, Holy Trinity Church, 267–74, 285, 288
Rothwell Charnel Chapel Project, 270
Rowling, J. K., 54–5

Royal Fusiliers, 181–2
Russell Court, London, 39
St Andrew's, Bishopthorpe, 179
St Andrews University, 245
St Cuthbert's, Edinburgh, 53
St Giles Graveyard, Edinburgh, 54
St Leonard's, Hythe, 274, 281–8
St Mary the Virgin
   Henbury, 202
   Whitby, 16–9
St Mary's
   Banff, 14
   Northchurch, 291–7
St Michael's Chapel, Austria, 288
St Michan's mummies, 275–81
St Olave's, London, 38–9
Sanders, Bridgitt, 301–4, 309–12
Sanders, Wayne, 301–4, 309–12
Sands, Bobby, 72, 90
Saoradh, 83
Sassoon, Siegfried, 186
Savage, Sean, 73–5
Sayers, Tom, 105
Schatt, Otto, 165
Scottish witchcraft panic, 243–6
Second Word War, 165–6, 170, 186
Sedlec Ossuary, Czech Republic, 288
Select Committee on the
   Improvement of Health in
   Towns, 1842, 41
serendipity, 35
sex workers, 135–42
Sharpham Meadow, Devon, 301–4,
   308–12
Shaw, Ethel, 11
Sheares, John and Henry, 278
Sheridan, Mark, 7, 10–1
Showers, Brian J., 214–6
Siddal, Lizzie, 106
Smith, Alexander, 64
Smith, Joyce, 322–4

Smith, Paul and Frances, 14–5
Smith, Richard, 322–4
Snow, John, 12
Society for the Abolition of Burials
   in Towns, 37
Son Of A Tutu, 23
Sophia, Princess, 34
South Lanarkshire
   Leadhills, 15–6
   Navvies' Graveyard, 13
South Shields, 254
Southwark, 135–42
Speirs, Douglas, 244, 246
Spence, Annie Paton, 65
Speyer, Josefine, 307
squirrels, 28–9
Stewart, Kate, 243–4, 246
Stirling, Old Town Cemetery, 3–4
Stoker, Bram, *Dracula*, 16–9
Stone, Michael, 88
stonemasons, 122–4
Stow, John, 137–8
Strachey, Lytton, 201
Sun, The, 74
Sussex, Duke of, 33–4
Swan River Press, 216
Sweeney, the Reverend Andrew,
   286–7
Swift, Jonathan, 293
Symonds, John Addington, 206, 207
Synge, J. M., 215

taphophile's credo, 82
Taslim, Gulam, 253–4, 255, 259, 261,
   262–3
Taslim Ali, 250, 253–4, 260
Taylor, John, 15–6
teleportation chambers, 26
Thackeray, William Makepeace, 35
Thesiger, Ernest, 26–7
Thiepval, 185–6

Index

Thorgerson, Storm, 127
tiger, first person in England to be killed by, 14–5
time machine, 26
time travel, 5
Tipton, Jim, 3
Tombstone tourism, 14
Torry Bay, 243–6
Torryburn, 244–5
Transport for London, 159–60
Treanor, Bishop Noel, 151
Trollope, Anthony, 35
Turner, Frank, 159
Twynnoy, Hannah, 14–5

U-110, 165
unbaptised infants, 142–55, 157–8
University College, London, 204
Upton, Byron, 36
Usher, Richard, 54, 56
Utting, Alfred, 319–20
Utting, Elaine, 320
Utting, Howard, 319–21
Utting, William, 319

Valhalla, New York, 58
Valiente, Doreen, 97
vampires, 111
vandalism, xiv, 4, 60, 109, 111, 113, 187, 322
Venus of Père Lachaise, the, 27
Verne, Jules, 60
Vernon, HMS, 172
Victoria, Queen, 24
Victorian period, London, 36–45
Vimy Memorial, 192

Wakeman, William, 145
Walker, George Alfred, 37–8, 39, 40–3, 138
Walker, Lynsey, 28

Walpole, Spencer, 138
war graves, 163–73, 181–92
    conscientious objectors, 173–81
Ward, Gerry, 76
Ware, Fabian, 166
Warriston Cemetery, Edinburgh, 58–65
Webb, Liz, 315–7, 324–5
weddings, 315–7, 324–5
Wells, H. G., 122
West, Ken, 302
Westbury-on-Trym, 203
Westwood. the Reverend Canon John, 267–8
Westwood, Vivienne, 140
Whalley, David 'Heavy', 166
Whelan, Liam, 223
Whitby, St Mary the Virgin, 16–9
White, Harry, 85
Wilde, Oscar, 5
Wilson, Margaret, 4
Wiltshire, Malmesbury Abbey, 14–5
witchcraft, witches and witch-hunting, 97, 243–6
Wombwell, George, 105
Wood, Corporal David, 89
Woods, Raga, 159
Woolner, Kate, 309
Woolner, Tom, 309
Worsley, Lucy, 293, 294
Worth, Adam, 105

Yeats, Jack Butler, 215
York, cholera graves, 12, 13
Young, Alexander, 9
Young, Isabella, 9
Young, John, 9
Young, Robert, 9
Young, William Fulton, 9

Zurich, 223–4